THE KIND OF
GUY I AM

Robert McAllister
WITH FLOYD MILLER

HV
7911
.M11K

McGRAW-HILL BOOK COMPANY, INC.

NEW YORK   TORONTO   LONDON

To my beloved Marie

who inspired me to

write this book

HV 7911
M 11 k

THE KIND OF GUY I AM

Library of Congress Catalog Card Number: 57-8013

Published by the McGraw-Hill Book Company, Inc. Printed in the United States of America

CONTENTS

Chapter One

THE BEER-BARREL

POLKA

I was a New York cop.

I've been an entertainer in speak-easies.

I've been an athletic champion, member of the U.S. Olympic Track Team.

Politicians framed me for perjury.

Gangsters framed me for murder.

I spent time in the Tombs, where they jobbed me.

Part of what happened was my fault, because I'm the kind of guy who can't stand being shoved around by mugs—whether they're from the Mafia, the "shoe-fly" squad, or City Hall. I'm also the kind of guy who can't keep quiet about it. Part of what happened to me was the fault of the times and the city in which I lived and worked.

I was a rookie cop in 1921 and a deputy inspector in 1953, and during every one of those years New York City was a wide-open town for those who could pay the tab. An honest cop was bound to run into trouble, and I wasn't the only one who did. But I'm a bullheaded Irishman—that made me louder, and my trouble worse.

Politicians play a large part in my story because politicians controlled the city. The ones who went after me and tried to make an example of me wouldn't have done it if I hadn't stuck my neck out. But in the beginning I was pretty dumb; I didn't even know my neck was out. When I first joined the force in 1921, my only ambition (other than becoming a champion sprinter) was to be a patrolman who kept a clean post and won the respect and maybe even the affection of those men, women, and children I was charged to protect.

I was a rookie, still learning my way around my first beat, when I received a call that was to alter my career and my life—it was a summons to appear before Police Commissioner Richard E. Enright. The commissioner occupied a position so exalted and so absolute that I was dizzy at the very thought of being in his presence. My destiny, along with that of 17,000 other cops, was in his hands, and a call to appear meant either something very good or very bad. And I didn't know which it would be for me. I could think of no infractions I had committed, . . . well, at least none sufficient to warrant the commissioner's personal attention. Still . . . ! I shined a shield that hadn't had time to get tarnished, pressed a uniform that still had the original creases in the trousers, and presented myself at Centre Street headquarters.

When I was ushered into the commissioner's office, he looked up from his desk and studied me for a long moment. He was a gray-haired veteran, and I felt the full weight of his authority. I stood at attention, trying not to breathe.

At last he smiled and said, "Congratulations on that race in Newark, son. What was it you won?"

"National A.A.U. 100-yard dash, sir," I said.

"The sports writers call you the 'flying cop.'"

"Yes, sir."

"Good publicity for the department. Now that we have a champion sprinter added to Matt McGrath and Pat McDonald, the weight men, I guess we have two whales and a cyclone." He laughed at his little joke, and I tried to laugh with him.

"Sit down," he said, his face sobering. I gripped my cap with moist hands and sat stiffly on the edge of the chair. He leaned forward. "How would you like to work on my confidential squad? I need good, tough young men. Inspector Bolan speaks highly of you."

The commissioner's confidential squad! This was a group of hand-picked men who performed secret assignments in plain clothes. This squad was not under the control of precinct captains, or division inspectors, or even headquarters deputy commissioners, but reported only to the commissioner himself. Even as a rookie, I knew the confidential squad was resented and feared by the rest of the department. The men on it were called "shoe-fly" cops, because part of their work was to go after dishonest police officers who made their shoes fly whenever they caught sight of a man from the confidential squad.

There was both an honor and a stigma attached to this job, but I didn't weigh them. I was too flattered and thrilled to have been chosen out of the thousands of men. Then too, you don't turn down an assignment in the police department. I drew myself up to rigid attention once more, snapped the commissioner a salute, and said, "Yes, sir. Thank you, sir." With those words, my fat was in the fire.

The commissioner introduced me to the man who was to be my boss in this new assignment. His name was George Faust, a first-grade detective. He was very neatly dressed, but his tailor couldn't completely conceal the powerful breadth of his shoulders. He looked like a man who could handle himself in a scrap.

Faust led me into Room 216, where his squad reported. Several of his men were busy there, reading official-looking documents or banging out reports on typewriters. They all wore plain clothes, and if they hadn't been in this building, few people would have guessed they were cops. Faust introduced me to them, and I heard a string of names: "Plagge, Yost, Coonan, Tuitt, McNamme, McMahon, Magrino, McCarthy . . . meet Bob McAllister, a new member of the squad."

There were shouted greetings and slaps on the back, and at once I felt a part of the group. They seemed to be good cops, tough cops. I liked their looks. Faust led me to a desk in a corner of the room, sat me down, and began to give me the facts of life about this assignment.

"You know, kid," he said quietly, "after a month on this job you won't have a friend in the department. The commissioner is going all out after the bootleg rings, which means we'll be making jump raids after the biggest bootleggers in town. Then, after we've knocked them over, the inspectors and captains in the precincts where we made the raids will be called on the carpet before the commissioner. He'll chew them out and say, 'My men can do it, why can't yours?' And that will make you and me and the rest of our squad real popular with everybody in those precincts. Get it?"

"I get it," I said.

"Let me spell it out a little clearer. I'm only a first-grade detective, but on our work I supersede all the brass in the department and report only to the commissioner. The rest of them can't touch me . . . or you. They may hate your guts, but they won't be able to break you. As long as you do an honest job, you're the commissioner's man. On the other hand, if you want to win a popularity contest, you're in the wrong slot."

"I never did consider myself much of a bathing beauty," I grinned.

"Good!" Faust snapped. "Let's go to work."

He took a large map of the Bronx from his desk and began to explain my first assignment. A new gang was trying to take over the beer racket in the Bronx, and its strong-arm men were beating up speak-easy owners who refused to buy from them. Our job was to find out who the gangsters were, how and where they operated, and eventually to bag them.

Faust put the point of his pencil on the map. "There's a garage here on West Farms Road near Tremont Avenue, and a stoolie reports that's where they're hiring drivers. You drive a truck?"

"I can."

"Go up there tomorrow morning and apply for a job." He reached into his pocket and pulled out a chauffeur's license and flipped it across the desk at me. It carried the name of James Finnegan. "Get your picture taken and put it on that license. From now on you're Jimmy Finnegan, and you used to work for Colonial Trucking. You met a guy named Tony Grecco, who also drove for Colonial, and he sent you up to this garage for a job. That's all you know. Okay?"

"Okay," I said. "But what happens if they give me a job?"

"Why, you go to work for them. You become a boot-legger."

I got home late that evening after further briefing by Faust—home being Peg Bradley's rooming house, where I lived with my brother George. It was not really a house, either, but a railroad flat on West 104th Street. Peg Bradley, a waitress of about fifty years, with snow-white hair and the sweetest disposition God ever gave a woman, slept on a day bed in the front room, George and I slept in the next room, and Peg's daughter Edna slept in the back room next to the kitchen. George and I were prac-tically members of the family.

George was stretched out on the bed reading the eve-ning paper when I came into our room. I began to remove my uniform and hang it up in the closet. I said, casu-ally, "I guess I can pack this uniform away in moth balls."

"Huh?" George grunted from the bed.

"I won't be needing it any more."

"What are you saying?" He was sitting up now.

"Gotta buy some work clothes."

"Bob, you're not fired from the department?"

I shrugged my shoulders. "Well, not exactly fired. It's just that I got a job driving a truck."

He jumped off the bed and pulled me around to face him. "You crazy? All your life you wanted to be a cop. Now you're gonna take a lousy job as a truck driver!"

"Not exactly lousy," I said. "It's for a ring of bootleggers and it pays real good."

Now he was speechless, and as I looked at his square, homely mug I was sorry I had teased him. George was more than my older brother, he was the only parent I had. People said we looked alike, but the resemblance was mostly confined to looks. George was the steady, hard-working, responsible one. He had gotten a job at Levy's Butcher Shop when he was ten years old and had been there ever since. He was the one who always supported me when I was out of work, gave me a roof when I had no home, and kept his nose to the grindstone while I bounced around half the world. He was the one who stepped in with ready fists whenever I got into a fight. He loved me the way a father loves his unruly child—with impatience, but hope.

I grinned and hit him playfully. "Don't you want me to be rich, George?"

"By God . . . ," he started.

Then I told him the truth, told him I'd been promoted to the commissioner's confidential squad, and that the truck driving was an undercover assignment. He let out a whoop that brought Peg from the kitchen, and when she heard the news she threw her arms around me and nearly smothered me in her bosom. Then Edna, young and pretty with her fair skin and big black eyes, kissed me on the cheek. Nothing would do but that we have a party in celebration.

After I had devoured half a cake, Peg fixed me with a stern eye and said, "Well, ya proved yourself, Bobbie, but there was a time when I wondered if ya'd ever be responsible enough for an officer of the law. Remember your target practice?"

"Peg!" I cried. "You promised you'd never tell!"

"Tell what, Ma?" Edna said.

George interrupted, "Come on, Peg, what was it?"

"You promised," I begged.

"Sure, I promised," she said with a nod, "but this is a celebration and a time to break promises. Besides, mebbe it'll keep ya from gettin' a swelled head over yer promotion." She looked around the room at her eager audience, and I could feel a blush coming. "George, remember when he was first appointed probationary patrolman, and you bought him his service gun? Well, I come home late one night that first week, and I smell somethin' burnin' like when I enter the room, but I don't think much about it and climb into bed. Well, saints above! It feels like there's gravel in my bed, and when I throw back the covers I find I'm sleepin' on a lot of bullets! Ya know what that guardian of the law had been doin'? Target practice right here in the flat. He'd put my mattress up against the closet door and shot into it, and some of the bullets stuck in the mattress, some come on through, and some went right into the door. I didn't discover the bullet holes in the door until a week later, because he'd plugged them up with soap!"

After they'd stopped hooting, George said, "You ever hear about his first pinch?"

"Here goes another promise broken," I said, with mock bitterness.

"That first week Bob was a probationary he kept searching for crooks. We couldn't even take a walk in the park without him looking behind all the bushes and trees. He was dead set to make his first arrest while still a probationary, but we never saw a thing goin' on that was against the law, and he was getting pretty discouraged. One time in the middle of the night, he wakes me outta a sound sleep and says, 'George, there's a thief outside the window trying to get in! I'm gonna arrest him.' He tiptoes to the window and looks down the air shaft and says he sees the crook crouching there, but he can't reach him. He tells me to hold his ankles and lower him out the window so he can surprise the crook and make the pinch. I lower him, just like he says, but suddenly there's a big uproar and he yells for me to pull him back up. His hand is all scratched and bloody. He'd tried to arrest a tomcat."

"Well," I said sadly, after the laughter had died down, "no danger of anybody getting a big head around here."

Peg soothed my ruffled feelings by drawing me over to the piano. She accompanied me while I sang some of our favorite Irish songs. I was soon back in good temper.

After we were in bed that night, George said, "We kidded you a lot, Bob, but everybody's real proud of you. You're going to make a big success of the new assignment."

A big success? Well, why not? I was young and strong and, if not the brightest guy on the force, certainly not the dumbest. And I wasn't afraid of any mug who ever walked. That night I was filled with a pleasant glow of confidence. What I didn't know was that the very mobsters I was to go after the next day were to become the real rulers of this city.

It was a bleak October morning eight hours later when I rode the subway up to the Bronx, my identification as Jimmy Finnegan in my pocket. I was feeling less glamorous and less heroic than I had the night before. I wore no uniform and I carried no gun.

I found the place on West Farms Road, a shabby four-story building that carried a sign, "Monarch Garage." I stepped inside. It was dark and smelled of grease and rubber. In the rear of the main floor was a tiny office, and through the dirt-streaked glass panels I could see a half-dozen thugs lounging about a desk. They watched me with expressionless faces as I made my way toward them.

"Wha' yer want?" one of them finally grunted at me.

"A job," I said.

"Job doin' what?"

"Driving," I said.

"Drivin' what?" the man at the desk persisted, a purposely stupid expression on his face.

"Driving a truck, for Chrissake!" I burst out. "What'd you think . . . an ice-cream cart? Tony Grecco passed the word along you were hiring, so I come up."

There was now a spark of interest in his dull face. He began to question me about Grecco, where I had known him and how long, whom I had worked for, where I was born. George Faust had rehearsed me well on the life of Jimmy Finnegan, and the answers came tripping smoothly off my tongue. As I talked, I began to wonder what had happened to Finnegan that made it possible for me to take over his life as my own. I prayed that the New York Police Department hadn't made any mistakes, and that the real Finnegan wouldn't suddenly walk into this tiny office.

At last the mug at the desk seemed satisfied with my story. "Wait with them others and we'll give ya a test." He jerked his head toward the other corner of the garage, where for the first time I noticed six or eight men leaning against a truck and smoking. I joined them.

An hour later I had passed the driving test and was again back before the desk in the garage office. This time a very dapper young man sat behind it and regarded me with cold eyes. He was dressed in the height of fashion, with a pearl-gray hat, a gray suit, pointed gray-suede button shoes, and a gray silk necktie that was tied in a small, hard knot in the style that was soon to be popularized by Jimmy Walker.

He questioned me again about Tony Grecco and the Colonial line where I had supposedly met him. Finally he said, "Okay, you're hired for a C-note a week. Just keep your mouth shut, unless you want to commit suicide." He laughed at his little joke. It was a thin laugh.

"When do I start?" I asked.

"Now. My name is Rocky. You come with me and I'll show you the main beer drop."

He led me across the garage floor, stepping delicately over the puddles of grease, and stopped beside a big Mack truck camouflaged as a butcher's delivery wagon. We climbed in, me behind the wheel, and backed the truck out of the garage to roll toward Southern Boulevard. We crossed a bridge over a ship canal and turned left on Whitlock Avenue to enter a neighborhood of corrugated-tin shacks. Here lived the city's down-and-outers, bums and winos, defeated men who huddled beneath their flimsy tin roofs while they drained Sterno through cheesecloth and then drank the poison. They couldn't afford the rotgut my new employers peddled.

In the middle of this wilderness was the beer drop. It was a block square and surrounded by a high tin fence topped by barbed wire. In response to our horn, a double gate swung open, and we drove inside. I stared about me in amazement. I don't know what I expected to find, but not this. We were in a junk yard—a graveyard of old bicycles, wagons, and automobiles! Wherever I looked there was nothing but twisted, rusting skeletons and scraps. A narrow, rutted lane wove its way among the grotesque mountain of metal, glass, and wood, coming to a stop in a clearing where I found several other trucks and drivers. Now I saw how the drop worked.

Hundreds of barrels of beer were hidden in underground storage rooms. The whole body of a wrecked car was carefully weighted and hinged to swing aside at a touch, revealing an entrance tunnel to the storage vaults. Rocky was watching me carefully, and when our eyes met, he smiled proudly. My honest amazement had convinced him that I was just what I posed to be, an ordinary truck driver looking for a job.

We entered one of the storage vaults and there, over a map of the City of New York, my route was laid out for me. I was to service the western edge of the Bronx that ran from Van Cortlandt Park south along the shore of the Harlem River to Randall's Island. Each day I was to pick up a truckload of beer here at the drop, then deliver it to those speak-easy owners who had been intimidated by the gang's beef squads. Twice a week, around midnight, my truck would join all the others in a caravan to the brewery in mid-Manhattan, on Twelfth Avenue between 18th and 22d Streets. This brewery was openly distilling near-beer, and secretly concocting bootleg beer of 5 per cent alcohol. On Tuesdays and Fridays we would load a new supply and bring it back to the drop in the Bronx. Every movement of every truck was plotted and checked with military precision. Nothing could go wrong.

Except something could, and would. *I* was there, leaning over the table with Rocky and learning the whole operation.

The first night, when I finally left the drop, I went back

toward my new rented room in the Bronx (I had been instructed not to continue at Peg Bradley's). I stopped at a candy store to telephone George Faust at headquarters and report everything I'd seen, particularly the location of the beer drop.

"Who's running it, Bob?" he asked.

"This Rocky seems the top."

"No, he's somebody's prat boy. We've got to know the big shots. Collect all the names you can, watch their cars for license numbers, get friendly with the other drivers, and keep your ears open for gossip. Nothing is too small or insignificant to report. Call me every night at this same time."

George Faust's instructions turned out to be surprisingly easy. The mobsters took childish delight in displaying their flashy cars. During the following days, I often saw them come wheeling arrogantly into the beer drop, and while they strutted about the place, I carefully memorized their licenses. Long black Packards were considered the classiest cars to have in those days, but every now and then a Stutz Bearcat appeared. The time was to come when no self-respecting hood would be seen in anything but a Cadillac. But that was several years in the future.

As the days passed, and I collected more and more license numbers and came to know the names and faces of the leaders, I felt a mounting impatience for direct action. I wanted to knock this gang over. How green I was! This gang was not only to consolidate its hold upon the Bronx, but during the reign of Mayor Jimmy Walker, it was to take over large sections of Manhattan. I was to spend the majority of my adult years fighting it and its allies, learning only late in life the bitter lesson that it requires more than honest cops to rid a city of crooks. It also requires honest politicians!

During those first weeks at the beer drop I met several young hoods who were to cross my path time and again in the coming years, sometimes with an exchange of bullets. One of them was a Harlem mobster named Joey Rao. He owned a piece of the beer racket and appeared about once a week to check deliveries and receipts. He was a sallow-faced, quiet-spoken man with darting, distrustful eyes.

Another, the opposite of Rao in appearance, was a handsome, open-faced, smiling Irishman. His name was Vince Coll. Within a few short years, he was to go on a killing rampage and become known as "Mad Dog" Coll. Nine years later I was to watch the medical examiner cut open the beautiful young body of Mae Smith, his sweetheart, to probe for the bullets he had pumped into her.

Rao used to nod to me, his eyes measuring and alert. Coll used to slap me on the back and demand, "How's it going, kid?"

"Fine, Mr. Coll," I'd say.

For almost a month I continued to deliver beer, reporting names and license numbers each night to the department and waiting eagerly for the moment we could knock over the whole mob. But George Faust made his first move without my knowing it was even planned.

It happened one night when we made our run down to Manhattan to load the trucks with freshly brewed beer. It was after midnight, and the caravan was weaving its cumbersome way back to the Bronx. Every trip was made by a different route, and we were instructed to stay in line and follow the man ahead of us. The big Mack rumbled and vibrated beneath me on its hard, rubber tires, and the chain drive clanked a steady rhythm through the night-shrouded streets of Harlem. Everything seemed drowsy and peaceful, but that was an illusion. Harlem never slept and was never peaceful. We came to 155th Street and turned east toward the bridge over the Harlem River. As we moved down the long hill toward it, I saw the bridge lights spanning the black water to the Bronx. I looked across to the spot where the Yankees were talking of building a modern, new ball park. They had just acquired Babe Ruth from the Boston Red Sox and were hailing him as a new home-run king.

Suddenly, as we approached the bridge, the whole caravan of trucks ground to a stop. One of the drivers came racing back along the line, shouting, "The Feds and the P.C.'s men just knocked us over. Ditch the trucks. Ditch the trucks!"

I jumped from behind the wheel and, with several other drivers, beat it back to Seventh Avenue where we hid in the door of a warehouse and waited and watched. Soon there came the distant wail of a siren, joined by another banshee cry, and another. The prowl cars, spindly model-T Fords, careened down upon the line of trucks. Blue-coated men and plain-clothed men piled out, guns drawn. But there was no fight; we drivers were huddled in the distant shadows.

Cops climbed into the trucks and soon the caravan was on the move again, this time headed for the High Bridge station house. I felt like cheering, but was careful to keep my face gloomy and to join the others in muttering curses at the Feds and the P.C.'s men . . . the police commissioner's men.

Later that night, when I was finally able to telephone George Faust at headquarters, I shouted exuberantly, "That takes care of them bums! Who do we go after next?"

George said patiently, "Take it easy, Bob. Knocking off a caravan of trucks doesn't mop up that gang. We're just trying to harass them, smoke out the leader, find his connections. You report tomorrow for work as usual, and keep your ears open."

Next day we drivers milled aimlessly around at the beer drop, waiting for orders. Everyone said that new trucks would be forthcoming, and that we'd be in business as usual before the day was out. Along about noon Joey Rao drove up and said we were all to appear that evening at a speakeasy on Southern Boulevard and 165th Street. This order was for the drop workers and guards as well as the drivers. His face was even grimmer than usual.

I appeared at the speak that night at about eight o'clock. The place had been taken over for this meeting, and nobody else was allowed in. After everyone had arrived, the doors were locked, and out of a back room stepped a man I had never seen before. I didn't know who he was, but I knew at once he was the boss. It was not only that he was surrounded by bodyguards; there was something about the man himself that marked him. There was an arrogance in the way he walked, a lithe, animal strength in his body, and a glitter in his eyes that suggested ruthlessness. He was very young. I judged him to be about twenty-four. His hair was light brown and his complexion healthily pink. His clothes were meticulously tailored. He might have been an up-and-coming businessman in midtown, rather than a gangster in the Bronx.

That is, until he talked. The moment he spoke he revealed what he was . . . a dangerous hood. His first words were a snarl: "Some sonofabitch in this room is a stoolie!"

He let his bleak eyes travel slowly around the room. I could feel sweat forming between my shoulder blades and trickling slowly down my spine.

"There was an inside tip," he said, his voice beginning to rise. "Some dirty bastard stoolie told the cops. If I find out who he is, I'll take a razor and cut his stinking skin off, an inch at a time. By Jesus Christ, I'll cut his tongue out and feed it to him!" He was screaming now and waving his arms hysterically. Then he stopped abruptly and got hold of himself. He was shaking with rage, but he controlled his voice. He spoke in a low, hoarse whisper. "The sonofabitch who squealed to the cops had better haul ass out, but quick."

Then he turned and marched out of the room, followed by his lieutenants. The rest of us sat there in stunned silence for several minutes, then stood up and began to shuffle toward the exit. No one spoke. Most of the men stared at the floor; some glanced suspiciously and fearfully at their neighbors. Several went to the bar for double whiskies, but I wanted to get out of the place.

I fell into step with another driver, and we walked quickly west on 165th Street. I said to him, "Who was that guy throwing all the crap at us in there?"

"That ain't no crap," was the reply. "That crazy Dutchman meant every word he said. That was Dutch Schultz, and I'd hate to be the guy who crossed him up!"

That evening Faust got the information he wanted; he learned the name of the leader of the new gang muscling into the Bronx. When I gave it to him on the phone, he puzzled over it and asked, "You sure you got it right? I never heard of him."

"That's the name, sir. His real name is Arthur Flegenheimer, but everybody calls him Dutch Schultz. And there's no question but he's the boss."

"I'll check him in C.I., and see if he's got a record. Call me again tomorrow at the same time."

The next day I called Faust and heard scorn in his voice when he said, "Yeah, he's got a record. But it's not much. He's a small-time punk, a sloppy flat burglar and a package thief. Three years ago he was caught trying to steal the silverware from a Bronx apartment and received fifteen months on Blackwells Island. After he got out, he heaved trunks for a moving-van company. Strictly a second-rater. We'll bust him, and soon."

"Yes, sir," I said.

How wrong could we be? In the next fifteen years Dutch Schultz was to take over all of the Bronx for his beer, and all of Harlem for his policy racket. We cops never did bust him. He was arrested fifteen times but never spent another day in jail.

Dutch was born in the Bronx on August 6, 1902, of respectable, hard-working parents. His father owned a livery stable and ran a small saloon. His mother was modest, devoted to her family, and deeply religious. The Flegenheimers tried to bring up their only son to be devout, but somewhere they failed. Dutch quit school in the sixth grade, and nothing could get him back. He sold newspapers, not because he wanted to help his family, but because there was adventure to be found on the streets. He was successively an apprentice roofer, an office boy, and a printer's helper, but he didn't work hard at any of his jobs. He began to run with the old Bergen gang, a bunch of hoodlums who hung out at Third Avenue and 149th Street in the Bronx. It was from them he learned what poor skills he had as a package thief and second-story man.

It was not surprising that my commander looked upon him as a small-time punk who could be easily disposed of. He didn't foresee that Prohibition was going to offer the opportunity for a lot of small-time punks to become big-time gangsters, and for a few of them, like Dutch Schultz, to become gang lords so powerful they couldn't be touched by the law.

And it wasn't only Faust who underestimated Schultz; all of us in the department did, right up to the end. We just never could figure out how it was that a guy like Dutch could rise to such power in the underworld. He was tough and mean, but not so much so as Vince Coll; he was smart, but not so smart as Joey Rao; he had courage, but there was more animal guts in the men who drove his trucks and did his killings. No, whenever we cops discussed it, we generally concluded that two other elements put him on top: he was lucky, and he had a native instinct for business. His gang prospered largely because of his efficient, businesslike methods. He left nothing to chance; even the careful routing of his beer convoys showed his passion for organization. He worked hard and kept careful track of all facets of the operation. I'm convinced that if he had ever gone into legitimate business, he would have made a success of that, too.

But all this is hindsight, of course. Things looked different when I was twenty-one. I was a rookie cop, and in my eyes the New York Police Department was the biggest, the best, the most powerful force in the city. When my commanding officer said that Dutch Schultz was a small-time punk, and we'd soon bust him, I believed it.

The following night I made a delivery of 20 halves to Bracker's Restaurant on City Island. It was a long run from the drop, and when we'd finished unloading, Charlie, my helper, was hungry. We went inside for a sandwich and coffee. As we entered the restaurant, I saw the Dutchman sitting at a corner table with a couple of friends and a handsome blonde. He recognized us and called out to the waiter, "Give them anything they want and stick it on my tab." Then he said to the blonde, "They're my boys."

Charlie and I ordered turkey sandwiches, apple pie, and coffee. While waiting for the chow, I glanced around the room. The wall directly behind Dutch Schultz was covered with sports photos . . . mostly fight champions, past and present. I let my eyes run idly over them, trying to identify them without looking at the printed names below . . . sometimes successfully and sometimes not. I worked over the pictures behind Dutch Schultz's left ear, then over the top of his head, and was working along behind his right ear when I saw something that made me freeze. There was a large picture of *me* . . . in a sprinter's crouch. The caption read, "Bob McAllister, the Flying Cop, National Sprint Champ."

I forced my eyes down to the sandwich that had been placed before me. I put the sandwich in my mouth and chewed on what tasted like sawdust. I tried to wash it down with coffee, but it stuck in my throat. I could feel a razor lopping off small pieces of my skin. At last Charlie was finished with his sandwich. We left the restaurant and climbed into the truck to roar back along City Island Avenue to the Bronx.

That night I called George Faust at the usual time and told him what had happened. "That was a close shave," he said.

"Don't mention razors," I begged.

"You pull out before the mob catches up with you. Report back at headquarters tomorrow afternoon."

When I left the phone booth I started to walk toward my rented room, but I suddenly thought better of it and took the subway back to Manhattan and Peg Bradley's. The next morning I went back to that rented room to pick up my things, and looked at a scene of complete destruction. All the bureau drawers had been pulled out and smashed, all my clothing had been cut to ribbons. The floor was littered with cigarette butts left there by my visitor. The Dutchman had seen the picture, but luckily for me, a little too late.

A month later the commissioner gave my squad orders to knock over the beer drop. We converged on the apparently innocent car dump in a half-dozen cars and jumped out with sledge hammers to batter down the corrugated-iron gate. By the time we got inside, the guards had fled. We hadn't come to make any arrests of small fry, but to destroy the gang's property, to harass them and cost them money, and to fray their nerves. The commissioner wanted the drop completely demolished.

We wanted records, of course, but found none, so we went to work with the sledges and soon were wading ankle-deep in bootleg beer. Over 300 barrels of suds bubbled into the dirt as we stove in bungs. We were about through with the job when a yellow Packard roadster roared up to the gate, and out jumped Dutch Schultz. Nobody recognized him but me. His face was impassive, ready to smile if he could make a deal, effect a payoff.

"Where you fellows from?" he said to George Faust.

"Who are you?" George snapped back at him.

"I'm just a trucker," he said. "I'm looking for one of my trucks and thought it might be here."

"That's a load," I yelled to George. "That's the Dutchman, Arthur Flegenheimer, alias Dutch Schultz."

He turned toward me, and recognition glittered in his eyes. "So you're the dirty sonofabitch who jobbed me!" he cried.

If I'd had more experience, or more self-control, I would have laughed in his face. But I was a kid and full of pride, and I didn't intend to let any mobster call a police officer a dirty name . . . especially if that police officer was me. My reflexes worked faster than my reason, and I threw a looping right that caught him on the jaw and draped him over the hood of his yellow Packard.

He came slowly erect, removed his silk handkerchief from his breast pocket, and dabbed at his mouth. It came away stained red. He looked at the blood and then at me. He said in a dead-level voice, "I'm gonna have a lot of influence in this town, copper, and I'll never forget you."

Every word he said turned out to be 100 per cent true.

Chapter Two

BLACK PADDY'S

"HAND O' GOD"

A few months after my encounter with Dutch Schultz, I was again summoned to the commissioner's office. He said, "This is a delayed Christmas present for your excellent undercover work on the Schultz gang. In the special orders published tomorrow, you will be promoted to the rank of acting detective sergeant, second grade. Your assignment remains unchanged. Keep up the good work." Then he handed me a new badge.

Alone in the hall, I sneaked a look. The badge glittered in my hand, the most handsome thing in the world. I had wanted to be a cop ever since I was a kid, just an ordinary cop on the beat keeping peace in the neighborhood, but I had never aspired to a gold shield. I wondered what the old gang of kids would think if they could see me now. There was Herby Farrell, Simp McGuire, Kid Wolfin, Meyer Powkowsky . . . the only kid on the block who could lick me. I wondered what had happened to them. I knew damn well they weren't cops.

23

The amazement was that even *one* kid out of my neighborhood had become a cop. In 1907, when I was eight years old and first decided to become a cop, my widowed mother, my brother, and I lived on West 98th Street near Columbus Avenue. It was a street of cold-water flats occupied almost entirely by us poor Irish. The buildings we lived in were ugly, and our lives, as observed by outsiders, must have appeared drab. Yet, we were convinced that our Irishness and our Catholicism gave us riches not shared by other people. Even as a child I felt set apart and a little special when I looked at the non-Irish, the non-Catholic. I suppose it was because the Irish stories I used to hear the adults tell had so much violence in them, such towering heroics. And as for religion, well, I went to a Protestant church with a pal of mine once when I was ten years old, and I found it drab and unexciting. Where were the beautiful vestments? the incense? the Latin chants? the whole dramatic ritual of the Mass? And where was the throat-tightening excitement (and fear!) when you stepped into the confession box to be alone with God and your own sins? No, I felt very glad to be spared the cold services of the Protestants.

As I look back on those days now, I can see that this feeling of superiority made us Irish-Catholic kids cocky, and sometimes even bullies. On Broadway to the west of us lived Jews, to the north were Negroes, sprinkled among us were Germans and Poles—we fought them all. I must add, however, that too often we didn't fight over any convictions of race or religion—often we fought just because there wasn't anything else to do.

My gang, the small fry, used to steal food from the grocery stores. Potatoes were the best thing to steal because we could make a "hot mickey" with them. This was done by putting some burning sticks of wood in the bottom of a tin can punctured with holes, and then swinging it on the end of a string. The forced draft soon turned the wood into charcoal, then we added the potato and swung it until the potato was cooked. A hot mickey made at twilight in the alley behind 98th Street is the most delicious thing I have ever eaten in my life.

When we weren't busy with our own devilment, we observed and admired the hell raising of the older guys. There was a teen-age group called the "Pearl Button Gang." They were not gangsters in the sense the city was to know gangsters after World War I. They were just young punks spoiling for a fight. They originally organized to keep the Negroes off our block, but that was just an excuse they used to look for trouble.

There were older toughs who hung out in Jordan's saloon at the corner of 98th Street and Columbus Avenue. Among these were the "cop fighters," men who went hunting for a uniform the minute they got drunk.

Here was where we kids looked for our heroes. These men weren't very laudable, but where else could we turn? In those days there was no radio or TV to give us ready-made heroes; we couldn't afford to go to the silent films; we wouldn't have been caught dead reading a book.

Toughness and daring were the things we admired, and it never occurred to us that we might find these qualities any place in our small world except among the Pearl Button Gang or the loafers in Jordan's saloon.

However, the summer I was eight years old I suddenly found it some place else—in the person of a round-headed detective named Quinn. I found courage, too, in a patrolman named "Black Paddy" Sullivan, a man who never avoided Jordan's saloon on his beat, though he knew that eight times out of ten he'd face a drunken cop fighter when he hove into view. But there was another quality in Black Paddy that changed my whole attitude toward cops, a very important quality I hadn't found among the Pearl Button Gang. Black Paddy was a man of his word.

I learned this one summer day when he came with slow and mountainous dignity down our street, saw me sitting on the curb, and motioned me to him. I approached, but not too close.

He said, "You're the laddie who's been takin' our night-sticks, ain't ya, now?"

"I don't know nothin' about 'em!" I cried.

I lied, of course. What had happened was this. The cops in our neighborhood were big but not fast, and so they had devised a method of dealing with us kids. Taking careful aim, they'd throw their nightsticks at us. Most of the cops could catch a running kid at 20 yards. The crack of a flying nightstick across your back . . . wow!

Since I was the fastest in our gang, it fell to me to execute the counterattack. I'd hang back until a cop threw his stick at a kid, then I'd dash in and grab it before he could recover it, and run like hell for Central Park while bellows of rage followed me. Once over the low wall and into the park, I'd bury the club. Within a month's time, I had at least ten clubs safely below the sod.

But I denied it to Black Paddy. I looked at him with wide-eyed innocence. "I don't know what yer talkin' about," I said.

"Yer name's Bobby McAllister and yer the fastest lad on

the block and ya do know what I'm talkin' about," he said. "Now what did ya do with them sticks?"

"I buried them in the park," I admitted reluctantly.

"Hm-m-m. Why don't ya be a good lad and dig 'em up and bring 'em into the station house?"

"Why should I?" I demanded.

"Well, now, because officers of the law ain't rich men. And every time you take one of them sticks, some poor man has gotta buy a new one for a dollar and fifty cents."

"Aw, the department gives them to you," I scoffed.

Black Paddy shook his head sadly. "The only thing the department gives us is this." He pointed to his potsy, the shield on his broad chest.

Money was something extremely scarce around our house and therefore something I had respect for. My mother worked six days a week as seamstress at Lord and Taylor's for ten dollars. Every day after school I sold newspapers at the 110th Street subway exit for a profit of maybe twenty-five cents a day. The cost of a nightstick deducted from our family's budget would have been a great hardship. My conscience began to hurt me, but I was still wary.

I said, "If I bring 'em into the station house, you'll pinch me."

"Bring 'em in and no questions asked," he said. Then raising his right hand in an oath, "Me hand o' God upon it."

I bargained further. "And the cops won't throw 'em no more at me?" He paused on that condition and rubbed his chin. I added, "If I ain't doin' nothin'?"

"If you ain't doin' nothin'," he agreed.

"And my brother neither, if he ain't doin' nothin'?"

"Yer brother neither," Black Paddy said.

One hour later I walked into the station house and deposited the nightsticks on the desk. The sergeant looked at them, then at me, and his face turned red.

"So you're the little sonofabitch . . . ," he cried, and made a lunge for me.

I turned to run but came smack up against Black Paddy, who had just come out of the muster room. He clasped me around the shoulders, and for a moment I struggled wildly, but I couldn't break his grip.

"It's all right, laddie . . . it's all right," he kept saying, until I calmed down. Then he turned to the enraged sergeant and said, "Sarg, I promised him immunity."

"Immunity!" the sergeant roared. "I'll give him some immunity . . . on the seat of his britches."

Black Paddy shook his head. "I give him me hand o' God on it."

There were more shouts and even threats, but Black Paddy would not be moved, and I left the station house free.

As I walked slowly home I thought about what I had just seen. All the sergeant's anger and all his authority couldn't shake Black Paddy in his determination to protect me. He had given his word and refused to go back on it. I had never before seen this sort of thing. The Pearl Button Gang often sent us kids on errands, for a pack of butts or a bottle of beer, promising us a nickel for the service. When we returned, like as not, they'd flip us a penny or maybe just give us a boot in the keister.

I had a new hero . . . and it was a cop!

As I look back now, I realize that everything about me as a kid seemed to indicate that I would grow up to run with the outlaws instead of the law. But one police officer gave his word and kept it! By such small things is a boy's future shaped. God bless Black Paddy Sullivan.

About a year later something else happened that was to have a great influence on my future. I won a foot race in the schoolyard. My brother George and I attended Holy Name School on 97th Street and Amsterdam Avenue, and there was one boy who thought he was the best runner there . . . his name was Gagliastro. One day he boasted, "There ain't nobody in this school can beat me."

My brother said to me, "Go ahead, Bobby, show him."

I hung back, and Gaggy sneered, "He don't dare race me."

Now a challenge was something you couldn't turn down . . . not in my neighborhood. A challenge to steal potatoes, to climb the elevated, to fight, to run . . . you just had to accept them all.

Gaggy and I lined up, while two boys held a string taut on the other side of the playground. At the word "Go!" I ran with all the speed I could drive into my legs. I ran headlong, blind, almost hysterical with a desire to win. I hit the makeshift tape at full speed, completely forgetting the school wall that now loomed up before me to receive the full impact of my body. When I finally fought my way back up out of the blackness, I was on my back, and there was my brother George laughing and dancing about me and shouting, "You beat him! You whipped him! You're the champ!" He didn't seem to care if I had a fractured skull, which I almost did.

"That kid's nuts," Gaggy kept saying after that. "I slowed up to miss that wall, but he run right into it, head first. If he ain't been nuts before, he sure is now, after that bump. And just wait till the Parochial School Championships. He'll be eatin' my dust."

At that moment I knew I wanted to beat Gaggy at the Parochial Championship races more than I wanted anything else in the world. But the races were to be run at Clason Point, way out in the Bronx almost to the Sound, and I didn't have the carfare. I might have held out some of my newspaper money, but I knew I just couldn't do that. Mom needed every cent of what George and I brought home. The Parochial Championships began to fade.

Then a miracle happened . . . a miracle in the form of a neighborhood dude named Frank Higbee. With his tightly nipped coats, cloth-topped shoes, and derby hat tilted far over his right eye, he was one of the sportiest dressers in the neighborhood. He was a lightweight, fighting for the New Pola A.C., at 116th Street. You could tell he was a boxer just watching him go down the street—light on his toes and occasionally dancing a couple of steps as if feinting at an opponent. We kids used to step aside real respectfully whenever he walked by.

I was shouting my papers at the subway exit one evening when he came up to me and said, "I hear you beat Gaggy in the schoolyard. That right, kid?"

"That's right, Mr. Higbee," I said.

"Okay, I'm takin' ya to Clason Point tomorrow. Get yerself some running clothes and shoes, and meet me here eight tomorrow morning."

The moment he turned his back I ran home, yelling as I went. "Mom! . . . Mom!" I burst into the flat. "I'm going to Clason Point for the championship races! Mom. . . ."

"Bobby . . . wait a minute! Tell me slowly, now."

I repeated the story more slowly and in detail, concluding with, "And Mr. Higbee's a fighter, Mom. And he heard about me and he's gonna take me . . . pay the trolley fare and everything."

"God bless him," she said quietly.

To squeeze the last bit of excitement out of it, I told the whole story over again, right from the beginning. "And then he said to me, Mom, then he said, 'Okay, I'm takin' ya to Clason Point tomorrow. Get yerself some runnin' clothes and meet me here at eight o'clock in the morning.' That's exactly what he said."

Running clothes! I hadn't mentioned that part before, hadn't even thought about it. How could I get running clothes? The same thought hit Mom, and I saw a look of sadness come over her face, and she turned abruptly away to stir the stew. Suddenly tears stung my eyes, and I was ashamed of them and walked quickly to the front room to stare out the window. I had never minded being poor, I didn't know what it was like to be anything else, but not to be able to go to Clason Point just because I didn't have any running clothes . . . !

This seemed to me to be unfair. I knew Mom was sad about it, and that too was unfair. Who arranged it so that some kids had running clothes and others didn't? Who could be that mean? As I asked myself these bitter questions, I kept my eyes guiltily away from the sky and on the street below. I knew my thoughts were wrong, maybe even blasphemy, but I couldn't help them. I swallowed hard to choke back a sob I felt pushing up in my throat.

"Bobby," Mom called from the kitchen.

"Yeah?" I muttered.

"I've got an idea. Come here a minute."

I ran to the kitchen to find her holding up her bathing suit and looking at it with a speculating eye. Then she held it up against me and saw that it came almost to my ankles. She said, "I think I can remodel this to fit you, Bobby. It would make a good running suit."

It would make a wonderful running suit, I thought, but. . . .

The one thing Mom had always loved to do was go swimming. When my Dad was alive, we used to make Sunday trips to the beach, and Mom would splash about in the breakers and giggle, and look as flushed and excited as a schoolgirl. After Dad died we couldn't afford to go to the beach, and Mom put her bathing suit away. But every spring she would take it out and hang it on the line for airing, as if we were going to the beach next weekend. We never did, of course, and every fall she'd lovingly repack it in sachet again. Now, if she cut it up for me, it meant the end of even that dim hope.

I knew I should speak out and tell her not to cut up her suit. I knew it was her most precious possession, but I couldn't say the words. Late that night, when George and I were supposed to be asleep, I heard the snip-snip of her scissors as she cut the suit apart. I put the pillow over my head to try to blot out the sound.

I met Mr. Higbee right on time the next morning and we climbed aboard a trolley that took us through the beautiful open country of the Bronx. How thrilling it was to ride through strange farmland, to see animals, to smell country air and feel a sun that seemed totally different from the one that filtered through the soot of 98th Street. Mr. Higbee filled me up with hot dogs and soda pop at the transfer

points, not a recommended diet for an athlete, but it didn't
bother my young stomach a bit.

When we arrived at Clason Point, there was so much
noise and confusion that I hardly knew what I was doing.
Mr. Higbee stayed right beside me to see that I didn't get
lost. I was given a number for my back and entered in the
midget-class 60-yard dash. I won my first two heats and
came up to the finals to discover my old enemy Gaggy in
the lane next to me.

He took one look at me, then turned to the other racers
and cried out, "Hey, what we doin'? Racin' *girls?*" He
pointed to me. "See . . . *she's* wearin' a *skirt!*"

I looked down and realized that Mom had failed to cut
the skirt off her bathing suit. Humiliation and rage filled
me, and I started for Gaggy. Mr. Higbee grabbed me and
said, "Don't lose your wind by fighting him. Run him. Run
his legs into the goddam ground. That's the way to whip
him."

At this moment the starter appeared, and we were forced
to take our marks. I eyed Gaggy with a hatred that was as
deep and unforgiving as a human being can feel. He had
not just made fun of me, but of my Mom's suit . . . and
therefore of my Mom.

"On your mark," came the crisp command. I crouched.
"Get set." I strained every nerve and muscle. "Go!"

I lunged forward. The vision of Gaggy's hateful face exploded me down the track and toward the distant tape.
Moments later, it broke across my chest.

When they presented me with the gold medal, I was so
happy there was no room left for hate. I would even have
shaken hands with Gaggy if he had offered. But he didn't.

I showed that medal to every passenger on the trolley ride home. When I hit my neighborhood, I was my own best advertiser. Mom must have heard the news when I was a block away. I ran up the stairs and burst into our flat.

"Here it is, Mom," I cried. "A gold medal. I'm champion. And it's for you, Mom . . . the medal. It's for you."

She was laughing and weeping at the same time. I told her all about the race, all about the whole amazing day. Then I told it to her over again. After we had both calmed down a bit, I said to her, "Do you like it, Mom? The medal?"

"I love it, Bobby."

"You like it . . . better than your bathing suit?"

She laughed and grabbed me into her arms and said, "I like it better than anything in the whole world, except my two boys."

Chapter Three

A COP'S BUFF

SHOULD NEVER DREAM

One way or another, a man has got to fight. My Uncle George Parker was a man who solved this problem in a unique manner.

Uncle George was himself unique. He not only had a great deal of money (or so it seemed to us), but he was a man of the world who wore impeccably tailored clothes with black braid around the cuffs and lapels of his coat. His manners were courtly, and he talked of things I had never heard before: of politics, the theater, and the famous people he knew.

Mom and my Aunt Nora, who lived with us off and on, both adored their brother, and his visits to our flat were great occasions for them. They would sit in rapt attention while he told of Broadway and downtown. They would laugh at his quips, blush and reprove him for his slightly naughty jokes, and nod in solemn agreement with his political opinions. Uncle George gave them a glimpse of the big, wonderful world that existed outside of 98th Street—he lent

35

drama and glamour to their lives. I used to look at his trim figure and erect carriage and wonder if I would ever be so witty, so masterful, and so successful.

After a time, however, I discovered I had made a wrong estimate of my uncle. He was witty, but he was neither masterful nor successful. He was a defeated man who didn't even practice his profession of law. He had married a rich woman whom he grew to hate, and he came to our flat to escape her.

His visits always followed the same pattern. He and his airedale dog, named Fighting Briar, would arrive in the early evening. He'd make a deep bow to kiss his sisters' hands, and then settle down to regale us all with his stories for a couple of hours. At about eleven o'clock he'd grow restless and begin to sneak frequent looks at a gold watch attached to an enormous gold chain draped across his brocade waistcoat. Between looks at the watch, he would scratch Fighting Briar's ear and murmur advice to be patient, though the dog showed no signs of impatience.

"You'll stay the night?" Mom would always say.

"Be delighted," he'd reply, then stand up and smooth his clothes. "Think Fighting Briar needs a walk before turning in. Just once around the block should do it." He'd snap the leash on Briar and walk to the door, then turn back with a half-apologetic smile and say, "Don't wait up. I'll let myself in."

The moment he was gone, Aunt Nora and Mom would exchange worried glances. "You don't suppose . . . ," Mom would say.

"I'm afraid so," Aunt Nora would answer.

"Maybe . . . maybe not this time," Mom would come back hopefully.

Aunt Nora would shrug her shoulders, sigh heavily, and make up a bed for Uncle George on the living-room sofa.

If I stayed awake long enough, I'd hear him come home around three in the morning. First would come the distant sound of drunken, stumbling steps on the lower stairs. Finally he'd burst open the door to our flat and reel into the front room, crooning softly to Fighting Briar, whom he carried in his arms. There would be a crashing sound as he flopped down on the sofa, then almost at once the sound of snoring as man and dog slept it off.

Uncle George's usual stay was three days; the entire time after the first evening's visit being spent between Jordan's saloon and the sofa in the front room. On the morning of the fourth day, his wife would appear and take him home.

Her name was Amanda, and she was a thin-lipped woman with eyes as friendly as two wet stones. She would arrive before Uncle George was out of bed, stand in the middle of the room, and glare at him until his eyes wavered and fell away. Then she would invariably say, her voice full of scorn, "Look at him!"

Uncle George seemed to shrivel up. He was no longer witty, nor masterful, nor anything at all except a man being whipped by a woman, a man with no courage or strength to defend himself.

She would hound him relentlessly. "All his fine manners, all his big talk . . . and what is he? A bum! A weak, spineless bum who can't even lick a bottle of whiskey. That's what I married!"

When Uncle George had been reduced to a pitiful thing, she would turn and march out of the room. He'd climb to his feet, smooth his rumpled clothing, and then follow meekly after her, his faithful dog at his heels.

But Uncle George fought back, in a way. It took several of his visits to our flat before I discovered just how. One night I heard him come home, but he didn't fall asleep at once; I heard him moving about and talking in a low, crooning voice to his dog. Finally I crept out of bed and into the living room to discover a most amazing scene.

Stretched out on the floor was the bleeding hulk of Fighting Briar. Great patches of hair were torn off, gaping wounds rent his chest and forelegs, and he was matted and soaked with blood. Uncle George knelt over him, his coat off, his sleeves rolled to the elbow, working quickly from a bowl of water and a small box of surgical instruments. While he worked, he crooned a low song of praise to his dog.

"The fightin'est dog that ever lived, that you are, Briar. No dog in this town can take you . . . no dog in this state. By God, there's no dog in the whole United States like you, Fighting Briar . . . do you hear me, boy? You're the best . . . the champion of them all. What you did to that other dog tonight! . . . man, o man . . . what you did to him!"

"Uncle George!" I gasped. "What happened?"

He gave me a quick glance and said, "Just patching up the champion a bit, boy. You can help me now you're here. Hand me the instruments as I call for them. The razor first. Quick, now."

I jumped to obey. First he shaved the hair off from around all the wounds where muscle and tendon showed beneath the parted skin. Then he sprinkled them with antiseptic and finally sewed them up with surgeon's needle and suture. All during this, Fighting Briar didn't make a sound. Though it must have been painful, he moved only his big brown eyes to follow his master's face.

The job completed, Uncle George washed his hands and then began to scrub the blood off the floor. "What happened, Uncle George?" I asked again.

"Little fight in the back room of Jordan's saloon," he said. Then, proudly, "Man brought a dog twice Briar's weight, but we whipped him. No dog that ever lived can whip my Briar. I bred him, raised him, and trained him to be a fighter, and he's the best in the world. The champion!"

I tried to understand all this, but it seemed terribly strange to me. I said, "Uncle George, you love Briar a whole lot, but you make him fight and get hurt. Why is that?"

Uncle George turned on me, and there was a fierceness in his face I had never seen. "In this world you have to fight to be anything. Remember that, boy. If you don't fight, you're nothing . . . worse than nothing. You think Briar feels those wounds? Not at all . . . because he's a fighter, a champion! It's when you're not a fighter that you hurt . . . then you hurt real bad."

Having said that, Uncle George lay down on the floor beside Briar and put his cheek on top of the dog's head. There were tears in his eyes . . . he was crying.

I was only thirteen, but I understood my uncle was talking about himself when he said how defeat could hurt; I realized that this airedale dog was doing the fighting for both of them.

It was Uncle George and Fighting Briar who were indirectly responsible for my becoming a cop's buff—something I'd had my heart set on but didn't know how to achieve. A buff is an errand boy for a police squad or a precinct, and since Black Paddy had become my hero I wanted to serve the force in this manner. Uncle George indirectly made it possible. One evening there was a knock on our door, and there was suave and immaculate Uncle George, and with him Fighting Briar. Mom and Aunt Nora came to greet him with fluttering cries and then sat wide-eyed for a couple of hours while he told them stories. Finally he pulled his big watch from his pocket, examined it seriously for a moment, and announced he'd better take Briar for a little walk. This time I crept out of the flat and followed him.

At Jordan's saloon I peeked through the window and watched my uncle at the bar, surrounded by a group of men who listened respectfully to his conversation. At this moment a group of Negroes approached the saloon from the direction of 99th Street, the tallest of them leading a dog by a piece of rope. It was the biggest, ugliest, meanest-looking dog I had ever seen, and I knew at once that here was a challenge to Fighting Briar. He was a bull terrier, I think, but with several other breeds mixed in, and he was deeper of chest than Fighting Briar and had a weight advantage of at least 10 pounds. My heart sank.

The men went into the saloon with their fighter and engaged my uncle in a conference. After a time I saw him nod his head and everybody except the bartender went into the back room. I couldn't see what was going on, but in a few moments there came the sounds of a dogfight such as I'd never heard. The excited, drunken shouts of the men joined the sound of the snarling and snapping dogs. Surely Briar was being torn limb from limb by that monster. Poor Uncle George!

Suddenly the door to the back room burst open, and a streak of white shot out through the swinging doors and past me. It was the bull terrier, running as if the hounds of hell were on his tail. The tall Negro came running after him, shouting curses at the top of his lungs. He paused on the sidewalk by me to watch his dog disappear from view down Columbus Avenue, then he spat out an oath and slunk off in the opposite direction.

A moment later Uncle George appeared with Briar in his arms. Blood was running from a dozen wounds and staining my uncle's fine clothes, but he was too happy to care. "The champion . . . the champion!" he cried over and over. "By God, he did it . . . the champion!" He spotted me and said, "Come on, boy, we've got to go home and fix Briar up."

"Yes, sir," I cried, and fell into step beside him, proud to walk with the champion.

Mom screamed when she opened the door, for the three of us were bloody by now, but Uncle George soon calmed her, and he and I set about our work with the surgical instruments.

After Briar was sewed up, I said, "Who was that man who brought the other dog, Uncle George?"

"His nickname is Freckles," my uncle said. "That's all I know about him, except the fact his dog can't lick mine."

Then I remembered that the Negro's face hadn't been an even brown in color, but blotched with pink. Thus his nickname. Freckles was a small-time stick-up man. He was to make me a buff.

Uncle George didn't come around for a long time after that, and the spring and summer days slipped uneventfully by. I sold my papers on the corner every day, and the headlines were full of things happening in all parts of the world, but nothing ever happened on 98th Street. In my soprano

voice I called out the fact that the Equitable Life sky-
scraper was on fire, but that was in downtown Manhattan.
Later on I shrilled the news that the *Titanic* had hit an
iceberg and sunk, but that was even farther away. At thirteen years of age, I began to think that nothing exciting
would ever happen to me.

It was on a sultry August afternoon that I heard the
shot. I was sitting on the fire escape outside our kitchen
window when the sound came from the tenement across
our back yard. Immediately a man leaped through one of
the windows, raced up the fire escape to the roof, and
streaked away through the forest of chimneys toward
Columbus Avenue.

I watched this with open mouth, not quite understanding
the meaning of it until I heard loud cries from the room he
had left. "Police! Help! Help!"

How often I had dreamed of being present at the scene
of a crime, and by my daring and resourcefulness appre-
hending the criminal! But now I could only stare, my
mouth agape. It just didn't seem real. Later—how long it
was I don't know—two cops stuck their heads out that
window and then climbed onto the fire escape.

"He went that way!" I yelled, pointing. "Over the roof-
tops."

The cops ran up to the roofs and made a search, but he
was gone. The criminal had escaped through some other
building to the street. I joined the crowd milling about the
street in front of the building and learned that the fleeing
man had committed a murder! There had been an argument
during a dice game in that flat, and he had pulled a gun and
killed a man.

At last the horse-drawn ambulance arrived, and a

shrouded body was carried down the narrow stairs and loaded into the van. The driver gave a crack to his whip, and the horses trotted off toward Central Park with their burden, releasing the spell that held us silent. Now we began to chatter, to speculate.

The murderer had been a big man, we all agreed, and a Negro, and . . . suddenly I was electrified! I knew him! I raced for the 100th Street station house.

"That murderer . . . on 99th Street! I know him!" I cried breathlessly to the lieutenant on the desk. "It was Freckles . . . that's his nickname! His dog fought my uncle's dog in Jordan's saloon. It was Freckles . . . I'm sure of it."

"Yeah, kid," he said with a wave of his hand, "we know it was Freckles. Now get the hell outta here."

Freckles was not apprehended for the rest of the summer. From time to time I'd see Detective Quinn prowling the neighborhood and asking questions, but Freckles had dropped out of sight. Detective Quinn looked like a bulldog and wore his derby hat low, resting right on his ears. He had the reputation of being fearless and relentless, and I had no doubt that sooner or later he'd track down Freckles.

As Thanksgiving approached, my brother got me an after-school job where he worked with Mr. Levy, the butcher. George and I were delivery boys, and we depended largely upon tips. The trouble was, however, that the majority of deliveries were in tenements where we had to send the meat to upper floors on a dumb-waiter. Without a face-to-face meeting with the customer, the tip was usually nonexistent. We figured a method of overcoming that. Each night we'd letter cards to be dropped in our hat and sent upwards with the next day's orders. The cards read:

> Thanksgiving is here,
>   Turkeys are fat.
> Don't forget to drop a coin
>   In the butcher boy's hat.

This scheme worked out pretty well. There were times, of course, when no tip was put in the hat. Sometimes, even the hat failed to come back down the dumb-waiter, and we'd have to climb upstairs to retrieve it.

It was the day before Thanksgiving and I was pushing the delivery cart loaded with a large order for Mrs. Block's boardinghouse on 97th Street when I saw a familiar figure slinking along Columbus Avenue, keeping near the buildings. It was Freckles!

With a pounding heart, I raced the delivery wagon up to Columbus, trying to keep him in view. As I made the corner, I saw him pause, look up and down the avenue, then enter Bruder's Pawnshop. I deserted the delivery wagon and headed for the station house.

Squat Detective Quinn was lounging on the front steps of the station house, puffing on a big cigar. I stammered out my story to him, and without question, he followed me back to the avenue. As we neared Bruder's, he said, "You stay back, kid. There may be trouble."

Then slowly and methodically Detective Quinn took a jackknife out of his pocket, opened it, cut the burning end of his cigar off, dropped the cigar butt and the knife back in his pocket, took his gun out of the holster, settled his derby hat firmly on his head, and walked into the pawnshop. Inside was a known killer, and I had expected the police would bring a riot squad and surround the place and shout for him to come out into the open. But no; Detective Quinn just walked in alone.

There was a long, terrible moment of silence, then a volley of shots. A minute later Detective Quinn walked back out, his hat still square on his head, his gun still in his hand. I ran up to him and saw that he was examining a bullet hole in the sleeve of his coat.

"Damnation!" he was muttering. "The Missus is gonna give me what-for."

I looked past him into the pawnshop. Stretched out on the tile floor was Freckles, his head lying in a spreading pool of blood. He was shot between the eyes. I stared in horror and fascination until Detective Quinn put his hand on my shoulder and turned me away.

"What's your name, boy?" he asked.

"Bobby McAllister," I said, "and I want to be a buff."

"You'd be a good one. Come around to the station house tomorrow and we'll put you to work." He pressed a dollar bill into my hand.

I became buff for the 9th squad: twelve men who worked from four in the afternoon until midnight to keep law and order along upper Riverside Drive and West End Avenue. They were on fixed posts with no time off for coffee or food, or to get warm, or to care for any personal needs. They worked twenty-seven days at a stretch before receiving thirty-two hours off. A good buff was a godsend for these hard-working men, and I tried to be a good one.

My job was to be an errand boy, rush them raincoats from the station house if it started to rain, bring them warmer clothes from their homes if it started to snow, sneak them coffee and sandwiches when they got hungry, and "lay chickie" for the sergeant while they consumed them. The very first night I was on the job big Mike Curtain, who was on fixed post at 102d Street and Riverside Drive, said to me, "Bobby, run get Pete and me some hot coffee to thaw us out."

I sped toward Broadway and swaggered into a delicatessen, conscious of the importance of my mission. I returned with the steaming coffee to find Mike and his partner stamping their feet and swinging their arms to drive out the chill of the sharp wind that blew off the Hudson River. They reached for the coffee eagerly.

"Ya know what Sergeant Mathewson looks like, don't ya, lad?" Mike asked me.

Everyone knew Sergeant Mathewson, a great round man of 250 pounds with a flowing, white handlebar mustache and blue eyes as cold as ice water. He was known as the terror of the 100th Street station house, because he imposed the most severe penalties on his men for the slightest infraction of the rules. The patrolmen who worked his tour of duty had to be on their toes at all times . . . or else! "Sure, I know what he looks like," I said.

"You lay chickie for him. Pete and me are goin' in the basement there to have our coffee and a smoke. You see him comin', sing out . . . and no delay!"

Mike and his partner disappeared into the cellar and I was left alone. Oh, the glorious weight of that responsibility! I stared about me, guardian of the world. Across the drive was the darkly mysterious Hudson River. From time to time a river boat sailed slowly and silently downstream, its navigational lights reflecting blearily in the water. What if one of these boats sprang a leak and began to sink, imperiling the lives of crew and passengers! Who would give the alarm? Bobby McAllister!

From down Riverside Drive came the crisp clop-clop of

horse's hoofs, and past me rolled a surrey drawn by a high-stepping mare. What if the horse should suddenly bolt and run away! Who would bring help? Me!

I glanced at the row of elegant buildings that stretched southward along the curving drive for as far as I could see. These were my responsibility, too. Fire? Murder? Rescue of the innocent and apprehension of the wicked would come swiftly because of that alert and stalwart buff attached to the 9th squad!

I leaned against a lamppost and tried to think up bigger and better disasters; I was lost in visions of my own heroism.

Suddenly my visions began to dissolve and something more concrete took their place. For a moment or so I was confused as to which was my imagination and which reality, but then it became clear and my stomach knotted with horror. Coming slowly toward me on his bicycle, like some majestic doom, was Sergeant Mathewson. He was still several blocks away, and in the darkness it was impossible to see his uniform, but I knew his shape. His great bulk was balanced on the slender wheel, looking at that distance like an orange stuck on a toothpick. But he was growing in size with alarming speed. Already he had assumed the proportions of a grapefruit . . . and in another few minutes, he would be Sergeant Mathewson himself! I turned and ran to the basement doorway and shouted into the darkness, "The sergeant!"

Out tumbled the two patrolmen, Pete running swiftly around the corner to his post, Mike taking up position by the street lamp I had just left. In another moment the sergeant came ponderously by, puffing a bit as he pumped the pedals. Mike gave him a smart salute, and he returned it. His cold blue eyes lingered suspiciously on Mike for a moment, I thought, but he moved on by and was soon out of sight.

Mike let out a sigh of relief, patted me on the shoulder and said, "Bobby, you're a good buff. Here's an extra dime for bein' so alert."

I blushed with pleasure, and with guilt, too. I didn't tell him how close to disaster we had come because of my daydreaming.

Chapter Four

SILK SHIRTS
AT SING SING

During the next few years the world was gathering itself for the convulsion of World War I, but I was unaware of it. In 1916, Pancho Villa raided New Mexico, and "Black Jack" Pershing chased him back, but the important thing in my life was the fact that I got a job as a truck driver.

The following year the 18th Amendment was voted by Congress and sent to the States for ratification. Prohibition was to play a big role in my life, but at its birth I was hardly aware of it. If I thought about it at all, I accepted the opinion generally held in my neighborhood—that it would never be ratified, never become law.

On April 6, 1917, however, there occurred an event I could not ignore. It reached right down into 98th Street, right into every other street across the entire country: America declared war on Germany.

We began to sing "Over There," and wherever I looked there was a poster of Uncle Sam with stovepipe hat, piercing eyes, and a long, bony finger that pointed directly at me. He was saying, "I want *you!*" I was only seventeen, but I lied about my age and joined the Army, humming the words, ". . . and I won't be back 'til it's over, over there!"

We had a family conference about it, George and I. He wanted to go as badly as I did—we were all red-hot patriots in those days—for President Wilson told us we were going to "make the world safe for democracy." But George and I had to consider Mom, and it was clear both of us couldn't leave her. George was now a butcher's apprentice with Mr. Levy, and making much more money than I was. Obviously he was the one to stay behind. He finally agreed.

Shortly after enlistment, I was sent to Kelly Field in Texas for training. On the first day, our sergeant lined us up and barked, "Who wants to volunteer for the air service?"

A thrill ran through me. I'd seen aviators strut about camp, carrying themselves like gods of the sky and wearing fitted blouses and Sam Browne belts and glistening leather puttees! And the riding crops they flourished with such a devil-may-care attitude! Oh, to be a pilot!

About a dozen of us volunteered, and the sergeant marched us out of our company street, across an enormous field, and toward a row of temporary hangars. There stood biplanes whose double wings glistened with silk and dope. Such frail things to carry a man aloft to battle, but we were game. We were the stuff aviators were made of!

The sergeant marched us around behind the hangars and then shoved an instrument into each pair of hands. The instrument was a shovel. "All right," he barked, "dig a latrine straight down the line there for about fifty yards."

We stood there too amazed to move. The sergeant barked the order for a second time. Some of the men began to scratch halfheartedly at the dirt. I spoke up:

"Sergeant, I thought we was gonna be aviators."

The sergeant was a grizzled career soldier with a face that was weathered and mean. He walked slowly up to me, waggled his head, and mimicked my words. "So ya thought ya was gonna be an aviator."

I gulped. "You said. . . ."

"I asked for volunteers for the air service!" he thundered. "You're in the air service! You're diggin' a goddam air-service latrine. And when you get through with this, you're gonna build a goddam air-service runway."

"But I thought. . . ."

"You *thought!*" he bellowed, his nose inches from mine. "With what? Don't ya know ya gotta be a college graduate to be an aviator? Tell me, smart guy, didn't yer thinkin' figure that one out?" Suddenly he dropped his voice real soft and sweetly sarcastic, and he screwed his mouth up as if he were going to kiss me. "Or maybe I mistook you," he purred. "Mebbe you got a college ejication. Mebbe yer a Haw-vahd man!"

The other guys began to snicker. I picked up my shovel and began to dig. I dug for the rest of the war . . . air-service latrines and air-service landing fields all over France.

In the spring of 1919, in the little town of Garden City, Long Island, I was discharged from the Army. When I arrived in New York, I saw that the town was fixed up for a great celebration. Fifth Avenue was hung with flags from end to end, and there was a huge plaster victory arch built over the avenue at Madison Square. In front of the Public Library at 42d Street, there was a shrine of pylons and lamps called "The Court of the Heoric Dead." Bunting hung from every building, and searchlights probed the sky after dark. All this was to welcome home the warriors, the heroes. I counted myself neither.

I watched on the sidewalk at 42d Street with the rest of the crowd as the 27th Division marched up the avenue. The crowds cheered, confetti filled the air, and the bands played "The Long, Long Trail." Across the street from me, on the library steps, was a reviewing platform, and from it the soldiers were welcomed home by a natty young secretary to Mayor Hylan. His name was Grover Whalen.

After the ceremony I went home to 98th Street. But it wasn't home any more. Mom had died while I was in France, Aunt Nora had moved out West, Uncle George had left his wife and disappeared entirely, and now there was nothing on this street but buildings. My brother was a full-fledged butcher with Mr. Levy, and lived in a rented room in Peg Bradley's flat on 104th Street. I moved in with him and started looking for a job.

There just weren't any jobs that spring and summer. The country was in a postwar slump, and there was little to do but hang out in front of the 102d Street firehouse. My old boyhood pals were there, Herby Farrell and Simp McGuire, and on those long, warm spring days, we refought the war. The monotony was broken every now and then by a Suffragette parade on Central Park West, and we'd go over and yell at the girls, but most of the time there was nothing to do but talk about the war and sports. There was a lot of argument about the coming heavy-weight championship fight in Toledo. Herby thought that the champ, Jesse Willard, was going to flatten the little guy, Jack Dempsey. The rest of us thought different because of the fact that Jesse was an old man . . . thirty-four years old! We were right. Oh, we were sharp on sports, I can tell you, but we didn't have jobs.

Some of the guys began drinking pretty heavily. Prohibition was scheduled to go into effect on June 30, 1919, and Jordan's saloon was crowded with guys who wanted to drink it all up while there was still a chance. They didn't know there would always be a chance.

I couldn't find forgetfulness in Jordan's saloon, however, because I neither liked whiskey, nor could I pay for it. There seemed nothing to cushion me from the facts of my life. I was no war hero. I was jobless. I was purposeless.

Then one day the newspapers announced that the police department was going to hire several hundred new patrolmen, and at that moment everything changed for me. I realized that I had always wanted to be a cop, and here was an opportunity. Suddenly I had a purpose. That night I tore the clipping out of the paper and stuffed it in my wallet. I didn't tell my brother because I wanted to surprise him. I had the idea that before he knew anything about it, in a couple of days at the most, I'd be standing before him, resplendent in my uniform. As it turned out, it wasn't all that easy.

The following morning I presented myself at police headquarters to announce I was ready to be one of New York's Finest. I was brusquely informed that, before I could even be considered for such an appointment, I had to pass a civil-service examination, and before I could pass that, there would have to be long weeks of study at the Delahanty Institute. I was disappointed, but not discouraged. Now that I had a bead on the future, nothing was going to stop me.

My brother George, God bless him, shared my excitement and continued to support me while I studied at the Institute. I had not had much formal education, and found studying the hardest work I had ever done in my life. But I was sure the reward would be worth it.

I took the civil-service exam at last and received a mark high enough to win appointment as a probationary patrolman. This meant that I had to attend the Police Academy for more study—law, rules and regulations, jujitsu, gunnery, and all the technical and physical skills necessary to keep a city of 7 million people from flying apart at the seams. It also meant that I could still flunk out of the academy and not receive my final appointment, but I didn't even consider that possibility. Having passed the civil-service exam, I knew I was destined to be a cop.

Though the months of study are long during the slow transition from applicant, to probationary, to rookie, there is a single, exact moment when you become a cop. That is when you put on your uniform for the first time. As it drew near, the anticipated thrill was tempered a bit by the cost, for a young cop's initial equipment costs him about $350 and often causes a great hardship. It certainly did with me. If it hadn't been for my brother George, as well as contributions from Peg Bradley, I don't know how I would have managed. But during my first week as a probationary patrolman, and while I was still studying at the Police Academy, George and I took the trolley down to lower Broadway where Smith and Gray, official uniform outlet, was located. There I bought my overcoat, winter blouse, winter trousers, summer blouse, summer trousers, cap, shoes, and necktie. Then we traveled back up to John Jovina's, licensed gunsmith, on Market Place, just behind headquarters, for the rest of the equipment.

The merchandise was in long glass cases, and a half-dozen clerks were standing about, but old John Jovina himself came to wait on me. He was grizzled and bent, having spent close to sixty years selling equipment, but he took his greatest pleasure in equipping us eager youngsters. From him I bought a club, nippers, headpiece, bullets, cartridge belt, holster, raincoat, rain hat, rain leggings, pen-and-pencil holder, memo-pad holder, and finally—the most important thing of all—the gun.

George said, "I want to buy the gun, Bob."

"Nothing doing," I said. "You've already loaned me money, and. . . ."

"That has nothing to do with it. I want to buy you your first gun."

"It's not fair to let you do that," I objected.

"Now look," he said, "I've watched you grow up from a snot-nosed kid stealing potatoes for hot mickies on 98th Street, and I've always known you were going to be a cop. I promised myself that when you made it, I was going to buy your gun. A graduation present, you might say. So shut up about it."

"What kind of gun you want?" John Jovina asked. "A .32? .38? .38 special?"

"The best," George said.

Jovina laid out on the glass counter a .38 special. It was a beautiful thing. Then he leaned close and said, "I make a present, too. The holster is from me . . . free of charge."

Our arms full of bundles, George and I took the subway

home where Peg and Edna Bradley were waiting for us. When we arrived, I went at once to the bedroom to put on my uniform. Carefully and solemnly I put on the black shoes, the pants, the bullet-studded belt heavy with holster and gun, the blouse and the badge, and finally the uniform cap, set straight and firm on my head. Then I stood in front of the mirror.

For a moment I thought I was looking at a stranger. That blue uniform created an existence of its own, and the reflection presented a man of dignity and responsibility. Then I grinned wryly. There was my square, homely mug grinning back at me, and I wasn't a stranger after all. But I wasn't entirely my old self. That uniform changed me; it wiped out the poverty and the meanness of my life, the lack of education, the fears and the defeats. A moment ago I had been a grown-up kid from the slums; now I was a police officer.

I took a last wondering look at the mirror, then marched self-consciously into the front room to stand before my brother and my friends. They smiled and began to applaud. I started to grin back, but something happened to that grin. It twisted, and my throat closed and my eyes stung with tears.

What a cop! I thought. Bawling my first minute in uniform!

Three months of intensive training flew by, and we held our commencement before a packed house of friends and relatives in the old Madison Square Garden. The class of '21 went through close-order drill, gave boxing and jujitsu demonstrations, and finally lined up to listen to Mayor Hylan and Police Commissioner Enright congratulate us and predict we would be a credit to the force. Commissioner Enright concluded the exercises, "You've been taught how to defend yourselves, as well as the citizens and the property of this great city. You carry a club and a gun for these purposes, but that does not give you the right to be aggressive or brutal. You wear a uniform that is both respected and feared. See that you honor that uniform. As long as you perform your duty honestly and fearlessly, I'll stand behind you through hell. Good luck and God bless you all."

We all cheered and broke for the exits, where I found George and Peg and Edna waiting for me. As we walked out of the Garden and up Fifth Avenue, George asked where I had been assigned.

"Twenty-eighth Precinct on West 68th Street," I said, "the heart of the Tenderloin."

My words were rather boastful, because this was one of the toughest areas in the city. It got the name of Tenderloin from the old days of Boss Tweed, when this area was juicy with shakedown rackets. I'd heard stories from the old-timers that, back in those Civil War days, the only way a cop could become a captain in the Tenderloin district was to buy the job from Tammany Hall, join in the shakedowns, and share the loot with Tweed. Things had changed since then, both in the city and in the police department, but it was still a rough neighborhood. I had the feeling (rightly or not) that to be sent there was an indication you had done pretty well in the academy, and showed promise of being a good tough cop.

George recognized the tone of pride in my voice and grinned at me. "You're gonna be a good cop, Bob, but don't try to lick the whole city."

I laughed at his joke. I should have taken it more seriously.

The next day I approached the precinct house with a swagger in my walk. I felt the pleasurable weight of the .38 special on my hip. I heard the faint jangle of the nippers. I was conscious of the neatness of my uniform and the brilliance of the badge on my chest.

The moment I stepped inside the station house, however, things assumed their true perspective—I was nothing but a rookie. Clustered around the alarm board were five- and ten-year men. Their uniforms were not as spanking new, nor so neatly pressed, and their figures had begun to swell around the middle; some of them wore glasses or had trouble with their arches. But they had something that was lacking in me—they moved and spoke with an attitude of authority. The years they had spent on the beat, the dangers they had faced and surmounted, the heartbreak they had seen . . . all these things gave them authority. They were the cops . . . I was only masquerading as one.

I stood in the middle of the room, not daring to go up to them, to mingle with them as an equal. They ignored me. Finally I gathered my wits together and reported to the desk, where a sergeant was on duty. I snapped him a smart salute and said, "Patrolman Robert McAllister reporting to the 28th Precinct for duty, sir."

He looked up slowly. "Yeah?" he said. "Transferred from what precinct?"

"Assigned from the Police Academy, sir."

"Oh," he said. The way he said that single word brought a blush to my face. I felt ridiculous standing at such rigid attention, and I wished I hadn't spoken in such a loud voice.

Some of the men at the alarm board turned to look at me and smiled. The smiles were not unkind, I'm sure. They were probably recalling with some fondness or sadness their own first days on the job. Still, they made me self-conscious. And what had happened to the dignity and self-assurance I had seen in the mirror last night? It had all been routed by a single word.

The sergeant leafed through the papers on the desk, found my academy records, handed them to me and said, "The captain wants to see you." I took the records with my left hand and with my right started to salute, but I stopped midway, unsure whether this was customary. But I realized I couldn't stand there with my hand halfway to the visor of my cap; it looked as if I were about to thumb my nose at the sergeant. I hurriedly completed the awkward salute and marched stiffly away, my face scarlet.

Shortly I was in the captain's private office and standing before a handsome, gray-haired man who looked more like a college professor than a policeman. He was Captain Mike Lyons. He nodded in recognition of my salute and extended his hand to receive my papers. He said, "Sit down, son."

I sat down, finding it strange to be called son when I wore the uniform of a police officer. But it was not unpleasant when it came from one obviously old enough to be my father. It was even reassuring, and I began to relax just a bit as he studied my record at the academy. Now I wished I had worked harder so he would be seeing better marks. At last he put the papers down and turned searching blue eyes on me.

He said, "Do you want to be a police officer . . . ?"

"Yes, sir," I said.

"Let me finish my question, please. Do you want to be a police officer, or did you join up only because there's a depression and you needed a job?"

"I want to be a police officer, sir. I've always wanted to, since I was a kid. I was a buff once, up in the old 100th Street station house."

He nodded and smiled. "Well, welcome home, then."

"Thank you, sir." I grinned.

He went on, "There's a few things you should know about this precinct, and about me. There may be some precincts in the city where you can do slipshod police work and get away with it, but not here. This is a big precinct and a tough one, and I expect every man to pull his own weight and a little extra. We play no favorites, and if you do good work you'll be commended, if you do bad work you'll be on the carpet. Make no mistake about this, Mc-Allister—if you're not an honest, hard-working cop, I'll give you a bad time. You're starting out clean, beginning your career, and what you do in the next few weeks and months will probably set the pattern for the next twenty years. Twenty years from now you may be a captain yourself, or you may still be a patrolman. The rank is of no importance, what will count will be your pride in your job, in your record. All those years will bear down on you and make you ashamed, or they will carry you with pride. Just remember, you'll never escape your record. Go out there tonight and start making it a good one."

At that moment I knew I was ready to go through hell for Captain Mike Lyons.

Later in the evening I entered the muster room to report for my first tour of duty, which was twelve midnight to eight in the morning. The lieutenant on my tour was a lean, pugnacious Irishman by the name of Mead. There was a habitual sneer on his face, and if Captain Lyons seemed to expect the best of his men, Mead seemed to expect the worst. When he came to my name on the roll call, he lingered over it, looking me up and down in a manner that showed he thought I'd never be a cop. I could feel my hackles rise. I determined to show him.

I was assigned to Post No. 12, a single block on 62d Street between Tenth and West End Avenues. When I heard Lieutenant Mead read it off, it sounded like any other post in the precinct; I was too green to realize that when you have but a single block to patrol, there must be something special about that block. My side partner, the man who was to patrol Tenth Avenue right next to me, was a five-year man named Dominick Quivigliao. He was a heavy-set Italian with big, gentle eyes and an easy grin.

As we began to walk toward our posts he said, "The lieutenant tossed you the hot one."

"You mean Post No. 12?"

"We call it San Juan Hill. You don't know about it?"

"One post is the same as another as far as I'm concerned," I said.

"Kid, you got a lot to learn. San Juan Hill is a battlefield. There were two murders here last month. This is where they break cops . . . especially rookies."

"What do you mean, Dominick?" I was beginning to feel a little uneasy.

"That's one of the toughest Negro neighborhoods in the city. When Mead can spare the men, he sends two cops to that post. They drop bottles on you out of the windows, throw stones from the doorways, sometimes they'll push a whole chimney off a roof on top of you. And if you panic, if you blow the whistle, they know they've got you. No matter what, you gotta stand your ground, ignore every brick or bottle until you *see* somebody throw it . . . then go after him. You gotta show 'em you're the boss of the block, then they'll let up a bit. But it ain't gonna be easy."

We walked in silence the rest of the way, coming at last to the corner of Tenth Avenue and 62d Street. I looked down the side street, down San Juan Hill, my beat. It was a narrow, squalid street lined with cold-water tenements and ending beyond West End Avenue at the New York Central tracks along the Hudson River. A single street lamp in the middle of the block threw a feeble light in a small circle, leaving the rest of the street in deep shadow. It looked quiet and deserted, but I knew it wasn't. Dominick patted me on the shoulder and said, "If you need help, just rap your stick on the sidewalk. Good luck, kid."

I started slowly down my beat. This was it. All the study at the Delahanty Institute, the civil-service exam, the work at the Police Academy, had been but preparation for this moment when I was a cop on a beat. I was alone, with what knowledge they had been able to pound into me, with what courage I could gather within myself. I was alone and in full charge. I looked at the sordid buildings and felt a great affection for them. They were not unlike the buildings I had grown up in, and now they were my responsibility. This might be a mean block, but it was mine, and I'd take care of it and keep it respectable despite itself.

Twice I traveled that block from one end to the other without seeing a thing. On the third trip they suddenly appeared. There were four of them, young toughs in their early twenties, and they gathered beneath the street light and began to pass a bottle of whiskey back and forth. As I came slowly toward them, they pretended not to see me but went on laughing and drinking and talking in loud voices. I remembered the lieutenant's last words to us in the muster room: "Keep it clean." He meant: Allow no congregating on your beat.

"All right, boys," I said to them, "break it up."

They all turned toward me, their brown faces impassive, but their eyes full of hate. For a moment there was silence as we stared at one another. Then the biggest of the four spoke up in a voice that dripped with politeness. He said, "Was you speakin' to us, mister policeman?"

"I was! I said for you to break it up. I want no congregating on my beat." They made no move, just stood there and stared at me. There was a thin smile on the big fellow's mouth. It spread wider and wider, and then he let out a long bray that was supposed to be a laugh. I felt my temper rise hotly but I choked it back down. I said, "I'm walking to the railroad tracks. When I get back, I want this street clear."

I turned from them and walked on down the street, my heels hitting hard on the pavement. Hoots of derision followed me.

"Crapper dick!"

"Go on, ya door shaker!"

"He's a yentzer! Wants our whiskey."

I didn't alter my pace by a single beat, but marched directly past West End Avenue to the railroad tracks, then turned about and started back. The four hoods hadn't moved from the light, and their admirers had begun to congregate on the surrounding steps. This was the show-down to see who was to be boss of San Juan Hill. I took a firm grip on my night stick and went forward. When I was 10 yards from them I called out, "Break it up . . . break it." I wanted them to know I was coming.

"Come on, crapper dick," the big one taunted. "I'm a bull buster."

Despite my resolution, I broke my stride and raced for them, swinging my club as I came. They parted just enough to receive my hurtling body and then closed about me, and the battle was on. I swung the club viciously and felt it land solidly on flesh and bone. There were cries of pain and rage, and for a moment they backed off, but then under the proddings of the crowd they closed again. This time they overwhelmed me and bore me down to the ground. I had an arm around the throat of the big one and I closed mercilessly, at the same time swinging at his head with my stick.

Through the grunts and the cries, I heard Dominick's voice as he charged to my rescue. The hoods suddenly broke and scattered, all except the leader; I had a death lock on his neck. Dominick stood above us, gun in hand, so I let go and climbed to my feet. I looked ruefully at my uniform. It was torn in a half-dozen places and covered with dirt. But the money this had cost me didn't really matter. I had made my first collar!

"I'm taking him to night court," I said to Dominick.

"Jesus, not in his condition," Dominick said.

My prisoner lay on the sidewalk, moaning and shaking his head, which had a deep gash in it. I said, "So I'll take him to the hospital first for some hemstitching, but I'm sure as hell gonna take him to court." I reached down and grabbed him by the collar to heave him to his feet, and off we started.

We arrived at night court on West 54th Street at about one-thirty in the morning, and by this time my prisoner had a bandage on his head and my uniform was brushed up a bit. Still, there was dried blood all over his clothes, and I had one eye rapidly turning black and closing. We two made something of a stir when we came into the courtroom.

Night court was quite a hangout for New York's sophisticated society people. They came there to watch the city's after-dark tragedies; it was all for kicks. But when I entered court, I saw that the first two rows of seats were occupied not by the thrill seekers, but by some well-dressed and extremely dignified-looking men and women. I found out later that they were civic leaders who were present to learn how night court operated.

When our case was finally called, my prisoner and I went to stand before the judge. Magistrate Fish was on the bench, and he looked down at us and said, "Well, officer, what is the charge?"

Before I could get a word out, my prisoner broke out in a stream of high-pitched words. "Yer Honor, please sir, there can't be no charge 'cause we wasn't doin' nothin' at all, sir. We was jest standin' there mindin' our own business when he come rushin' at us, swingin' his club and knockin' us down. We wasn't doin' nothin' at all, Yer Honor, sir, we was law-abiding citizens and. . . ."

That last comment made me burst out, "That's a lot of bull, Your Honor. They're all a bunch of no-good punks, and when I tell 'em to move on. . . ."

The sharply rapped gavel silenced me. Magistrate Fish

spoke in a quiet but firm voice, "Officer, the court is not interested in your opinion of the prisoner's character. Just tell what happened."

I told him exactly what happened, not being unduly modest about my part in it, either. I thought I'd give those well-dressed spectators an idea of how the men in the 28th Precinct handled mugs. When I finished my story, Magistrate Fish leaned over the bench to stare at me. He said in an incredulous voice, "You mean to say you just walked up to them and began swinging your night club?"

"I told them to move on," I said, "but they just jeered. A police officer has got to be respected, Your Honor. I intend to keep a clean beat and when I tell the mugs to do something. . . ."

He rapped his gavel and said, "Court is adjourned for ten minutes. Officer McAllister, will you come into my private chambers, please?"

I followed the judge out of the court and, as he passed the civic leaders, I saw him glance embarrassedly at their frowning faces. When we were alone in his chamber, he said, "How long you been on the force, officer?"

"About an hour and a half, sir."

He shook his head sadly. "I thought so. Now look, son, you can't beat up people any time you feel like it. You call them hoods and perhaps they are, but they're also citizens and they have rights under the law. You can't beat a man unless he commits an overt act, unless he attacks you first, or resists legitimate arrest. I have no choice but to release the prisoner. Let's hope he doesn't bring assault charges against you."

I sneaked out of court the back way and, as I walked slowly across town, I cursed myself for a bonehead.

As I walked, there came to me memories of my boyhood hero, Black Paddy Sullivan. I realized I had acted tonight in the way I had seen Black Paddy act when he kept the Pearl Button Gang in line. But Black Paddy's day was gone. This was another age and perhaps the old methods could no longer be used.

The next night when I entered the muster room, Lieutenant Mead looked at me with his cold blue eyes and I knew he'd heard all about my trouble at night court. "McAllister," he said, "didn't they teach you nothing at the academy?"

"No, sir," I said. Then, blushing as the other men began to snicker, I said, "I mean, yes, sir."

"Well, have you got anything between your ears besides lard?" I stood silent, my face scarlet. He went on, "You got yourself something of a record. Less than an hour on your beat and you're in trouble." He shook his head and muttered, "I always get 'em. If there's a prize boob in the class, he'll be sent to the 28th Precinct. I'll be damned if I know what I do to deserve it. Somebody at headquarters must have it in for me."

When I got to my beat that second night, I started slowly down the long block and saw that they were there again. The mob of idlers was gathered under the street light waiting for me. There was to be a showdown all over again. What could I do now? One thing I couldn't do was avoid them. I walked right up to them and they eyed me, not with insolence this time, but with speculation and perhaps uncertainty. The big guy was there, the bandage still on his head. He alone swaggered a bit.

I spoke directly to him. "I made a mistake last night," I said. "I should never have taken you to court. I should have beat the crap outta you and dumped you in that vacant lot over there. Okay, now I've learned, and we'll start over again tonight. I want you punks to break it up. There's gonna be no knifings, no holdups in this block while I'm on post. I'm gonna walk to the railroad tracks and when I come back, I don't want to see any of you. If you're here . . . well, this time we won't bother with the hospital or the police court. We'll just settle it among ourselves."

I marched on down the dark street to the tracks, my heart pounding with both fear and anger. If they didn't break it up, and if there was another fight, it would probably be the end of my career in the police force. But I couldn't back down now. I made the turn at the end of the street and started back, not daring to look ahead at the street light, fearing to face the terrible choice I might have to make. When I was a half-a-block away I looked . . . and the street was empty.

Black Paddy, I breathed in a little sigh of relief, you were right! It worked!

That night I made a choice that was to hold firm for the rest of my life: I chose being a tough cop instead of a cautious cop. There were to be a lot of people who said I was wrong, but I didn't see it that way. I believe that if more cops answered toughness with toughness in our cities, there would be less crime committed. I hold with the old saying, "There's a lot more law in the end of a night stick than in all the legal books."

With all the work and excitement that entered my life when I became a cop, I still devoted a lot of time to athletics. I ran and boxed in the police gym several hours each day when I was off duty. The Police Field-Day Games were due in September, and I intended to enter them, either as a sprinter or a fighter. Events shaped my decision on that question. I was to get in another jam.

It started out innocently enough when I ran into Richie Ryan one afternoon on Tenth Avenue. He was an old army buddy of mine and had won the A.E.F. lightweight title in France. He was the only man to win a decision over Benny Leonard when Benny was on his way up.

"Mac!" he cried, throwing his arm around me, "You're a cop!"

"Better than digging latrines for the air service," I said.

"Oh man! But what about the boxing you used to do. Did you give that all up?"

"Hell, no. I still throw some leather."

"Look, I got a ten rounder coming up at Jimmy De Forrest's club in Long Branch. How about being my sparring partner and helping me work out?"

I agreed on the spot. It wasn't only that I loved to box; I figured it would be good for my wind and help me train for the police games. Richie and I worked out every day during my off-duty hours. I was eager and strong and young, and I pressed him hard. He liked that. He won the New Jersey fight by a knockout in the third round.

After the fight he said, "Mac, there's a charity show for the Prisoners' Mutual Welfare League up at Sing Sing in a couple of weeks. I'm on the main go. Why don't you come along and fight a six-round prelim?"

"Sure," I agreed. I should have realized that a cop fighting in Sing Sing might well cause some trouble, but I didn't. And also, I had no way of knowing that Sing Sing in that summer of 1921 was not run by the warden, but largely by the prisoners themselves. In a few short months

the State Legislature was to launch an investigation of Sing
Sing, resulting in the indictment of the warden for homosexual relations with some of the prisoners. But I didn't
know about any of the conditions there. I was still only a
rookie.

Richie and I were riding the New York Central on our
way to Sing Sing when I said, "I forgot to ask you who
I'm fighting, Richie."

"A bum named Kid Breslin," he said. Then, grinning,
"On second thought, he's not a bum. He'll give you a
fight. But you can take him."

"Sure," I said.

"Owney's lined up a pretty good card."

"Who's Owney?"

"He's running the show. Owney Madden."

"Owney Madden!" I exclaimed. "You mean the head
of the Winona Club? The guy called 'Owney the Killer'?
That the one?"

"Yeah, that's him."

"But he's a prisoner up there. You mean he can run the
fights while he's serving time?"

Richie threw back his head and laughed. "Mac, you
got a lot to learn. Owney not only runs the fights, he runs
Sing Sing."

"Richie, you're kidding me."

"The hell I am."

"But why should the guards let him get away with anything? It doesn't make any sense."

"For two reasons. First, he's got control of the prisoners,
and that makes him pretty strong. Second, he's got a lot of
the folding stuff, and that makes the guards pretty rich."

"You mean he *bribes* them?"

Richie turned toward me and snorted, "For Chrissake, Bob, you're a cop. You know the score!" The surge of anger I felt must have shown on my face, because he put a restraining hand on my arm and said, "Now take it easy, Bob. I didn't say *you* were on the take. There's a few honest cops around, and you're probably one of them. But don't try to bull me about Sing Sing."

What could I say to him? Call him a liar? I could only pray that when we got to Sing Sing I'd find out he was all wrong. I slumped back in my seat and thought about Owney Madden. Although Owney's heyday as a gang lord had not yet arrived, he had already built up a formidable mob on New York's West Side, and his Winona Club controlled the pilfering and shakedowns in that waterfront area. When Owney had arrived in New York at the age of twelve, he knew all the tricks of the Irish in Liverpool, where every man had to fight for a job on the docks. He devised the tricks of sewing a razor blade into the peak of his cap; during the fight, he could merely bob his head to slice his opponent's jugular vein. He was reputed to have killed five men before his first arrest.

He was serving his first term in prison for the killing of Little Patsy Doyle, who made the mistake of announcing his intention to take over Owney's mob. Owney lured Patsy into a West Side saloon and shot him down, but to the amazement of everyone, there were a couple of witnesses willing to testify to that fact, and Owney was sent to Sing Sing for ten to twenty years. Now, according to my friend Richie, he was running the prison.

The train stopped at Ossining, and we taxied to the vast, gray stone pile of Sing Sing. Just inside the gate we were greeted by our host "Owney the Killer." He was small, dapper, and quite young—about twenty-five. He was dressed in a silk shirt and custom-made flannel slacks. His blue eyes were penetrating and intelligent. He spoke in the quiet voice of a modest man, but his manner soon revealed him to be just the opposite. Owney never raised his voice, because he didn't have to; nobody disputed the fact he was boss.

"How ya, pal?" he said, shaking Richie's hand warmly.

"Swell, Owney, how's yerself?"

"Okay, okay. Who's yer boy?"

"This is Bob McAllister. He'll fight Kid Breslin in the sixer."

Owney and I shook hands, then he motioned us to follow him. There were uniformed guards present, but they didn't act like guards so much as servants. They opened the doors for Owney and then trailed along behind him, waiting to do other services. With a sinking heart, I knew that Richie had been right. I looked at the guards, thinking that their shame must show on their faces, but it didn't. They only looked bored. I just couldn't understand it. If nothing else, their pride should have kept them from taking Owney's money.

We arrived in an office where a uniformed clerk sat at a desk. Owney said to Richie and me, "Gotta check your personal belongings here." Then he grinned. "Ya might be smuggling in some guns and the warden wouldn't like that."

At that moment I dropped my gun and my badge on the desk. They seemed to make a terrific clatter, and everyone in the room turned to stare at me. Finally the clerk found his voice. "What the hell is this?" he demanded.

"I'm a police officer," I said. "New York City, 3d Division, 28th Precinct."

One of the guards said, "Jesus Christ! *He's* gonna get in that ring?"

"Owney," the property clerk said, "I don't like this."

Owney stepped forward and looked me up and down. "Richie," he said finally, "gimme the score."

"You asked for a prelim fighter; I got ya one. That's all there is to it. He's a cop . . . so what?"

"So what?" snapped one of the guards. "He's goin' into a room with a couple of thousand cop haters. We don't want a murder . . . !"

Everybody began to talk and argue at once, everybody but Owney who continued to stare at me. Finally he raised his hand for silence and they all stopped talking. "Can this gee give us a good fight?" he asked Richie.

"He'll give you a good fight," Richie said.

"Okay, he goes on."

"But, Owney . . . ," one of the guards started to protest.

Owney silenced him with, "I'll see nothing happens. But maybe it would be a good idea not to pass the word he's a cop."

Everybody agreed. I agreed double.

When it was time for my bout, two keepers escorted me through the crowd of convicts to the ringside. The ring had been set up in the mess hall, and the prisoners sat at the benches and tables ordinarily used for eating purposes. The first three rows at ringside were occupied by men dressed as Owney was, in silk shirts and custom-tailored slacks. They all smoked big cigars, and were talking and laughing together like any fight crowd. You'd never know they were prisoners, but they weren't ordinary prisoners, they were the elite of Sing Sing, they were Owney's boys. Ordinary prisoners sat in the back rows and wore regulation prison uniforms.

I climbed into the ring and was conscious of a sudden increase in the buzz of conversation. Billy Joh, the referee, motioned me to my corner, and I danced a bit, eyeing Kid Breslin in the opposite corner. Then Billy introduced us, and my name brought on a hurricane of boos and catcalls. I knew then that the grapevine had received word I was a cop.

"Okay," Billy was saying, "give us a good clean fight. Go to your corners and come out fighting."

I was nervous and rusty. Aside from my sparring in gyms, this was the first time I'd had a fight since France, and when Kid Breslin charged me with a flurry of punches, I reeled backward. I didn't see a left quick enough to slide it, and it caught me flush on the ear and knocked me flat.

The dining hall went crazy with screams of elation. I could barely hear Richie shouting at me, "Stay down, Mac, take nine. Stay down."

I climbed to my feet unsteadily at the count of nine, the referee wiped my gloves, and Breslin was on me in a fury, hoping for a quick knockout. Blood was flowing from my nose and a cut on my mouth. My ear felt like it was on fire. Through the tumult I heard Richie's voice crying, "Stay in close . . . in close!" I clinched, and the bell saved me.

Richie flopped me on a stool, snapped an ammonia capsule under my nose, and began his instructions. "Keep in close, Mac. And work on his belly . . . he's wide open. I'll let you know when to start punching over his left, but now walk away from it."

Involuntarily I glanced over my shoulder at the ringside of silk shirts. Richie caught my expression and said, "Stop worrying about them bums. You got a fight in the ring, not out there. And besides, look up at the balcony."

I looked up to see a dozen guards standing with submachine guns cradled in the crooks of their arms. They were prepared to protect me, but they seemed awfully far off. I could receive a shiv in the back any minute, and they'd never know who did it. Still, I knew Richie was right. I had to concentrate on the fight in the ring.

During the next round, I danced a lot and stayed in close. My ring knowledge was beginning to return to me, and though Kid Breslin was working on my bleeding nose and cut lip, I finished the round stronger than I began it.

When the third round started, the ringside heckling increased. They didn't like the fact that I had been boxing instead of slugging it out. "You yellow bastard," they screamed, "you couldn't fight your grandmother."

In the middle of the round we were fighting right over the ropes, and I looked down into their contorted faces as they yelled their hatred of me. They wanted blood, did they? I decided to give them some. I blew my bleeding nose at them, spraying their clean silk shirts with my own gore. They jumped to their feet in a frenzy, screaming obscenities at me. The guards on the balcony unlimbered their guns. Their foul words filled me with the anger I needed to win. Yellow, was I?

I went after Kid Breslin in such a fury that he backed away, amazed at the sudden change in me. As he started a left hook, I hung a fast, short right on his jaw and moved in, working his belly with a flurry of lefts and rights. I heard him gasp, saw him take a staggering step backwards, and I crossed a right to his unprotected jaw. I put all I had into that punch, all the hatred and scorn I felt for those silk-shirted hoods who were crying for my blood. When I felt the blow land, I knew it had done the job.

Kid Breslin's eyes glazed over, his knees began to buckle, and he sank down slowly. He grabbed at my legs for support, but I stepped aside and he pitched forward on his face. His legs twitched once, then he lay quite still while the referee intoned the count to ten.

For a long moment there was a stunned silence in the room. Then a spattering of applause started at the back, among the ordinary prisoners. The applause caught fire and spread and swelled, until even the front rows, the men in the spattered silk shirts, were on their feet cheering. The world loves a winner—even if he's a cop in Sing Sing.

Back home, Peg Bradley stayed up half the night putting ice packs on my swollen face and right ear, but all it seemed to do was lose us some sleep. The next morning I couldn't have looked worse. I put some face powder on to try and cover the worst bruises and went out to breakfast before reporting for duty.

The counter man looked at me and said, "What the hell happened to you, Mac?"

I said, "Even if I told you, you wouldn't believe it."

When I entered the station house, I tried to sneak by the desk, but the sergeant saw me and said, "Ya got yerself in a jam again, huh, McAllister?"

"I . . . I don't know, sir," I said.

"You'll know soon enough. The captain wants to see you."

"Yes, sir," I said, feeling all gone inside. "Now?"

"He said the minute you come in. I guess that would be now, wouldn't it?"

"Yes, sir," I said, and walked toward the captain's office.

"Officer," Captain Lyons said, "how'd you get your face banged up?"

"Boxing, sir."

"In the gym?"

"Well, sir, yes, sir, a sort of a gym. Just a few of the boys."

"You were fighting at Sing Sing," he said sternly.

"How'd you know?" I blurted out.

"It's a captain's job to know everything that's going on in his command. Now start at the beginning."

I told him the whole story and when I finished, he said, "Son, don't you know what a chance you took by going up there to fight? I'm not only thinking about your safety, but the safety of those prisoners. You might have started a riot."

"Yes, sir," I said. "I'm sorry, sir. I didn't know it was against the rules or I never would have gone."

"Damn it all," he snapped, "there are no rules on it. Who in his right mind would have ever thought of such a thing?"

"I'm sorry, sir," was all I could think to say.

He shook his head and sighed. "All right, son, but use your brains next time. When you're a police officer, you must always think of the welfare of others."

"Yes, sir," I said. Then I had to say it. I had to tell somebody, and my own captain seemed the best one to tell. "Captain, did you know that Owney Madden runs Sing Sing?" He looked at me without any change of expression, yet the temperature in the room dropped several degrees. I couldn't stop now. I said, "Owney Madden has bribed the guards and he has his clothes tailor-made and he has whiskey in his cell and he runs the gambling games there as well as the fights."

"Officer," Captain Lyons said in a cold voice, "that's a very serious charge."

"Sir," I cried, "I was up there. I saw it with my own eyes."

He leaned back in his chair and his face now looked very tired. "Sit down, son. Now, exactly what do you want to ask me?"

"I . . . I just wondered if you knew about it, sir. That's all."

He gave a sad smile and said, "Suppose I tell you what's really on your mind. You were up at Sing Sing and got your first look at a grafting cop. And now you're a little sick and a little scared. You don't know who to trust. You don't know if your side partner is honest, or the sergeant, or even if I am."

"Oh no, sir," I protested.

He held his hand up to silence me. "As long as human nature is the way it is, there's going to be some crooked cops, just as there are dishonest businessmen, and bankers, and doctors. But we don't have many of them and when we find them, they stop being cops. Don't ever get cynical or distrustful of the men you work with, because that's the first step toward letting down your own standards. You just take good care of the record of Officer McAllister; I'll take care of the record of the 28th Precinct; we'll both forget about Sing Sing because there's nothing we can do about it. Any more questions?"

"No, sir." I snapped him a salute and left his office with a little prayer of thanks for having gotten off so easily. It turned out not to be so easy, however. For two weeks I assisted the attendant, which meant I cleaned the spittoons and scrubbed out the toilets—all to the loud guffaws of my fellow officers.

If I thought of myself as a hot shot up in Sing Sing, I sure was no hero in my own precinct house. I decided then and there to give up fighting and concentrate on running.

The police games went off on schedule in September, and I beat Jack Eller for the department championship in the 150-yard dash. When I presented myself at the winners' table, the photographers snapped my picture as Police Commissioner Enright presented me with a beautiful trophy— a clock mounted on an ebony base, with a bronze eagle on top spreading its wings in free flight.

"Congratulations," the commissioner said to me. "You're a great sprinter and a credit to the department."

His words made me feel wonderful, of course, but I wasn't at all sure that Captain Lyons and Lieutenant Mead shared the sentiment. I vowed to do better on the job. No more bonehead jams, just good, by-the-book police work. I went back to my beat.

I was still on San Juan Hill, and after that first night, the hoods had never tried to break me or drive me off my post. I got things thrown at me from time to time, but they were mighty careful to keep out of sight when they did it. No, it was something quite different that was finally responsible for removing me from San Juan Hill.

There were some Negro prostitutes living at the top of the hill, and white men, midtown playboys out for a new thrill, began to visit them. A couple of them got rolled and knifed, and we knew a bad new trouble spot was developing. Captain Lyons finally issued orders that we were not to let any white men prowl around the hill after dark.

His words were, "Chase them the hell out of there before they get hurt by something worse than a dose. No legitimate businessman is there after dark, only white trash trying to change their luck. Keep that hill clean of them."

I determined that no white man was going to change his luck on my beat!

A few nights later I was standing post on the corner of Eleventh Avenue and 62d Street when I saw a tall, dignified white man of about fifty-five years begin to climb the hill. I shook my head and thought, what would your grandchildren think if they knew what you were up to? You should be ashamed. Then I took out after him.

He stopped at my hail and turned to face me calmly. I said, "Mister, are you in good health?"

"I am," he said stiffly.

"Then keep it and stay out of this neighborhood." I took him by the arm and started to escort him back to the avenue, but he jerked away from me.

"Officer," he said, "I'm just going to stroll down West End Avenue."

"The hell you are," I cried. "You're out for a piece of tail, but you're not getting it on my beat. I got orders to keep you guys from getting hurt up here, and I'm gonna do it whether you like it or not."

I reached for him again, but at that moment he whipped a leather wallet out of his pocket and flipped it open before my nose. There was a beautiful gold shield with a spread eagle.

"I'm Inspector Bolan," he said, eyeing me up and down.

"I understand there's been numerous assaults in this area and I want to look it over."

"I . . . I didn't know, sir," I muttered. Then I stood there dumbly while he turned and slowly climbed up the hill and disappeared into the night. Good Lord, I wondered, what have I done now?

When my relief reported, he had already heard about it. "You picked on Inspector Bolan, the boss of the Tenderloin," he said in amazement. "You'd better look for another job, Mac. Boy, how dumb can you get?"

When I signed the return roll call at the station-house desk, the sergeant said, "Just a second, kid. I have a notification for you."

He handed me a slip of paper, and on it was typed: "Report in full uniform 2:00 P.M. Tuesday, September 27, 1921, to the commanding officer, 3d Division."

The commanding officer of the 3d Division was, of course, Inspector Bolan.

As I walked home that morning, I was already job hunting in my mind.

When I presented myself to the division commander's outer office the next day, a lieutenant told me to be seated. While I was waiting, a redheaded giant burst into the room, waved to the lieutenant, and went into the inspector's private office. I wondered who it was who could enter such an exalted place without being screened by the lieutenant. I soon found out.

When I was at last instructed to enter, I found Inspector Bolan sitting at his desk, the redheaded man sitting beside him. The inspector put my worries to rest with a warm smile.

"I hope you weren't worried about having to report to me," he said.

"Oh no, sir," I lied.

"Well, meet your new plain-clothes boss, Lieutenant Red Walsh."

I gave the redheaded man a salute and then shook hands with him, all the time trying to figure out what all this meant.

"I like your spirit, McAllister," the inspector was saying, "and I like the way you carry out orders." Turning to Red Walsh, he said, "Think you can use him?"

The plain-clothes lieutenant had been studying me, and now he grinned and said, "Take the uniform off that kid and he'll look like an altar boy instead of a cop. He ought to be just about perfect for plain-clothes work."

Chapter Five

THE END OF INNOCENCE

On my first day as a member of the 3d Division's plain-clothes squad, I was introduced to my partner, Mike de Luca. He was a slightly built man with a large nose and a mop of coarse, black hair. You'd never pick him out of a crowd as being more important than an elevator operator, which was a great advantage for a plain-clothes man. He was one of the smartest cops I ever worked with.

"How about a cup of coffee while we get acquainted?" he said.

"Sure thing, Mike."

We went to a lunchroom, and over two thick mugs of coffee he began to question me about myself. I told him what there was to tell about my police career, which wasn't much, but he seemed satisfied.

"You want this assignment, Bob? You *want* to be a plain-clothes man?"

"Sure I do. Why?"

"Your attitude makes a difference how we'll work to-

83

gether. You've never before had a partner, and I can tell
you it's a very intimate thing. You gotta know all about
the other guy. There might come a time when your life
depends on it. A good partnership is where you can an-
ticipate what the other guy will do in every situation.
But the perfect partnership is where the other guy acts
and thinks like you do."

"I hope ours will be like that, Mike," I said.

He grinned. "We'll see, kid. In the meantime, how'd
you like to see your beat?"

"The 3d Division? Hell, Mike, I grew up in New York.
I know this town."

"But you've never looked at it through the eyes of a
plain-clothes man. Come on. I've got to teach you to see
all over again."

Fifth Avenue was the eastern boundary of our division,
and we now headed for it. This was 1921, and the avenue
had no Empire State Building, no Radio City, no big department stores or office buildings, but consisted of long
blocks of stately marble and stone mansions owned by the
city's financial and social leaders. The Vanderbilts, Car-
negies, Morgans, Astors—all lived here in grand estates.
We stood on the corner of 45th Street and looked north.

Mike said, "Well, what do you see?"

Maxwells and Franklins and Stanley Steamers were moving past us at a stately pace. I said, "There's hardly any
carriages left on the avenue. Everyone is riding in automobiles."

He shook his head. "You're not a traffic cop, Bob. You're
a plain-clothes man, and that means you look for people,
not for automobiles."

I looked at the sidewalks, thronged with people. "They're

all going about their business in a law-abiding manner," I said defensively.

Mike said, "Let's just walk along with them a bit. We'll see."

We started slowly north on the west side of the street. The men were dressed mostly in black suits with peg-top pants, button shoes, and derby hats. The postwar style revolution hadn't touched them the way it had the women. Women's skirts were shorter, a full 9 inches above the ground, and for the first time in generations the female ankle was a common sight. These women were wearing rouge and lipstick, too, something that only their fallen sisters had previously applied. When we reached the fifties, a high-wheeled taxi pulled to the curb in front of us, and a beautiful young woman stepped out, revealing a delicate calf encased in a new garment fast gaining popularity— flesh-colored silk stockings.

"A whore," Mike said in a low voice.

"Mike! You crazy? She's beautiful . . . and she doesn't dress any different from other women!"

"They don't, any more. That girl's name is Lucy Manners, and she makes fifty dollars a night. She's just as much a whore as the girl who makes two dollars."

"But she's going into that mansion. Doesn't that belong to . . . ?"

Mike nodded and mentioned the name of one of New York's most prominent families. "That guy prefers to buy it from whores. Gives him a different sort of a thrill, I guess."

We walked on up the avenue and came to an apartment building. The doorman was talking to a handsome, well-dressed man, and writing something on a slip of paper which he then handed to him. The man tipped him with a folded bill and walked away. Nothing unusual about that, I thought; merely a man asking directions and tipping liberally for the information. But I was wrong.

"That doorman's name is Fred. He's a pimp for queers," Mike explained. "All across the country there's a grapevine of queers who know about Fred. These men are often respectably married in their home towns, but like to go lacy when they hit New York and won't be recognized. Fred supplies them with addresses."

As we passed him, the doorman touched his hat and said to Mike, "Good evening, sir."

"Hello, Fred," Mike replied.

We turned west off the avenue and looked down a block lined with quiet, brownstone, four-story houses. Mike said, "More speak-easies in this block than any other single block in New York. There, see that basement door with the peephole in it? That door is reinforced with steel plates, and behind it is a fortune in bootleg liquor."

As we stood there, two young people—they couldn't have been over eighteen or nineteen—walked down the three steps and knocked at the door. After a moment, I heard the peephole slide open. The boy held up a card for identification. He wore a raccoon coat that came to his ankles, and the girl had her hair shingled right up the back of her head. There was a new word being applied to her and her kind, it was "flapper." The door opened, and they disappeared inside.

Mike growled, "They'll be in there all night, drinking rotgut whiskey and necking. They think they're damn smart and sophisticated, but they can't see where they're headed."

"Where are they headed, Mike?"

"You can take only so many hangovers without hitting the bottle when you first wake up. And for some of them, even whiskey won't be strong enough. That's what *he's* waiting for."

Mike jerked his head toward a slender figure moving along the opposite side of the street, a man wearing a pinched-in suit with pointed lapels. His face too was pinched, and his eyes darted among the passers-by. Mike said, "That's Soapy Randal, a dope pusher."

We came to Broadway, and I saw a theater marquee ablaze with lights spelling out, "Ziegfeld Follies of 1921." The music that poured into the street from the open windows of the clubs and restaurants had changed over the past two years to match the mood of the times. What I heard was not romantic violins playing waltzes; now the music was dominated by trumpets and saxophones wailing for dancers who clutched each other in a syncopated embrace called the "bunny hug."

As we crossed 46th Street going south, Mike nudged me and said, "There in the doorway, that's a gambler named Arnold Rothstein."

I looked quickly to see a gray-faced man who stared expressionlessly at the passing crowd. Mike said, "He's part of a gang known as the 'Broadway crowd,' along with Nick the Greek, Nigger Nate Raymond, George Mc-Manus, Al Levy, Gus Mayor, and Dollar John. They got a floating game here on Broadway, play a different hotel each night with their rigged dice. If some sucker ever wins in a Rothstein game, he usually winds up in the East River."

There was something evil about Rothstein that revealed itself at once. I remember that Bill Fallon, "the great mouthpiece," once said of him, "Rothstein is a man who dwells in doorways. A gray rat waiting for his cheese."

Mike and I cut south and then west to Seventh and Eighth Avenues, the heart of the garment area. Here was where the new flapper fashions were being turned out, sheath dresses with short hems and the waistline low on the hips. Mike stopped in front of one of the loft buildings and cocked his ear. "What do you hear, Bob?"

I listened. "Power sewing machines. Lots of them."

"Yeah, but behind that sound is another one, real faint. It's a sort of clanking."

"Now I get it," I cried. "What is it?"

"A printing press. Out of that building come counterfeit Scotch and Irish whiskey labels so perfect that only a Treasury man could spot them. They'll go on bottles over in Jersey."

We continued west to Ninth, Tenth, and Eleventh Avenues, to Hell's Kitchen and the grinding poverty of the slums. Cold-water tenements were crowded between reeking slaughterhouses, and out of them came pinch-faced adolescents, trigger-happy kids who were the recruits for the growing gangs.

We came to the Hudson, to the vast docks that fingered the river. Here was violence for its own sake; the longshoremen and sailors who worked here had a code and a law of their own, and it was enforced with blackjacks and brass knuckles. Smuggling was the industry here. Narcotics, jewels, or human beings—they were all smuggled into the city through the docks.

At last we came back to the 3d Division headquarters. Mike said, "There's your beat, Bob. What do you think of it?"

"You made me see it like I never had before," I said. "But Mike. . . ."

"Go ahead. I know what you're going to ask me. When do we make a pinch?"

"Well, yes."

"It's one thing to know what's going on. It's another to prove it in court. And remember, we're just two small cops. But we'll do our share of work. Don't you worry."

Mike educated me slowly and painstakingly, always impressing upon me the fact that a good plain-clothes man must develop an extra sense; he must take what his eyes and ears report and then add to this information an extra instinct of his own. I worked hard at it, and I think I eventually developed that instinct, but I was never in a class with Mike de Luca. He could watch a stranger walk down the street and tell whether or not he had something to hide.

All during this training period I was eager for action, I wanted to make a pinch. Well, the time for my first collar finally arrived, and did I louse it up! What I did became a legend in the department, and it took me years to live it down.

Lieutenant Walsh called the squad into his office one afternoon to give us the setup. The squad consisted of twelve men in all, including Mike de Luca and me.

"We got another complaint from the Committee of Fourteen," Red Walsh said, frowning at a departmental communication in his hand. The "Committee of Fourteen" was an anonymous group of civic leaders who had banded together to fight crime in New York. They had their own staff of investigators who went around looking for crimes, and then reported them to the police. The police department didn't relish the idea of a civilian group doing its work, of course, but we always had to follow down the leads.

"A committee investigator by the name of Stevenson," Red Walsh was reading from the paper, "reports four Spanish girls committing acts of prostitution at 358 West 57th Street." He looked up at us, frowned and said, "None of you men had a lead on this?" There was silence. The Committee of Fourteen had scooped the 3d Division again, and Lieutenant Walsh didn't like it a bit. He said grimly, "All right, let's go."

On the way to the 57th Street address, he said to me, "McAllister, with that Irish kid's face on you, they'll never suspect you of being a cop. You go on up, use Stevenson's name to get in the place, and when you've collected the evidence, raise the shade on a front window and the rest of us will raid the place. Got it?"

"Yes, sir," I said.

The address turned out to be an old brownstone mansion that had been converted into apartments, one to the floor. It was quite a plushy setup. Lieutenant Walsh and the rest of the men scattered themselves up and down the street while I walked into the lobby, found the name Letita Lopez, and punched the bell.

The door released with a buzz, and I entered the building to climb a curving marble stairs. At the head of it, standing in an open door and silhouetted against the room light, was a young woman wearing the sheerest negligee—and nothing else.

"Hallo," she said in a softly accented voice. "Who you wish to see?"

"Letita Lopez," I said, "or any of her friends. I'm looking for a good time."

"Oh?" she said, a provocative smile on her red lips. "What makes you think you get good time here?"

"Mr. Stevenson sent me."

His name was the right one, for she smiled and stood aside for me to enter. Business must have been slow that night for all four girls were there in the living room. There was Letita and Inez and Conchita and Agnes. How Agnes got in there I'll never know.

The girl who had let me in cuddled against me and purred, "Which wan you like, honey?"

"I like 'em all," I said. "But first, Letita, I'll like you."

I paid her the ten dollars in marked bills and thereupon began collecting my evidence. It took me about an hour, and I must say that the last twenty minutes of that hour was very hard work. At last I staggered to the front window and ran up the shade. In a matter of seconds there was the sound of pounding feet on the stairs, then my squad burst into the room while the girls screamed shrilly.

Lieutenant Walsh came up to me with a dark expression on his face. "What in hell took you so long?" he demanded.

"Long?" I said, outraged. "There were *four* of them. How fast could you do it?"

His mouth fell open, then closed, then fell open again. Finally, hoarse words came out. "You . . . all of them?"

"You ordered me to collect evidence against them, didn't you?"

"Oh no!" he cried, pounding his forehead with the palm of his hand. "I've got an idiot on the squad! An idiot! Oh my God . . . !" Finally he got control of himself and shoved his nose against mine and growled, "A police officer

is supposed to collect evidence of an offer to commit prostitution . . . *an offer to commit* . . . only an *offer!* Didn't
you ever read that regulation?"

If I had, I'd forgotten it.

"I . . . I thought you wanted me to . . . ," I stammered.

"You thought!" he shouted. "Don't you see the jam
we're in now? We take those girls to court, and all they
have to do is tell the judge what you did, and *you'll* be the
one sent to jail, not them. And what I'll hear from that
goddamn Committee of Fourteen! The commissioner will
probably transfer me to Staten Island. McAllister . . . you
bonehead!"

Finally he stopped chewing me out and took Letita into
a corner for a whispered conference. At the end of it, he
motioned to the rest of the squad to follow him, and we left
the apartment. Down on the street, he explained, "I made a
deal with them. We don't make the pinch and they won't
talk about McAllister, and they set up business in some
other district. Okay, let's forget the whole thing."

I was ready to forget it, but the big grins on the faces
of the rest of the squad told me it wouldn't be easy. I'll bet
that to this day the story of bonehead McAllister and the
four Spanish girls is told in the locker room of the 3d
Division.

After that episode I spent a lot of time studying the *Code
of Criminal Procedure*, for I knew that with another error
I'd be off the plain-clothes squad and back pounding a beat.
In the following months I began to run up a good record
of arrests and convictions. The important part in an officer's

record is convictions. Any man can make a collar, but to make it stand up in court is something else again.

In court you not only have to know the rules of evidence, you not only have to defend your actions against the often savage attack of defense attorneys, but often have to contend with the open hostility of the judge. I don't know why it is, but some judges seem to take the attitude that the arresting officer is on trial. I had two close brushes with "their honors" during this early part of my career.

The first episode was, in terms of some of the newspaper headlines, "The Case of the Framed Actress."

It started on a blustery March day when Lieutenant Walsh called me into his office and tossed me a complaint to follow up. He said, "Some big-shot politician got himself a dose of clap from a girl at the Somerset Hotel. The boss wants you to handle it. Read the complaint carefully and go to work."

I studied the letter sent in by the politician and noted that his escapade with the whore at the Somerset had taken place almost two months before. Hell, I thought, that cheater has probably been many places since then, and could have picked up his dose from a dozen girls, but he wants to pin the rap on the Somerset. Still, I had an assignment, so Mike de Luca and I went to work.

Using the name of Robert Pope together with a Detroit address, I registered at the Somerset and at once began demanding a lot of room service. I ordered cigarettes and ice setups and food. I let it be known that I was a businessman in town for a brief vacation and that I was a big spender.

For three days nothing happened except that Jimmy, the Negro bellboy, always kidded about women whenever he

answered the room-service calls. He'd tell a couple of dirty
stories and then remark that there were sure a lot of nice
girls around town. I'd laugh at his jokes and roll my eyes
at the thought of a woman, but I never asked for one. I had
to wait until he *offered* a girl, otherwise I might be charged
with "entrapment."

On the third evening, when Jimmy responded to my call
for a bowl of cracked ice, he looked at me closely and said,
"Mr. Pope, you're all alone in the city and pretty lone-
some. I know a little charmer who would like to keep you
company and give you a real good time. What do you
say?"

"Sure," I said. "I'd like company."

"Okay. I'll send her around in a little while."

A half hour later there was a knock at my door and I
opened it to find a beautiful young woman who looked
more like an actress than a whore. She put an unmistakable
smile on her face and said, "My name is Estelle."

"Hello, Estelle."

"A little bird told me you wanted to play some tricks.
Am I in the right room?"

"Was it a little black bird, Estelle?"

"It was," she said.

I stood aside and she came into the room with a slow,
hip-rolling walk. "Honey," she whispered, "it will cost you
twenty dollars for a beautiful trick."

"Take off your clothes, sweetheart, and let me see what
I'm getting for my money."

"First the money," she smiled, "then I'll be real nice to
you. You won't be disappointed, honey."

"I guess I know a bargain when I see it," I said, peeling
off twenty dollars in marked bills. She tucked the money

in her purse, then pulled her dress off over her head. Beneath it, she wore nothing. She curled up on the bed, small and kittenish. I leaned over her and said, "Estelle, I've given this advice to plenty of beautiful girls on Broadway: Don't go whoring in the hotels. I'm a cop, and you're under arrest."

She sprang upright in bed, her eyes glittering with hate. "You dirty cop bastard," she breathed.

I picked up the phone to call Mike de Luca, who was covering me from a room down the hall. "I made an arrest, Mike. Come right over."

When he arrived, we demanded the money back from Estelle, then both of us signed it for identification. I left Mike with her while I went downstairs to get Jimmy, the bellboy. Perhaps the phone operator had heard my call to Mike and tipped him off, anyway, he wasn't to be found. The desk clerk stared at me balefully and said he didn't know where Jimmy was.

I went to the basement and found him changing his clothes in the locker room and getting ready to skip. "What do you want me for?" he whined with the look of injured innocence.

"Procuring a female for the purpose of prostitution."

We took the prisoners to the 47th Street station house, and Estelle was detained in a back room under the watchful eye of a matron. As I was standing at the desk giving the details of the arrest to the desk lieutenant, the front door burst open and a young man rushed up. He held a blanketed infant in his arms. He exploded in a torrent of words: "Where's my wife? Where's the dirty, framing, cop sonofabitch who arrested her? It's a frame-up . . . a lousy frame-up and by God, I'll. . . ."

"Now just a minute, mister," the lieutenant said. "Take it easy and you'll learn the truth."

"The truth!" he screamed, his eyes bulging crazily. "I know the truth. I was home minding our baby while she went down to the drugstore to get some paregoric. How could the mother of a nursing baby be a prostitute? You crazy? Who did this to her? I'll kill the framing bastard."

"Easy now," the lieutenant said, "and we'll let you talk to your wife." He motioned to a patrolman. "Take him back to see the girl the division man arrested."

When the wild young husband was gone, the lieutenant said to me, "Okay, I've got everything needed for the arrest record. You'd better leave now before the husband spots who you are."

The next morning, before arraignment, as I was signing the affidavit in the Women's Court, Assistant District Attorney John C. Weston approached me and said, "Is this the case where a show girl with a nursing baby was arrested for prostitution at the Somerset Hotel?"

"Sure, it's the case," I snapped. "She's an out-and-out whore, so what's all the excitement?"

"Well, her husband is a fairly well-known actor and he's telephoned all the newspapers, crying frame-up. Haven't you seen the morning papers?"

"No, I haven't and I don't give a damn what they say. This was a direct case."

"Okay . . . okay, Mac. We'll prosecute it."

The case was called at noon before Judge Jesse Silberman. The defense lawyer, Mr. Abe Karp, gave a long and impassioned plea about the innocence of his client. He alleged that she was in the hotel elevator when the bellboy told her there was a baby with convulsions in one of the rooms, and the mother needed help. When she knocked at the door where the sick baby was supposed to be, I grabbed her and falsely charged her with being a prostitute. I did a slow burn, listening to all those lies.

At last I was on the stand, sworn and under oath, and I told the true facts of the case. The bellboy's action in trying to run away certainly helped prove my case, but the minute I tried to mention him, Mr. Karp objected. "Your Honor," he cried, "nothing was said or done by the bellboy in the presence of the defendant."

The judge gave me a stern look and sustained the objection.

"Now, officer," Mr. Karp purred at me during cross examination, "the defendant never mentioned sexual intercourse in her conversation with you, did she?"

"Not those exact words, if that's what you mean."

"What words did she use?" Judge Silberman interrupted.

" 'It will cost you twenty dollars for a beautiful trick.' "

Karp shouted, "She told you it was a beautiful trick you played on her to get her into your room. Isn't that the truth?"

"No, sir," I said. "Prostitutes use indefinite phrases: good time, party, fun, trick. This woman used the word trick, and she meant by that she was offering to commit an act of prostitution."

Karp went after me in a savage cross-examination for almost an hour, making me appear to be a monster who framed innocent women in order to build up my own record of arrests. Then he went after Mike de Luca in the same way.

When Estelle took the stand, she told all those lies, punctuating them with gentle sobs. Oh, she was making an impression on the court, all right. As for newspaper reporters, they were eating it up. I could see tomorrow's headlines, unless something happened to show the judge I was telling the truth.

Then it came to me . . . the clincher. I grabbed the D.A. excitedly and whispered into his ear. He nodded and stood up to address the court. "Your Honor, the arresting officer has just remembered a mark of identification that will establish beyond doubt that the defendant disrobed in front of him. She has a jagged scar on her lower abdomen. It may have been made by an appendectomy. The People will insist upon a physical examination to establish this fact."

There was an uproar in the court, but the judge gaveled silence and said, "There is a conflict of testimony in this case. I order an examination of this defendant by a physician. Court is adjourned until tomorrow morning at eleven o'clock."

The next morning Judge Silberman called the court to order and said, "After examining medical reports, I find that the arresting officer described in detail a scar on the defendant's abdomen. The defendant is found guilty and remanded for sentence."

So it turned out all right. I had my collar and I had my conviction. But it might have so easily been different. Leaving the courtroom, I said to Mike, "What if she hadn't had that scar on her stomach? What then?"

"Well, the way things were shaping up, I'd say we would have faced a perjury charge."

"But there must be hundreds of hustlers without a blemish."

"That's why we gotta be very careful."

"I still don't get it. Why should anybody ever take a prisoner's word over a cop's?"

Mike grinned at me. "Bob, you've still got the idea that the minute a man puts on a police uniform he becomes a hero. Cops are human beings, some of them are weak, some of them are lazy, some of them are liars. Among 17,000 men there's bound to be a few. A judge can't automatically take a cop's word. He's got to have evidence. Your job is to give him that evidence, all the evidence you can collect, and if he doesn't think it's enough, well, that's *his* job. You shouldn't take things so personally. Develop a thick skin."

I tried but I was never completely successful. I was to have my own troubles within the department over the next thirty years, but right to the end I continued to worship the force, and I could never get over the belief that the men in blue deserved better of the courts and the public.

A week after this hearing, a complete medical report was issued on Estelle, and she was found to be suffering from a virulent case of gonorrhea. Without doubt, she was the one who had infected the big-shot politician.

Six months later I had my second run-in with a judge who believed one of my prisoners rather than myself. Four members of our squad, including Mike and me, were sent to raid an apartment on West 96th Street where, according to an anonymous tip, a gang of teen-age girls were doing business with the Navy.

In answer to our ring, a big, sultry blonde who had not seen her teens in many a year answered the door. "What's your pleasure, gentlemen?" she said, with a meaningful smile.

"Our pleasure is to look over your apartment," Mike

said, pushing past her. The blonde shrilled her protests, but could hardly stop four cops. She had a real lavish setup, with brocaded walls, thick rugs, and French antique furniture. By now I had discovered that the better whore houses in town were furnished to look like a millionaire's apartment. Polly Adler, particularly, spent a small fortune on the furnishings of her houses. I've never been invited to visit the apartment of a duke or a duchess, but if it ever happens, I'm sure I'll feel as if I'm raiding another house.

"Who pays the rent on this place?" Mike asked the blonde.

"Do you mind telling me who you are?" the blonde demanded.

"We're cops, honey, and we got word that you've hired yourself a bunch of teen-age girls for immoral purposes with the fleet."

By this time we had made our way to a door opening off the living room, and we went through it into a luscious bedroom all of silks and satins and smelling of perfume. Huddled together there were four young girls, their bodies showing through the most transparent of gowns and their eyes wide with fright. Not a one of them was over eighteen, and it made me choke up with anger to think of this cynical blonde selling their bodies. These kids should have been in high school, and having dates with nice boys.

Mike rang the telegraph bureau for a pie wagon, and we all went downstairs. As usual, a small crowd was waiting with morbid curiosity. We began to load the girls into the wagon when a voice behind me said, "You dirty dogs."

I turned around to find an admiral standing in the hallway. He wasn't of the American Navy. I didn't know what

Navy he belonged to, but he was loaded down with gold braid, epaulettes, a glittering sword, and a Van Dyke beard. His hat was a work of art, being one of those fore-and-aft affairs with a great plume of feathers. He was so gorgeous that I immediately got the idea that he didn't belong to any real Navy, but was dressed up for a masquerade.

"What'd you say?" I asked.

"You have no right to arrest those girls without a warrant," he proclaimed grandly.

"You run your Navy, bud, I'll take care of the girls."

"That's an insult, sir," he cried. "I should run you through." With a flourish, he whipped out his sword.

I thought to myself, this boy's got a short circuit some place. I moved fast, sending a whistling right that landed flush on his Van Dyke. Down went the Navy.

Mike bent over to pick up the sword and run his thumb along the blade. "Hey, it's sharp as a razor," he said. "This guy's a real psycho!"

The admiral came to in the pie wagon as we pulled up to the 100th Street station house. He rubbed his beard. "God-damn you," he said to no one in particular.

Into the station house we went, follow-the-leader, Mike and the other squad members, then the girls, then the admiral, and finally me. The admiral stormed up to the desk and shouted, "Let me speak to the official in charge."

The desk lieutenant squinted through his glasses at the gaudy uniform and said mildly, "Speak your piece."

"Sir, I am Count Louis Bourbon, direct descendant and heir of King Louis Philippe of France. I am a duly accredited representative of the French Embassy in Washington. This man," he pointed a majestic finger in my direction, "assaulted me. This, sir, is an international incident."

The lieutenant looked puzzled and scratched his head. "There must be some mistake."

"No mistake, sir," the count said. "He assaulted me."

"I hit him all right, Lieutenant," I said. "He pulled his sword on me."

"Ah!" the count cried. "He admits the assault, and not only did he assault me, he arrested me. You must know that the diplomatic corps is immune to arrest. I demand satisfaction."

"I dunno . . . ," the lieutenant said, sweat breaking out on his forehead.

"Kindly notify the French Embassy at once," the count said.

The lieutenant motioned to the attendant and said, "Escort the count to the rear room and extend him every courtesy." After the count had left, the lieutenant said to me, "All right, kid, give me the whole story."

I gave it all to him, and when I finished, I demanded that he lock up the phony count on the charge of assaulting an officer during the performance of his duty.

"Now look," the lieutenant said, "maybe we can talk the count into forgetting the whole thing."

"To hell with him," I said. "I want him locked up."

The lieutenant shook his head. "This whole case is loony. If I don't go along with you division men, the inspector will chew me out. And if I do, and this guy turns out to be an honest-to-God count, then I'll never make captain. My ass is in the sling either way. Where do you guys dig up cases like this? Jesus!"

"We don't dig up anything," I said. "We just take 'em as they come."

"Okay, okay," the lieutenant said with a resigned shake of his head. "But let's reduce the charge here—more chance of making it stick. I'll book the girls as wayward minors and send them to the Florence Crittendon Home. As for the count, we'll give him disorderly conduct."

Count Louis, scion of the Bourbons, heir to the crown, was fresh as a dauphin when he appeared in court the next day. It was miraculous how a guy could be so starched and glittering after a night in the can. The Honorable George Simpson was the presiding judge, and he got to our case about twelve-thirty when everybody was tired and hungry.

Maybe I shouldn't blame things on the impatience of everybody to get things over with before lunch, maybe I just made a lousy showing. In any event, it was clear to me from the moment I took the stand that there was an air of skepticism in the court. I told my story in detail, but somehow when you say that a man called you foul names, and the words turn out to be "You dirty dog"—well, it did sound a little ridiculous.

I leaned heavily on the fact that he had drawn his sword. Surely this would impress the judge, I thought. It didn't.

"Officer," Judge Simpson interrupted, "did he point the sword at you?"

"No, sir," I said.

Judge Simpson shook his head dubiously. "I'm not certain we have a case of disorderly conduct in a public place. It is even questionable whether the apartment hallway is a public place."

As I prepared to step down from the stand, I could see the count grinning with satisfaction. I knew exactly what was going through his mind—there was opening up a chance for him to sue me for false arrest. Taking a desperate chance, I blurted out, "Your Honor, I think he's a phony."

Judge Simpson looked at me with shocked surprise on his face. "Officer," he said sternly, "are you suggesting that this gentleman is not bona fide?"

I mumbled some sort of an apology and climbed down from the stand. The count was grinning wider. I could see him adding "defamation of character" to the previous charge of false arrest. Me and my big mouth!

The count took the stand and hardly finished reciting his titles when Judge Simpson dismissed the charge. Then, as the photographers snapped pictures, the judge leaned over the bench to shake hands with the count and apologize for the embarrassment caused him. I slunk out of court. Now I was a sitting duck for any proceedings the count might choose to bring against me. I went to bed that afternoon wondering why I had ever chosen to be a cop.

The phone rang during the early evening and I came out of sleep slowly, resentfully, and mumbled into the instrument. In another minute, however, I was totally awake. On the other end of the wire was a man named Hickey, a keeper at the Blackwells Island prison, and he had electrifying information for me.

When he finished his story, I exclaimed, "Hickey, are you sure of this?"

"Damn right I am," he said. "Meet me tonight and I'll give it all to you."

"In front of Dinty Moore's at nine," I said. "But how will I know you?"

"I'll know you," he said. "I've seen you run and I'm one of your fans."

When I reached Dinty Moore's, I was greeted by a big

Irishman who swallowed up my hand in his. "You see the *Journal* tonight?" he asked. He opened the paper, and on the second page was a picture of Judge Simpson shaking hands with the count. The caption read, INTERNATIONAL INCIDENT AVERTED. The villain of the story was, of course, me!

Hickey then pulled out of his pocket a picture and a slip of yellow paper. One glance at them and I pounded him on the back. "Hickey," I cried, "you're going into Dinty Moore's with me and have the best meal in the house."

I was so excited, I didn't have much appetite, but I enjoyed watching Hickey stow it away. As we parted, I headed for the office of the *Daily News*. The only man I knew there was the sports writer Jimmy Powers. I used his name to get in to see the editor. Soon I was telling my story to a reporter and giving him the picture and the slip of paper I had received from Hickey.

The reporter whistled and grinned and said, "This is gonna be one hell of a story."

That Saturday night, in the dim light of an oil lamp hanging inside a corner newsstand, I saw the count's face staring at me from the front page of the *Daily News*. He was smiling, resplendent in uniform, sword, and plumed hat. The caption read, COUNT DE BUNK. The story revealed that he was one of the smoothest confidence men who ever tried to muscle the city. He had a criminal record a yard long and had just finished a thirty-day stretch on Blackwells Island, where good old Hickey had spotted him.

I bought a copy of the paper and, in the small hours of Sunday morning, I found a friendly milkman about to enter the apartment building where Judge Simpson lived.

He agreed to deliver the paper with the judge's milk. Attached to the paper was a note that read, "Dear Judge: Sorry I had to do this, but it was self-defense. Bob McAllister."

Two days later I was in court with a homosexual case, and who should be sitting but Judge Simpson. I began to sweat, wondering whether perhaps I had been too bold with that note. Could that constitute contempt of court, I wondered? After the case was disposed of, Judge Simpson invited me to come into his chambers. When I entered, he clasped my hand and smiled and said, "Some of my associates on the bench have given me quite a ribbing about that phony count."

"I'm sorry, Judge . . . ," I started to say.

"Nonsense, my boy. It was my own fault. He just took me in. But let's catch up with him, shall we? I'll give you a warrant and you bring him in. I'll throw the book at him."

I sure wanted to make that collar but I never got the chance. The count blew New York and headed for Hollywood. I later read in the papers about his capers out there and noticed that he had given himself a promotion. He called himself a prince.

Despite winning the two cases I just recounted, as well as a great many others, I found being a plain-clothes man a rather unpleasant assignment. Most of our work was in prostitution, and after handling several hundred cases, I became discouraged. As fast as I arrested one prostitute, two more seemed to go into business. And the other men in the division seemed to look down on us plain-clothes men. Part of it might have been jealousy over the fact we didn't have regular hours and regular beats, but there was scorn, too. I heard their jibes in the muster room. I'd walk in and one patrolman would say to another in a stage whisper, "That guy's got a real big arrest record . . . all whores. He couldn't collar anybody else. They might shoot back."

Finally I went to Inspector Bolan and asked to be transferred. He listened patiently to my complaints about the assignment. Then he said, "Bob, when you enlisted in the Army, were you ready to give up your life in the battle?"

"Yes, sir," I said.

"Well, you're in a battle now . . . a battle to make this a decent and law-abiding town. Yet you haven't got the guts to listen to a few bellyachers. Is that it?"

"Well, sir . . ." I could feel myself blushing with shame.

The inspector smiled and said, "Bob, you're a damn good cop and an honest one. Your record of stand-up arrests is excellent. If men like you lose your guts, what do you think will happen to our squad? To this town? Pimps and whores and bootleggers would turn it into a wilderness. The people depend on you, Bob. I depend on you. The commissioner depends on you. You going to let us down?"

"No, sir," I said, saluted and left the room.

After that I tried to shut my ears when I heard the locker-room taunts.

Chapter Six

DEAL

A STACKED DECK

Nineteen twenty-three was a momentous year for me. I established four world track records, I met the girl I was to marry, and unknowingly I became entangled in a political feud that was to send me to prison. Any one of these events would have supplied enough adventure for a single year; I got them all together. Let me recount them in the order in which they happened—my running triumphs first.

You've heard the phrase "natural born athlete." Well, I don't believe it. One man may be endowed with greater muscle, or better reflexes, or more heart than another, but these qualities alone don't make him a champion. To be a winner, an athlete has to learn his trade, and I never knew one who learned by himself. Behind every champion there is a trainer, a man who is not only a teacher, but a friend, providing a source of courage and inspiration as well as technical advice. The man who was all these to me was Jake Weber.

I met him in 1922 through Al Copeland, a sports writer

for the *Daily News*, who recognized that I had many faults in my running style and knew that Jake could straighten them out. Jake was a trainer for the New York Athletic Club and Fordham University, and had trained such diverse athletes as Jake Ruppert, Frankie Frisch, Willie Hoppe, and Eddie Farrell. He had trained the great Homer Baker, and now he was to train the obscure Bob McAllister.

Jake altered my style radically. I was a notoriously slow starter, and I ran with flailing arm motions that not only looked awkward, but wasted power as well. Jake got me to thrust fast and hard out of the starting holes, and to hold my arms parallel with my body and use them as pistons for greater momentum. And Jake knew more about nervous tension than all the doctors in the world. Before every race, when giving me a rubdown, he'd talk softly and continuously in my ear to unravel my nerves, drive off the stage fright. "You can do it, Bobbie boy," he'd croon. "Keep them arms parallel and drive . . . and nothing can touch you. Just breathe deep now, son, and relax. Pretty soon you'll be flying down that track, leading 'em all, but not now. Now's the time to relax and let old Jake loosen up them muscles. That's the boy. You're a beauty boy, Bobbie, and you're gonna lead them all. Just remember that, and relax."

As the starting time neared, Jake would lead me out to the track, talking softly to me all the time. "Jog a bit, Bobbie. That's the boy. Take a few slow fifties, then a few starts. Keep your sweat clothes on, Bobbie. Just take it nice and easy."

I'd jog and make starts and warm up, then at the last minute he would strip me out of the sweat clothes and bend over with me as I dug my holes. Then as the starter took his place, Jake would whisper tensely, "Okay, Bobbie, this is it. Fast outta them holes, drive hard . . . drive . . . drive. It's your race!"

Jake was like a starting motor. When he stepped back from me, I'd be crouched there with every nerve and muscle ready for the supreme effort. At the crack of the starting gun, I drove!

A dash race is like a physical spasm. It lasts only for seconds, during which time you are seized in a special sort of agony. You see nothing but the straight sweep of track narrowing in the distance to that precious white tape. To get there first, to break that tape before anybody else, can seem the beginning and end of life.

Under Jake Weber's careful handling I steadily improved my style and my time. On the eve of George Washington's birthday, Jake entered me in a meet at the 13th Regiment Armory in Brooklyn. I was probably as nervous for this meet as any of my career. This was the first time I had run for Jake, and I wanted desperately to prove that his confidence in me was not misplaced.

When my event was called, the 150-yard dash, Jake led me out to the track, talking softly as we walked. I was in a daze of excitement and I didn't hear a word he said, but his calm, confident tone came through and helped me control my nerves. There were six of us running. We adjusted our starting blocks, crouched and tried a few starts, then were ready. One hundred and fifty yards away was the white tape marking the finish line. I fastened my eyes on it, and never removed them. At the sound of the starting gun, I surged forward from the blocks, completely unconscious of the other runners, deaf to the roar of the crowd, blind to

everything but that slender white tape that came closer
. . . closer . . . then burst across my chest.

When the times were announced, it was revealed that I
had set world records for the 110-, 120-, 130-, and 150-yard
distances. I hugged Jake and cried and laughed. Only now
did I hear the cheers of the crowd. On the following day
the *Herald Tribune* headlined the story on the sports page
and said:

> His times for the distances mentioned above were
> 0:10 3/5, 0:11 4/5, 0:12 3/5, and 0:14 3/5 respec-
> tively. The fastest previous time made indoors for
> the 150 yards is 0:15 4/5, the record having been held
> jointly by Jack Eller and Alvin Meyer.
>
> Because of his recent fine performances, McAllister
> has become an idol with the followers of the sport
> and every time he appeared on the track he received
> vociferous applause. When he sped home in record
> time the ovation accorded him by the 10,000 fans in
> the armory resembled that which Melvin Sheppard
> and Martin Sheridan used to receive when they were
> athletic heroes.

That night Jake threw a party in celebration. That night
I met my wife.

Now, I'd been to Jake's house many times before and
never felt quite comfortable there. I loved Jake, but his
wife Emma was something else. Emma always spread newspapers over her carpets and chairs to keep the dirt off them,
and whenever company would arrive, she'd remove the
papers with great reluctance, acting as if human contact
with her furniture were going to ruin it. Also, her first
husband had been a rich man and she never let anybody
forget that fact. I never knew whether he died or divorced

her, but all she had left from that golden period was a
grand piano and a collection of twenty-four hats. She wore
a hat in her own apartment whenever she entertained,
sometimes even changing hats in the middle of the party.
The collection was kept on pegs in a hall closet, and that
closet door was always left open. Whenever I'd pass down
the hall, I'd swing that door shut, and she'd have to find
some excuse to go into the closet so she could open the door
again. I guess she didn't like me much more than I liked
her.

At this particular party, even Emma Weber and her
hats couldn't bother me—I was too excited. Jake had invited a lot of sports celebrities, and when I arrived at about
eight o'clock, the place was jammed. Emma greeted me at
the door, a big hat on her head and a pained expression on
her face. The poor woman was being torn by a terrible
conflict: she didn't like all these people standing on her rugs
and sitting on her chairs, still, their presence gave her an
opportunity to display her hats. I introduced her to my
date, a big, placid chorus girl who never had anything to
say.

"Aunt Emma," I said, "this is Flo Floman."

"How do you do," Emma said, her voice coming through
her nose the way it always did when she put on her hats.

"Hullo," Flo said. That was the only complete sentence
in her vocabulary.

"The powder room is down there," Emma said, gesturing
along the hall and past the open closet door.

Flo went slowly down the hall is if she were on a runway
at Minsky's, and never even looked in the closet. I felt kind
of sorry for Emma. I went into the living room where Jake

cried out my name, and everyone turned my way to applaud. This was my day—even more than I knew.

Jake hugged me and cried, "The Champ . . . by God, the Champ!" Then he whispered in my ear, "Follow me, I've got somebody I want you to meet." He led me through the crowd and to the grand piano in the corner. A young woman was playing it, but she stopped and smiled up at us. Jake said, "Bob, this is my niece, Mabel Smith."

She had wavy brown hair piled high on her head (the shingle craze hadn't touched her) and an oval face with enormous brown eyes. I'm not saying that I fell in love with her at first sight, but I knew at once that here was something very special. She was small and delicate, yet there was strength about her, and certainty. At once I wanted to show off in front of her. I searched desperately for something to keep her attention. I couldn't very well run a race right there in Jake's living room.

"You play the piano?" I finally asked, stupidly. She had been playing when we came up.

"She plays like an angel," Jake declared. "And all them fancy things, like Chopin and Paderoofski."

She smiled and said nothing. I blurted, "I sing a little bit."

"Oh, how nice," she said. "Would you like to sing something now and have me accompany you?"

"Well, if we know any of the same songs," I said.

She leafed through the sheet music on the piano. "Here's one of the new hits," she said, holding up a song. "Do you know it?"

The title of the song was "Ten Thousand Years Is a Long, Long Time to Wait for the End of the World." I

knew it. Jake quieted the others as I began to sing. I'm a
tenor, and I can sing awful high and awful loud. Never did
I sing higher or louder. If the chandeliers didn't crack, it
wasn't my fault. I was determined to give Mabel Smith an
earful. When I finished singing, everybody applauded and
I bowed, but I turned quickly to Mabel.

"How'd you like it?" I asked.

She smiled and said, "Your fortissimo is quite remark-
able."

I took this as a compliment. I thought I had wowed her
and sat down next to her on the piano bench to sing some
more songs. It wasn't until weeks later that I discovered
that what she really had meant was that I had nearly shat-
tered her eardrums. But that disillusionment was yet to
come. This day was still mine.

When the party broke up around midnight, I sent Flo
Floman home with another guy and announced I'd escort
Mabel home. I didn't ask her, I just told her. This was my
day to be masterful. Down on the street I looked for a taxi,
but she protested.

"Let's take the trolley," she said.

"Nothing doing. Tonight we travel in style."

"Please, the trolley would be fine."

"Look, I can afford to take a girl home in a taxi."

"Maybe so, but I really *prefer* the trolley."

We argued about it, but I was stubborn. When a cab
came rolling down the street, I hailed it and pushed her into
it. She huddled in a corner of the seat, and I saw that her
face had gone white, and that she was trembling.

"Mabel, what's the matter?" I asked.

"N-nothing," she quavered.

"Are you sick?"

"I'm all right."

I reached over to touch her hand, and she shrank away from me with a little cry. Suddenly I realized what was wrong. "For gosh sakes," I said, "are you afraid of me?"

She managed a small smile and nodded. "A little."

"But why?"

"Well, Aunt Emma warned me about you."

"She did what?" I shouted.

"She told me you're a vice cop . . . told me all the things that vice cops do . . . and. . . ."

At that point I exploded. It was bad enough to be sneered at by the other cops on the force, but to be feared by decent women, well, I was sore. I'm not sure that my violent reaction reassured Mabel, but at least she knew I wasn't going to rape her in the taxi. But behind all my loud talk was a trace of guilt. I didn't know what Aunt Emma had told her about vice cops, but could it have been any worse than the things I had done? Probably not.

Fortunately, the summons to the commissioner's office and my transfer to his confidential squad came soon after I met Mabel. Even so, it was some time before she felt safe with me. It took her months to say "yes" to my urgent pleas that she marry me. Happy as I was when she finally did say the word, I couldn't foresee that, within a few short months, she would become my only hope and strength. We didn't plan a long engagement, three months at the most, but before even that short time elapsed I was caught up in an amazing sequence of events that was eventually to land me in prison.

I found myself in the cross fire between two rival factions in Tammany Hall. One of the factions, comprising some of the most powerful men in the city, reached into the police department and chose me to railroad to prison. Unimportant though I was, certain events drew me to their attention, and they decided that I'd be perfect for their purposes.

For those readers who don't understand much about Tammany, let me briefly trace its history and methods. Tammany Hall was first established in 1789 by an Irish upholsterer named William Mooney. He based the name and the rituals on Indian lore, and divided the organization into various tribes, each tribe being led by a "sachem," and the entire organization being led by a "grand sachem." Mooney founded Tammany as a patriotic and benevolent lodge; his successors turned it into a political organization, making it the New York City wing of the Democratic party. The rest of the Democratic party was not entirely happy about this, but needed the votes Tammany controlled. When the great Irish immigration hit New York in the nineteenth century, Tammany took the foreign-born under its wing, fought for their rights, and won their political loyalty.

By 1842, Tammany had developed a method of assuring its victory at the polls; it organized flying squads of Irish thugs who descended upon any precinct that threatened to defeat a Tammany candidate and stuffed the ballot box with a lot of phony votes. Anyone who dared to protest got his head bashed in.

The most powerful and infamous Tammany grand sachem was William Tweed, who was at the peak of his power in 1870 and plundered the city of close to 60 million dollars. He was finally sent to jail, where he died, and for a time the reform forces of the city took over the government. But Tammany was not long out of power, primarily because it championed the foreign-born and the poor, and there were always a lot of both.

Once, when I was about ten years old, my brother and I went swimming naked in the Hudson River, diving off the New York Central tracks. The railroad bulls caught us, hauled us off to the 100th Street precinct house, and charged us with trespassing. Word was sent to my mother by other kids, and, within an hour, she arrived at the station house bringing with her, not a lawyer or even our priest, but our district Tammany leader. He had a brief conference with the captain and we were released, despite the loud protests of the railroad cops.

There was no charge for this service, it was merely expected that my family would vote for Tammany candidates, which I'm sure they did. We kids grew up thinking that Tammany Hall was our friend and protector, and in many ways it was.

The Hall had such control of the voters that almost every serious and honest man who wanted a political career had to join. Consequently, there developed a series of internal disputes between reform groups and the traditional bully boys. It was into just such a struggle that I was plunged.

John Hylan was the Democratic mayor of the city when I became a cop. He ran a clean administration, and the newspapers soon nicknamed him "Honest John" Hylan. His police commissioner, Richard Enright, was another incorruptible man.

During my first days on the force, some of the old-timers advised me to get myself a "rabbi," the name they gave to a political sponsor. In the past, policemen had won advancement or good assignments only if they were sponsored by a Tammany district leader, or alderman or assembly-man. The old-timers were wrong in their advice to me, however, for under Commissioner Enright's regime, the rabbi influence was at a minimum. True, Tammany had elected Hylan and had been rewarded with a lot of patron-age throughout the city government, but all things con-sidered, the mayor and the police commissioner were sur-prisingly independent. Then came Prohibition to drive a wedge right down the middle of Tammany Hall.

Mayor Hylan and Police Commissioner Enright had a simple and forthright attitude toward Prohibition: as long as it was the law, it should be enforced. They did their best. There were those in Tammany who didn't see it that way, and when Hylan refused to listen to them, they vowed to deny him another term in office. The anti-Hylan forces within Tammany eventually selected Jimmy Walker as their front. Walker was speaker of the assembly in Albany at the time, and receiving a lot of attention because of his stylish dress and his ready wit. But Walker didn't have Hylan's scruples.

When I became innocently involved in this fight among giants, it was 1923. The mayoralty primary was still two years away. Tammany Hall was not openly divided into factions, but there were powerful forces determined to get rid of Hylan if the opportunity presented itself. I became that opportunity. It started as a routine police assignment.

That spring, Supreme Court Judge Mullin issued a search warrant for a Water Street boardinghouse suspected as a drop for bootleg whiskey smuggled from the nearby East River. The raid was assigned to the commissioner's con-fidential squad, consisting of First-Grade Detective George Faust, Second-Grade Detective Plagge, Patrolmen Yost

and Coonan, and Acting Detective Sergeant Bob McAllister.
That fateful afternoon we piled into the cars and headed
for Water Street.

We found a shabby, three-story building, the kind
merchant seamen room in when they're ashore. George
Faust pounded on the door. After a time the door was
opened a crack by a surly young man who demanded to
know what we wanted. George showed him the search
warrant.

"Go ahead and search," he said. "We got nothing here."

The front room on the first floor was a recreation room
with two pool tables and a half-dozen easy chairs. No place
to hide whiskey here. We found nothing in the big dining
room, or the kitchen, or the upstairs bedrooms. We went
down into the cellar, and there found only six cases of liquor.

George scratched his head and said, "It doesn't figure.
Our tip was that they had almost 200 cases and were paying
protection to the politicians and the precinct house."

At this moment a tough-looking blonde came screaming
down the stairs. "You can't touch that liquor. My husband
got it before Prohibition. Get out of here, you bastards."

"What's your name?" George demanded.

"I'm Mrs. Castro," she shouted, putting her nose against
George's. "I own this boardinghouse and if you don't get
outta here, you're gonna be a sorry sonofabitch. I got pull
and I can have you busted."

"Do you own this liquor?" George demanded.

"My husband does. He's had it for years."

"Where is your husband?"

"At work, and I'm gonna go get him." She stormed back
up the stairs and out of the house.

George looked around at us and said, "Something screwy

here. Our tip was fourteen-carat. Let's take this liquor upstairs and then give the joint another shakedown."

The next time around we flushed a dozen bottles out of various hiding places, but that was all. We had just put them on the pool tables, along with the cases we found in the basement, when Mrs. Castro burst in the front door. She was accompanied by two beefy-looking men in regular business suits. She pointed to us and shouted, "There they are. Find out who they are. Get me their shield numbers."

One of the men stepped up to George and said, "I'm Detective O'Hara from the Oak Street squad. This is my partner, O'Leary. Now, what the hell is going on here. Who are you?"

George said quietly, "I'm Detective Faust. We're from the commissioner's office."

"The commissioner's office," O'Hara gulped. "Oh, I . . . I didn't know. Mamie Castro said some guys were tossing her place, and we thought . . . well, it might have been some drunken sailors, or something." He licked his lips and tried to smile. "Any way we can help you fellows?"

"Not unless you know where the rest of the stuff is hidden."

"I'm afraid not. Well, I guess we'll be going." O'Hara and his partner made it fast out the front door.

George said, "Okay, Bob, you take the arrest. I'll call the wagon."

We took the evidence and the surly young man who had opened the door down to the Oak Street station house and booked the young man. When the desk lieutenant asked him his name, he snarled, "Tom Foley."

That name made no impression on me. Politics hadn't

entered my life, and it never occurred to me that this name belonged to one of the most powerful men in the city. The desk lieutenant was asleep at the switch too, because he didn't even bother to check if this was the man's real name. And so, while the lieutenant and I stood there dreaming, the name of Tom Foley went on the blotter, and there was created the first ingredient of a monstrous plot to smear Mayor Hylan and Police Commissioner Enright with charges of graft and corruption.

The real name of our prisoner was "Snakes" McGrath. The name he gave us belonged to "Big Tom" Foley, a district sachem in Tammany Hall and an anti-Hylan man.

Faust left me at the Oak Street station, saying he was going back to headquarters to try and get more information about Mamie Castro's house. He was back in an hour with another lead and a new search warrant. We went back to Water Street and this time entered a vacant house next door to Mamie's. We crashed the cellar door and there found 170 cases of whiskey wrapped in burlap sacks. We had hit the jackpot, all right, but we had no prisoner. It was evident that Mamie had stored the stuff here and then moved it to her house a few cases at a time, but we couldn't prove it. Needless to say, no one ever claimed the liquor.

We loaded the stuff into a wagon and carted it down to headquarters where it was later destroyed. That was the end of that case . . . I thought. There was nothing to indicate that this was not a routine bootleg pinch, like dozens I had made before and would make afterwards. I didn't know that I had lit the fuse for a bomb that was to rock the department. Nor was the Mamie Castro case to be the end of my trouble. The very next raid was to add to my growing list of powerful enemies.

On the morning of April 9, 1923, George Faust informed me there had been a complaint that $50,000 worth of contraband liquor was in a basement storeroom at 300 Central Park West. The complaint alleged that this liquor belonged to a Mr. Charles F. Zittel, publisher of the Broadway magazine entitled *Zit's Weekly* and proprietor of the Casino Restaurant in Central Park. Faust directed Jimmy McMahon, Frank Magrino, and me to assist him in investigating the complaint.

At three o'clock that afternoon we were in the basement of the elegant apartment house and looking over the various storage rooms. Sure enough, we came to one bearing the name "Zittel." The superintendent of the building, John Harris, admitted that cases of liquor were taken out of this room almost every day. Presumably, they were transported to the Casino in the park. As we looked over the door, the super went back to his workshop. There were two Segal locks on the door.

"Let's kick it in," I said. I put my back against the cement wall opposite the door, pulled up my right foot, and let go. The door barely quivered. I tried again and almost broke my leg.

Hearing the crashes, the super came running with his assistant, a man named Alfred Music. "You can't break that door down," Harris said. "It's reinforced with steel plates."

"How do you know it is?" I demanded.

"I reinforced it myself, at Mr. Zittel's orders."

I whispered to Faust, "Take them back in the workshop and keep them there. We'll get in, somehow."

When the super and his assistant were gone, I went outside the building to look around. There was an alley eight feet below the sidewalk on the south side, and storeroom windows looked out upon it. I climbed a 7-foot safety fence and dropped down into the alleyway, only to discover that the windows were screened with iron bars. They were screwed to the frame, and I sent for a big screw driver to remove them. I soon had them off, then broke a small hole in the window to reach in and unlock it. Inside the room I found cases of liquor stacked to the ceiling. Fifty thousand dollars was a modest estimate of its worth. I unlocked the door from the inside and let the rest of my squad enter. I told the super that he'd better send for Mr. Zittel.

Mr. Zittel turned out to be a small man who wore glasses and was neatly dressed in a pin-striped blue suit, a striped blue shirt that sported huge diamond studs. He replied quite frankly to Faust's questions.

"Yes, I run the Casino in the park under a concession from the city. Since 1919, I've run one of the finest restaurants, serving the best food and liquor. Before 1919, I solicited theatrical advertising for William Randolph Hearst. I'm a respectable businessman and this is a disgraceful way to treat me. There is something behind this complaint and I'd like to know what it is."

"We are informed," Faust said, "that this liquor is contraband, having been delivered by bootleggers."

"That's untrue," Zittel said. "This liquor is legal; I own it by purchase six years ago, before Prohibition was passed. I bought it from James B. Regan, proprietor of the Knickerbocker Hotel."

Faust turned to me and said, "You heard him admit ownership of the liquor. Lock him up."

As I led Zittel away, he said to me, "I suppose you're

doing what you think is your duty, officer, but you're headed for trouble. This is a political squeeze play by men who want to get my restaurant."

"Sour grapes," I snapped at him.

I was wrong and Zittel was right. There was a close friend of Mayor-to-be Jimmy Walker who wanted this restaurant very badly. His name was Sidney Solomon, and he had a conversation with Walker that was recorded by Gene Fowler in his biography of Walker, *Beau James*.

It went like this.

Walker: "Sidney, is there anything I can do for you?"

Solomon: "Well, yes. I'd like to take over the old Casino in the Park."

Walker: "I'll see what can be done."

No one knows exactly how Walker maneuvered everything, but shortly after he became mayor, Zittel lost his restaurant and Solomon got it. Walker and his current girl friend, Betty Compton, personally directed the remodeling and redecorating of the Casino. It became their hangout, and consequently the hangout of the Tammany leaders all during the golden days of the Walker administration. Though I locked up Zittel for having liquor which he served in the Casino, after Solomon got the restaurant it continued to serve liquor without any trouble from the law. That's the way things were. Prohibition was a racket, a tool for blackmail and shakedowns. And the cops were caught in the middle.

As I marched Zittel out to the police car waiting at the curb, he shook his head almost sadly and said to me, "Son, there's going to be a stink on this one, and you're going to be right in the middle."

Chapter Seven

"THE BOFF" AND ME

Our squad worked late that night in the basement of the West 100th Street station house, sealing and labeling each bottle of the huge cache belonging to Charles Zittel. By the time we left the place, the early edition of the *Daily News* was on the street. The headline story read:

ZITTEL IS ARRESTED!
HIS LIQUOR SEIZED
WITHOUT WARRANT

Enright's Squad Forces Way
Into Publisher's Home and
Carries Away Private Stock

Charles F. Zittel, editor of Zit's Weekly and concessionaire under the Hylan Administration of the Casino Restaurant in Central Park, was arrested at 5 o'clock yesterday afternoon by Detective Robert McAllister of the Headquarters "rum squad" for an alleged violation of the Mullan-Gage law. McAllister declared that "Zit" had concealed $50,000 worth of choice liquors in the cellar of the apartment house in which he lives at 300 Central Park West, at Nine-tieth Street.

The editor . . . charged that McAllister with two other detectives had entered his apartment house without a search warrant and that they had broken into a locked storeroom to seize the liquor. He added that he intended to fight the case to the limit. . . . McAllister . . . broke through two locks, according to Zittel, and forced the door open.

Except for the part about my being able to break through those locks, the story was an accurate account of what happened. I went home to sleep without any misgivings.

My appearance in court the next morning couldn't have come at a worse moment. Inspector Bolan, my old boss in the 3d Division, had cracked down the day before on speakeasies and cabarets in his area, and the courtroom was full of night-club owners who had secured a warrant charging Bolan with the crime of "oppression," of "persecution," and of "depriving businessmen of the right to make a living." The presiding judge was the Honorable Joseph E. Corrigan, a man who made no effort to hide his dislike of Prohibition. The muttered conversation in the court was full of barbed references to the police department.

The Zittel case was called and the judge swore me in. I testified to the facts, saying about the door only that, "I opened it and let the squad in."

"Let me see the letter of complaint," Judge Corrigan snapped.

I gave it to him and he studied it a moment, then said, "I understand that some bottles seized in the raid were broken. McAllister, have you any more regard for a whiskey thief than any other kind of thief?"

"No, Your Honor."

"Neither have I," said the judge. "Who sent you to the house? Was it Commissioner Enright himself?"

"No, sir, he did not."

"You testified in direct examination that you opened the door and they walked in. Did you break down the door to get in?"

"No, sir."

"Did you kick down the door to gain entrance?"

"No, sir."

"Step down," His Honor said, a faint smile on his face.

The superintendent of the building was then called to the stand. The judge asked, "Did you see McAllister, the arresting officer, kick down the door?"

The super almost shouted, "Yes! I saw him kick the door in!"

Judge Corrigan turned and faced the courtroom, crowded with speak-easy owners and their arresting officers. He spoke in slow, weighted words that carried to every corner of the court: "I order that the warrant officer place this detective under arrest on a charge of perjury."

For a moment there was a stunned silence in the court, then, as the significance of the judge's move became clear, an explosion of excited voices. I sat with an open mouth, not really believing what I had just heard.

Alexander Rose, counsel for Mr. Zittel, shouted over the hubbub, "Your Honor, what about the defendant, Mr. Zittel?"

"The charges against him are dismissed," the judge said.

Now the court was really in an uproar, because every speak owner there saw a chance of winning his freedom. The judge gaveled for silence, and when he finally got it, he addressed the courtroom in general, and the reporters in particular. He said, "It is disheartening for a magistrate to sit on the bench and daily learn to what depths of degradation the police department of this city has dropped on the attempted enforcement of this liquor law. I disapprove of the methods the police use in handling the liquor question." Then he gave a cold glance in my direction and said, "Bail set at five hundred dollars."

Five hundred dollars! I didn't have that much. Out of the confusion that swirled about me there stepped a professional bondsman who put up the money. The next thing I knew I was out on the street with Faust. I turned to him and cried, "My God, what happened?"

"You got a raw deal, Bob."

"But why? I told the truth. How could that judge do that? My name will be in the papers . . . charged with perjury. He's got no right to blacken my name that way when I was only doing my job!"

"Bob . . . take it easy!"

I looked at him and said, "Don't you know what this means to me? To my record in the department?"

He said quietly, "I know." He put his hand on my shoulder. "You want my advice? Don't pop off, don't do anything until you see the commissioner."

"I'm going to see him right this minute," I said.

When I entered his office, I discovered the commissioner had already heard about the charge. He put his arm around my shoulders and said, "That's a tough break, kid. Sit down and let's talk about it."

"Commissioner, you don't think I. . . ."

"That you're guilty of the charge? Not for a moment."

"Thank God," I breathed fervently.

"When Corrigan made that charge, he wasn't trying to get you, Bob. He was trying to smear the entire department, trying to discredit me and the mayor."

"I still don't get it, sir."

"I'll be frank with you, son, but this is just between us. There are some powerful politicians in town who don't like the way we've been enforcing the liquor law. They're out to get the mayor, and they'll use innocent men like you to do it."

"But why *me?* I'm not important?"

"In a way, you are. Because of your athletic career you're well known in town, and anything that happens to you will make headlines. If Corrigan had charged Faust with perjury, it wouldn't have gotten half the publicity it will with the charge made against you. This is the beginning of a dirty campaign. Last week they charged Inspector Bolan with oppression; this week they charge you with perjury; next week it will be something else . . . but all of it is aimed at me and the mayor. You see the pattern?"

"I'm beginning to, sir."

"And now that they've got their hooks into you, they probably won't rest with a perjury charge, they'll try to dig something else up. I'm going to stand behind you, Bob; the mayor is going to stand behind you. But in return, I want you to be absolutely candid with me."

"Yes, sir. I will, sir."

"Tell me, do you have any big money? Any real estate or stocks? Any other income they can find out about?"

I couldn't help smiling. "Commissioner, my worldly wealth is a little over three hundred and eighty dollars, deposited in the Dime Savings Bank."

"I was sure of that," he said. "I knew you were an honest

cop and a credit to the department. Now, I'm not going to be stampeded into suspending you just because Corrigan slapped a perjury charge on you. Still, I don't think it would be wise to keep you on liquor cases. I'll transfer you to the gangster squad under Lieutenant Sheridan. In the meantime, I'll request the corporation counsel to assign a lawyer to your case. Good luck, Bob, and don't worry. We'll lick them."

The attorney assigned to defend me was Mr. Tarbox, an assistant corporation counsel, and he accompanied me to the West Side Court when my case was called the following week. We entered a scene of wild confusion, with the reporters and photographers all but mobbing me. I knew a lot of them from the times they had covered me at the track meets, and ordinarily I was happy to talk to them and pose for pictures, but not today. As I worked my way into the packed courtroom, I referred all questions to Commissioner Enright.

Mr. Tarbox stood up before Judge Corrigan and asked for an adjournment of my case so that another magistrate could hear it.

"No," snapped His Honor. "I've heard this from the beginning and I'm going through with the rest of it."

"Your Honor," Mr. Tarbox said, "I submit that for the reason you brought the charges against the officer, you should not hear them."

"I'm going to hear them," Corrigan said grimly. "I'm setting it down for the first of May in Harlem Court. I will continue the defendant on five hundred dollars bail."

As we left the court, Mr. Tarbox assured me, "Don't worry, Bob. He won't hear the case. For the past nine months he's been causing nothing but trouble for every cop who makes a Mullan-Gage arrest. But he won't hear your case."

I tried to find reassurance in his words, but I was now beginning to understand the political scope of the case. I wasn't at all certain that the Honorable Joseph E. Corrigan would not be my accuser, my judge, and my jury. But meanwhile I had work to do. I was on the gangster squad and mercifully relieved of any more liquor arrests. I tried to forget my troubles in my new assignment.

Roving bands of young hoodlums had begun to infest the streets of New York, preying upon merchants and taxi-cab drivers, demanding protection money. Later on, in the mid-twenties, all this sort of racketeering was to be organized by the major mobs, but now it was a hit-and-run affair of small neighborhood gangs. Half a dozen of these punks would come up to a taxi stand outside a first-class hotel and demand ten or fifteen bucks from the drivers in line, and if they didn't receive the money, they'd ice-pick the tires or pour sugar in the gas tanks. By the time the cops arrived, they would have disappeared.

The city was concerned over the effect upon out-of-town visitors, and the police department was given the assignment of cleaning up the situation. But it wasn't easy to catch them, or to collect evidence for a stand-up case that would send them to jail. So the gangster squad was created. The purpose of the squad was quite frankly explained to me the first day by our commanding officer, Lieutenant Sheridan.

He had been a middleweight boxer in his time, and carried the face to prove it—a broken nose and scar tissue around the eyes. He looked me over carefully when I reported and then growled, "They tell me you've done some fighting in the ring."

"Yes, sir," I said.

"When ya got pillows on your hands and a referee to watch . . . well, it's different from bare knuckles with a bunch of hoods in a back alley. You got guts, McAllister?"

"Yes, sir," I said.

"If you haven't, we'll soon find out. Now lemme tell ya what we're gonna do. We're going after the shakedown mugs, the tough guys, the muscle guys. But we're not gonna collect any evidence against them, we're not even gonna arrest them—we're gonna give 'em some of their own medicine—we're gonna work 'em over. We're gonna search this town from one end to the other and wherever we find 'em, we're gonna beat 'em up. This isn't according to the book, but we're gonna forget the book. When we get through with them, they're either gonna be too scared to shake down the storekeepers, or they're gonna be in the hospital. Now, come on into the other office and I'll introduce you to your partner. His name is Johnny Broderick."

At this time Johnny Broderick was unknown. In another ten years he was to be the most famous detective on the force, and his name enough to strike terror into the hearts of gangsters. He scorned the use of a gun but charged the enemy with flailing fists. The cry "Broderick is coming!" was enough to empty many a poolroom and bootleg dive. His name was used to coin a new phrase in the department: to "Broderick" came to mean to "muss up a tough guy." Jack Dempsey was quoted as saying, "Broderick is one man I'd hate to meet in a dark alley. Matter of fact, if I knew he was waiting for me, I'd walk the other way." The under-

world nicknamed Johnny "The Boff," and he was so
pleased by this tribute that he adopted the name.

But all this was in the future, and when I met Johnny
Broderick, he was a stranger to me, though an impressive
one. He was somewhere between a middleweight and a
light heavyweight, with massive shoulders and powerful
arms. His square face was already scarred from numerous
fights he'd had as a kid and in labor wars, and his square
jaw was thrust forward in habitual belligerence. But his
eyes smiled a welcome.

"Hi ya," he said when we were introduced. "Sit down,
kid."

We were about the same age, yet it seemed natural for
him to call me kid—beside him, I looked so innocent and
untried. We began talking easily, as if we were old friends.
It turned out we were both born and raised in the Tenderloin, both of us had come from desperately poor families,
had always had to fight in the streets, had always wanted to
be cops.

"Well, we made it," he grinned at me.

"Yes, sir," I said. We were of equal rank, still I called
him "sir."

He looked me over and said, "You're in shape."

I couldn't help boasting a little. "I'm a sprinter. I hold
the indoor records for the 110, 120, 130, and 150 yards."

"I know. I've read all about you in the sports pages."

"Thanks," I said, real pleased.

"But tell me, you ever do any fighting?"

"In the Army, and a little amateur work."

"This is a fighting assignment. You know that?"

"Lieutenant Sheridan told me all about it. And it suits

me fine." Broderick leaned forward and tapped me on the knee for emphasis. "Let me give you some advice, kid. Always remember that you're a better man than any six of the underworld rats we'll be going after. You're better because you're a cop and they're crooks . . . just as simple as that. They're yellow, or they wouldn't be trying to knock over cabbies and shopkeepers; they don't have the guts to make an honest living, to work and sweat, and they don't have the guts to stand up to you and me. I don't carry a gun, I only carry these two weapons." He held his fists in front of my face. "And they're scared of these, and they'll be scared of your fists, too. Always remember, you're tougher than any of them."

"Yes, sir," I said. I wasn't at all sure it was true, but it sounded nice to hear him say it.

Broderick said, "Okay, now go out and buy yourself a pair of gloves, kid gloves that fit kinda loose." I did as he told me without even asking why.

Our first assignment came the following day when Lieutenant Sheridan stepped out of his private office and said to us, "A shopkeeper on Rivington Street was just beaten up. Looks like a case for us. Let's go."

Rivington Street was on the lower East Side in the heart of New York's ghetto. Here was the city's disgrace, a slum even worse than the one I had grown up in. Packed into a few square miles of rotting tenements were more Jews than in the city of Jerusalem. The narrow streets were jammed with pushcarts that supplied all needs from pots and pans to mezuzahs. Skullcapped patriarchs cried their wares in shrill old voices while housewives bargained fiercely in their native language. Far down the street we saw a police car and an ambulance. There was our trouble.

It was in a second-hand clothing store, narrow, dingy, and smelling of dust. Now it was crowded with police. Stretched on the floor was the ancient proprietor, one side of his face gory and torn. His attackers had apparently tried to rip his beard off, taking part of his cheek in the process. His wife sat on the floor by his head, and while the doctor worked to patch him up, she rocked back and forth to the rhythm of muttered prayer, her eyes streaming with tears.

"Any identification?" Lieutenant Sheridan asked of the precinct man in charge.

"None," he said. "The old man is in no condition to talk and his wife is pretty incoherent. All we know for sure is that somebody tried to shake them down for ten dollars-a-month protection. They've been paying it for several months but this time they just didn't have it."

"This is Kid Dropper's neighborhood, isn't it?" Sheridan asked.

"That's right. He and his gang hang out at the pool hall down the block, corner of Willett Street."

"I brought a mug shot of him along. Let's see if she recognizes it."

Sheridan leaned over the old woman and held the picture in front of her. "Is this the man, mother? Did he do it?"

She took one look at the picture, then let out a piercing cry and covered her face with her hands. A police interpreter discovered through her broken sobs that it had indeed been Kid Dropper and his gang. We also found out that she was so terrified that she wouldn't formally identify him, and certainly wouldn't appear in court against him. The police were up against the familiar stone wall, unable to get a stand-up case.

But this was what the gangster squad was for. We filed grimly from the shabby store and climbed into the car to head for the poolroom at the corner of Willett.

This Kid Dropper we were going after had a record as long as your arm. He had started out, back during the war, as a member of Paul Kelly's "Five-points" gang. He was a degenerate, and had a reputation as a shiv man, that is, a knifer. He was sent to Sing Sing along with another member of the gang named Johnny Spanish. They became enemies in prison, and when they were released, formed rival gangs of their own. The bad blood between them became worse when Kid Dropper's girl fell for Johnny Spanish. The Kid lured her into his car, took her for a typical gangster "ride," and dumped her bullet-riddled body into a swamp near Maspeth, Long Island.

This resulted in declared war between the two. In 1919, Johnny Spanish was found shot dead on Second Avenue. Kid Dropper was charged with the murder, but no witnesses could be found with enough courage to come forward and speak the truth. From that time on his gang specialized in labor disputes, hiring themselves out to beat up pickets or employers, depending upon who paid them. Things had been slow on the labor front recently, so now he was beating up defenseless old men too poor to pay tribute. I felt real eager to meet Kid Dropper.

Johnny Broderick and I were riding together in the back seat, and he said to me, "In a poolroom, watch out for the pool cues, they'll use them as clubs. And watch for brass knuckles, they can cut you up."

"Brass knuckles!" I exclaimed. "Why don't we have some?"

He grinned at me. "It's not according to regulations, Bob. But we'll manage." He pulled a roll of adhesive tape out of his pocket and two half dollars. "Here, let me fix up your hands. "What's your best punch?"

"Right cross."

He nodded and took my right hand and began to tape it, the way a boxer's hands are taped. There was a difference, however. After a couple of turns of the tape, he laid the two half dollars across my knuckles and then taped them in place. When he was finished, he said, "Now, put on your kid gloves." I pulled them on and they were a perfect fit. I pounded my right hand in the palm of my left one and grinned.

The pool hall was two steps down from the street, and the dirt-streaked window pretty well concealed us until we were inside the place. We had been instructed that there was to be no fight unless Kid Dropper himself was there, and that the first man who recognized him was to give the cry.

Johnny Broderick led the way in, then stood spread-legged to glare around the room at a dozen men who had frozen at our entrance. We were in plain clothes, but they knew we were cops, just as we knew they were crooks. We could smell each other out.

Suddenly Johnny pointed to a hulking man with lank black hair at a far table. "There's the bastard," he said. Then speaking directly to Kid Dropper, he said, "We're cops but we didn't come here to make a pinch. We didn't bring our guns. We're gonna show you that any cop can take you over at any time, and with nothing but his fists.

And this is what you're gonna get every time you try to shake down anybody."

With that, we charged.

It was bedlam for the next few minutes. I took a pool ball above the ear, and for a moment I was blinded with exploding stars, but when my head cleared I was in a cold rage and bore into the nearest man. I caught him flush on the throat and heard him gag as his Adam's apple swelled and choked him. He sank slowly down and I kneed him in the face as he went.

The odds against us were about two to one, plus the fact that they had pool balls as ammunition. I saw Johnny working around the side of the room toward Kid Dropper, who was standing in a far corner, behind two of his hench-men. Suddenly Johnny sprang on top of a pool table and from there took a flying leap over the heads of everyone to land on the Dropper. I understood his plan—pick off the leader and the others will be demoralized. But now he was surrounded, and at least a half-dozen men were throwing punches at him. I charged the circle, screaming my rage as I came. I rabbit-punched one of them, and he gave a little sigh and sank from sight. Johnny's nose was bleeding and there was a dewlap of torn flesh over his right eye, but he was flailing out with his fists, causing havoc wherever they landed.

I worked my way toward Kid Dropper. He had a cue in his hand, the weighted end raised as a club. He waited for an opening, saw it, and began to swing. I shouted a warning to Johnny, who shifted enough to take the cue on his shoulder instead of his head. The blow should have broken his arm, but he came back with a left and a right deep in the Dropper's stomach. The cue clattered to the floor, the Kid's eyes bulged as his tortured lungs gasped for air. Johnny brought a vicious right to his slack jaw, leaving it a smear of red.

A shrill whimper, a frightened animal sound, came from Kid Dropper. He turned and bolted for the door. In another moment the room was empty except for us cops and for those gangsters too hurt to move from the floor.

Johnny and I looked at each other and grinned foolishly. We were both cut and bleeding but we didn't seem to hurt. He said, "We took 'em, Bob. By God, we took 'em!"

I nodded, feeling a lot better about the old man with the torn face.

Chapter Eight

A WRONG BEEF

Work on the gangster squad kept me so busy that I developed the illusion everything was normal; that I was an ordinary cop doing his job, planning to get married to the girl he loved, looking to the future with optimism. Commissioner Enright had said that I was a pawn being used in the struggle for power among politicians, but as the days passed the impact of his words faded. That perjury charge had all been a bad dream, something to forget about.

But the battle in Tammany Hall between the forces for Hylan and those for Jimmy Walker was deepening all the time, and another bolt by the Walker camp was aimed at me on April 22d.

That evening the *New York Telegram* hit the stands with the headline:

McALLISTER TOOK $600 BRIBE FROM HER AFTER RUM RAID IN HER HOME, SHE TESTIFIES

Mamie Castro, the proprietor of the Water Street boardinghouse I had raided, was accusing me of shaking her down! Accompanying the story was a big picture of me with the caption:

> Detective McAllister, accused of grafting by woman, shown here in running togs in one of the events in which he earned his nickname the "flying cop."

I read the nightmarish headline over and over, not believing the words could possibly say what they did.

This headline was only the beginning of a one-two punch. The second one came almost at once, with an announcement from the district attorney's office that it was conducting a full-scale investigation of me and the entire police department. The D.A. was a man named Joab Banton, who owed his job to Tammany leader Foley. In announcing the convening of a grand jury for my case, he lashed out at what he called "bluecoat bootleggers." Thus the enemies of Mayor Hylan and Commissioner Enright were to be in full control of my case. Things looked pretty black.

And in the midst of it all, there arrived the day Mabel and I had set for our wedding. I kept postponing any decision on my personal life right up until the last moment, but two days before the wedding date, I felt I had to speak out.

"Honey," I said, "let's postpone the wedding awhile."

She grinned at me and said, "It won't do any good, Bob. You'll have cold feet a month from now just the same. The only thing to do is hold your breath and plunge right in. You'll be glad when it's all over."

"You don't understand what I mean, Mabel. Good God, I want you for my wife more than anything in the world, but it's not fair to ask you to marry me with this trial hanging over me."

"Not fair to whom?" she asked softly.

"To you! All sorts of lies may be said about me, I may be smeared in the press until no self-respecting woman would want to be seen with me."

"I would," she said firmly. "I love you and I know you're innocent. And you'd better show up at that altar on time, or you'll be in some *real* trouble, Bob McAllister."

"But, honey. . . ."

She took hold of my hands and looked me straight in the eyes and said, "We're going to lick them. Don't you understand that, Bob? You're innocent, and we're going to fight every inch of the way and win."

So we were married. I needed her love and her strength. If she hadn't been at my side in the days that lay ahead, I'm certain I should have gone under.

Shortly after our wedding, Mabel and I had dinner at Uncle Jake Weber's. We all tried to be gay during the meal, but my troubles hung over us, stifling conversation. Finally, with coffee, Jake brought into the open what had been weighing on our minds. "Bob, you got two charges pending against you—attempted extortion and perjury."

"That's right," I said.

"What you need is a bang-up lawyer."

"The department will supply me with a lawyer," I said.

"And you'll accept just anybody they assign you, I suppose," he said scornfully. He pointed his cigar at me and continued, "You're in serious trouble and you've got to conduct your own fight."

"Jake! I'm going to fight with everything I've got."

"And what you haven't got is a good lawyer, a man who knows all the angles on these criminal cases. You need somebody really big . . . like William J. Fallon."

"Oh . . . sure."

"I'm serious, Bob. I've talked to Fallon and he's interested in you."

"You . . . know Fallon? You . . . you've talked to him?"

"He's a Fordham grad. We been friends for years. I told him about your bum rap, and he's interested in the case."

"Well, I'll be damned," I said, and leaned back in my chair to think about William J. Fallon. He was about the best-known criminal lawyer in the city. He was called "the great mouthpiece," and his spectacular courtroom performances were famous. He was equally famous as a man-about-town, a Broadway playboy, rumored to be the love of Gertrude Vanderbilt, and a man of such brilliance, charm, and prestige that it seemed ridiculous to think he'd bother to take my case.

"Jake," I said, "we've got a couple hundred dollars in the bank. I've heard of Fallon getting as much as fifty thousand dollars for a single courtroom appearance."

"Does it hurt you to talk to him?" Jake demanded.

Mabel put her hand on my arm and said, "Jake's right, honey. What can you lose by talking to him?"

"Okay . . . okay. I'll see him."

Later that night, when Mabel and I had left Jake's and were walking slowly crosstown to the subway, I said, "Hon, do you remember my telling you about my first tour of the beat with my partner Mike de Luca when I was

a plain-clothes cop? Remember my telling you about seeing the gambler Arnold Rothstein standing in a doorway
on Broadway?"

"Yes, dear, I remember."

"I wanted to arrest Rothstein right there on the spot, but
Mike explained to me that we had to take things slow, had
to get stand-up cases. I've since discovered that Rothstein
has been arrested several times but never spent any time
in prison. Do you know why? Because his lawyer is William J. Fallon. Fallon always gets him off."

She hesitated a moment. "That proves he's a good lawyer."

"But he's on the other side," I burst out. "He's for the
crooks, not the cops."

"I can see what you mean, Bob, but I think you're
wrong."

"I don't know whether I'm right or wrong, but. . . ."

"Please, let me say something, dear. And try not to get
angry. Try to understand my point. You keep thinking
that because you're a police officer, everyone must know
you're honest. But it just doesn't work that way. When
you stand trial, your uniform won't protect you . . .
you'll be just an ordinary man who is an accused perjurer,
an accused extortionist. You need a lawyer who is an expert
in criminal law . . . because you're accused of being a
criminal. I know it's hard for you to accept that fact,
honey, and it's hard for me to say it to you. But it's the
truth."

I reached for her hand and squeezed it. She was right,
of course. But, oh God, it was hard to accept it.

The next day I went to see "the great mouthpiece," just
as dozens of famous criminals (and innocent men too, I

suppose) had done before me. His office was in the Knickerbocker Building at Times Square. His secretary greeted me
cordially and then announced me over the phone. Fallon
didn't wait for me to come into his private office; he came
out and greeted me. I was quite overwhelmed when I saw
him. I'm not sure what I expected, perhaps a man whose
shrewdness would show on his face, but Fallon's coun-
tenance was completely open and guileless. He was 6 feet
tall, weighed 190 pounds without an ounce of fat, had
wavy, apricot-colored hair and the voice and gestures of
a Shakespearian actor. He generated an electric atmosphere
about him that convinced you he could accomplish miracles.

He greeted me by my first name in his booming voice
and took me into the sumptuous office overlooking Broadway—his street.

"Bob, I've watched you run many times. It's a real
pleasure to meet you. Jake Weber is an old pal of mine,
you know. He tells me you're now a member of the
family."

"Yes, sir. I married his niece."

"Congratulations. I always advise young men to get married and settle down. I don't take my own advice, of
course."

I laughed, knowing that Fallon's fame as a nonchalant
Lothario was fully as great as his reputation as a lawyer.

He became serious and said, "Bob, tell me what happened
at Zittel's and down in Tom Foley's bailiwick."

I told him all the details. When I finished, he ran his
hand through his long hair and muttered, "Incredible.
Politics is a mighty dirty thing."

"I'm learning that," I said.

"You know what happened to my partner, Joe Shalleck?"

"No, sir."

"He was campaign manager for Jimmy Hines a while back, and Jimmy had a falling out with Murphy and Tom Foley. Joe went to a polling place on 17th Street, 100 feet from Charley Murphy's home, and found a number of erasures on the poll list and complained to the chairman. Next thing he knew he was hit with a lead pipe from behind. He fell to the floor and then the boys began to use him for a football. His friends outside heard the commotion and came charging to his rescue, whereupon one of Murphy's men pulled out a gun and shot Shalleck in the breast. Damn near killed him." He shook his head and said, "You're in rough company, son."

"I guess I'm in a worse jam than I thought," I said glumly. "And I never even heard of Tom Foley until all this happened."

"I'm sure of it, Bob, but Foley thinks differently. I got a tip that Foley is out to bust you because that convict you booked after the Mamie Castro raid swears you forced him to use Foley's name."

"That's a damn lie," I exploded.

"Of course, but to prove it is the problem."

"Why should he take a crook's word instead of a cop's? I don't get that!"

"Bob, I know a lot of politicians and I know a lot about them. Their greatest weakness is vanity. Tom Foley believes that everybody in town knows him and therefore, even if you didn't force that convict to use his name, you knew what he was doing and didn't stop him. Believe me, Foley will never forget this. He's your sworn enemy for life, and you might as well face that fact."

Here was the second powerful man who was my sworn

enemy for life—the other being Dutch Schultz. Fallon could see my depression, I guess, for he slapped the desk and said, "You're mixed up with a bunch of bastards, Bob, but I'm going to defend you and see you get a fair shake."

"But, Mr. Fallon . . . ," I started.

He held up his hand. "If you're going to talk about money, forget it. This case is strictly on the muscle."

I tried to thank him, but he interrupted me with instructions to get the transcript of the testimony on the Zittel and Castro cases. He ushered me to the door, his arm around my shoulders, with the final instructions: "Every booze peddler and dope pusher on the East Side knows Mamie Castro. What I want you to find out is how well she knows those two bulls out of the Oak Street station—O'Hara and O'Leary. I want to know what the connection is there. Dig it up as soon as you can. And, Bob, if you run short of cash at any time, I'll lend you what you need."

When I left Fallon's office, the old spring was back in my step, I was back in fighting trim. The misgivings I had felt when I came now seemed ridiculous. There was something about the warmth, the vast self-confidence of the man, that gave me the courage I needed. Fallon could absorb your troubles, make them his own, and dispose of them. Whatever his reputation, he was a great human being.

I carried out Fallon's assignment the next day and discovered that Howard O'Leary and Frank O'Hara had grown up with Mamie Castro, gone to the same school, shared the same friends. Fallon chortled at this news and said it wrapped up the case. I prayed he was right.

But the day the case opened, the newsstands carried the big black headlines:

McALLISTER THE STORM CENTER
OF BOOTLEG INQUIRY

I was the storm center, all right. It didn't feel good.

The trial was routine until Mamie Castro was on the stand and about to be cross-examined by "the great mouthpiece." At this moment the courtroom atmosphere became taut, with everyone straining to hear each word. Bill Fallon advanced toward the woman with smiling courtliness. He might have been addressing a grand duchess when he said, "I'm so sorry, Mrs. Castro, but I'll have to ask you a few questions." The following exchange is from the court records:

Mr. Fallon: Mrs. Castro, do you remember being questioned by Mr. Hirschfield at the Municipal Building?

Mrs. Castro: Yes, I do.

Mr. Fallon: Do you remember your answer to the question, "Will you pick out all the policemen who were in your place on the morning in question"? I refer to page 278 of the minutes. You picked out Officers Faust, Plagge, Coonan, Yost, and McAllister.

Mrs. Castro: Yes, that's right.

Mr. Fallon: On the same page by Commissioner Hirschfield, Question: "Now, you are sure you didn't see anyone else there, or did you send for anyone?" And you answered, "I sent for my brother to take the arrest."

Mrs. Castro: That's right, Counsel.

Mr. Fallon: Did you call Detectives Frank O'Hara and Howard O'Leary at the Oak Street station house and ask them to come over to find out who the men were who raided your place?

Mrs. Castro: Yes, now I remember.

Mr. Fallon: Then it wasn't your brother you called; it was Detectives O'Leary and O'Hara? Be careful how you answer, Mrs. Castro; perjury is a serious crime.

Mrs. Castro: Yes.

Mr. Fallon: O'Hara and O'Leary came right over to your place and made the officers identify themselves?

Mrs. Castro: Yes.

Mr. Fallon: Did you hear Detective Faust say they were from the Police Commissioner's office?

Mrs. Castro: Yes.

Mr. Fallon: How long do you know Frank O'Hara and Howard O'Leary?

Mrs. Castro: A long time.

Mr. Fallon: You went to school with them?

Mrs. Castro: Well, yes, they came from the same neighborhood.

Mr. Fallon: You call them Frankie and Howie, and they call you Mamie. Isn't that a fact, Mrs. Castro?

Mrs. Castro: Yes.

Mr. Fallon: Do you consider O'Hara and O'Leary honest police officers?

Mrs. Castro: Yes, they are honest.

Mr. Fallon: Do you trust them?

Mrs. Castro: Yes.

Mr. Fallon: Now then, when McAllister took the $600, part of it belonging to the sailors, all your rent money, did you make a protest to Detectives O'Hara and O'Leary?

Mrs. Castro: No.

Mr. Fallon: Did you say, "This crook [pointing his finger at me], this betrayer of his sacred trust took the sailors' and my money"?

Mrs. Castro: I didn't say anything.

Mr. Fallon [He was no longer polite; his voice thundered and vibrated through the hushed courtroom.]: You were hurt! You were wronged! Your money was taken from you! Yet you made no protest, no outcry to your life-long friends?

Mrs. Castro [almost inaudibly]: No, I didn't say anything.

Mr. Fallon: Your brother was there?

Mrs. Castro: Yes.

Mr. Fallon: Did he say anything to the two detectives whom you called, who came at your request?

Mrs. Castro: No.

Mr. Fallon: Nothing was said about the money to anyone?

Mrs. Castro: No one said anything.

Mr. Fallon: When did you first tell anybody about the $600 extorted from you by McAllister?

Mrs. Castro: After I heard there was an investigation, my brother told me to go down and make a complaint.

Mr. Fallon: Your Honor, there's not a scintilla of corroborating evidence in this case. The State has failed to produce any evidence that McAllister asked for or received a bribe from Mrs. Castro. Four officers besides McAllister were present. Two detectives, friends of Mrs. Castro, were called by her to the scene. She admits no complaint of any kind was made to anyone until after she heard there was an investigation and her brother told her to make a complaint. Is this the action of a normal person? All this after almost four months to think it over. Mrs. Castro's story is fantastic, without corroboration or one single strand of evidence to lend it authenticity. I respectfully move for dismissal of the charge.

Judge Crain: I agree. Case dismissed.

Later, Bill Fallon talked the case over with me and said, "This is the old routine used to get hunk on a cop who steps on somebody's corns. All they need is one phony witness to make a charge and the wheels are set in motion. The district attorney knows damn well he can't get a conviction on an extortion charge on the unsupported testimony of the person who allegedly gave the bribe. Yet the case has a great nuisance value; it puts a man on the defensive, and a political hireling of this great sovereign state can pauperize a man, and destroy his reputation."

Now the score was one down and one to go. Mamie

Castro's story of extortion was washed up. But there was still the little matter of the Zittel case—a time bomb that could wreck my chances and career in the department. On June 8th, the hearing on the perjury charges began before Judge Crain.

Mr. Zittel testified that he found the door of his storeroom open and pieces of cement and plaster on the floor. Officers seized his liquor and "that man"—he pointed at me—arrested him. He signed the complaint, he said, at the behest of Corrigan.

As soon as Mr. Zittel finished his direct testimony, Bill Fallon moved in. Eugene McGee and Joe Shalleck, his aides, sat at the counsel table and frequently handed him notes.

I did not understand immediately what Fallon was trying to develop. Then it dawned on me as I listened to his adroit questioning of Mr. Zittel.

> *Mr. Fallon:* After you were arrested, Mr. Zittel, the charges against you were dismissed by Magistrate Corrigan?
> *Mr. Zittel:* Yes.
> *Mr. Fallon:* Was all your liquor returned to you, Mr. Zittel?
> *Mr. Zittel:* Yes, every bottle.
> *Mr. Fallon:* About how many bottles would you say, Mr. Zittel?
> *Mr. Zittel:* I would say, roughly a little over three thousand bottles.
> *Mr. Fallon:* Thank you, Mr. Zittel, that's all.

The building superintendents were the next witnesses. Both men swore that they saw me put my back to the wall, raise my foot, and kick the door in. Fallon said, "No questions."

Fallon then made a request that the perjury charge be

dismissed on the grounds of insufficient complaint. "The charge," he said, "was illegal inasmuch as the defendant admitted raiding the Zittel cellar without a search warrant, thus negating the defendant's testimony as to what happened in the raid." He again made a motion that the charge be dismissed "because it made no difference how the defendant gained entrance into the Zittel cellar; whether he used a sledge hammer, a pinch bar, or by any means or methods, it was still immaterial. The defendant had no business in that cellar without a search warrant."

"Motion denied. Proceed with your defense," ordered Judge Crain. Fallon said, "The defense rests. No witnesses."

I was worried and I searched Fallon's face but found nothing to indicate he was upset. Who was I to question the way "the great mouthpiece" conducted a case, but still, this case happened to be *me*.

The jury retired and thirty minutes later indicted me for perjury and instructed that I be held for trial.

As we walked out of the courtroom, I turned to Fallon and said, "You didn't put me on the stand. I didn't have a chance to tell my side of it."

"Bob," he said, "I had good reason for not putting you on the stand. With all due respect for Judge Crain's knowledge of the law, this is one case where he is 100 per cent wrong. The whole case hinges on the word *immaterial*. Zittel was dismissed, his liquor returned, no one was hurt but you. You can't be convicted under the law, and I'll be damned if I'll put you on the stand and give the press a Roman holiday. Most people hate a cop, Bob. And in these days particularly, God help the cop who goes before a jury on a liquor case, no matter what the charge. Just you have patience and trust me. We'll beat the rap."

Later that afternoon I reported back to headquarters and told Commissioner Enright what had happened.

"Don't worry, Bob," the commissioner said. "You have the best lawyer in the country. He knows what he's doing. Just keep your chin up."

"Yes, sir," I said, snapping him a salute and turning to leave.

"Bob," he called after me, "you know I'll have to suspend you from the force."

"Suspend me . . . from the force, sir?" I stammered.

"It's the law. Any police officer under indictment must be suspended. I'm sorry."

It was a heartbreaking moment when I stood before the main desk of the detective division and turned in my gold shield and gun. Something very precious had gone out of my life. Worse was the feeling that we had somehow given up without a fight. Was "the great mouthpiece" wrong when he gambled on the word *immaterial?* All I could do was wait and pray.

Mabel was waiting for me on the main floor. I went to her and told her what had happened.

"We'll lick them, darling," she said with that indestructible courage of hers.

"But in the meantime, I'm out of a job."

She laughed and squeezed my arm. "I didn't marry you because you were rich. And you'll get another job. It's not the end of the world."

Around her, I could never feel sorry for myself.

Chapter Nine

THE COLD HEART
OF JOAB BANTON

What does a suspended cop do?

He walks the streets, block after block, hour after hour, wondering what has happened to him. There had been a time when he walked these streets in pride, with responsibility, with badge and gun and a firm step—but now he is nothing. He thinks the disgrace shows, like a brand on the forehead. When he meets old friends on the force, they are ill at ease with him, sympathetic, but seemingly eager to be rid of his company. He is a pariah, a leper whose disease might infect those who come too close.

A suspended cop looks for jobs, but what kind? A man under indictment for perjury is not in high demand.

Chet Bowman, the sprint star of the Newark Athletic Club, tipped me off that Davega's sporting goods store on Nassau Street had a job open as a clerk, and hoped to hire a champion athlete. I rushed down there. Six months before, the manager would have ordered drinks on the house if I had walked in the front door. Now he gave me the fish eye and said, "No, I don't think I remember you. However, if you wish to fill out an application form, something may open up." It never did.

Johnny Broderick sent me to a detective agency where I got a job, not as a private eye, but as a guard for scabs imported to break a strike at the Figge-Hutweiker slaughterhouse in the heart of Hell's Kitchen. The job wasn't pretty, but it paid fifteen dollars a day, and that was enough to keep the honeymoon furniture from being put on the street by the sheriff's men. The strikers, the scabs, the guards—we were all the poor and dispossessed fighting each other.

One night as I walked slowly home after work, full of self-disgust, I picked up a copy of the *Daily News*, and on page two saw a picture of the strike. An arrow picked out a tiny figure—it was me! The headline on the picture read WHERE THE "FLYING COP" HAS LIT. Sickened, I threw the paper into the gutter.

The strike ended and there were no more such jobs for me. I was too notorious and focused too much attention on any job I might be given.

And all the time the district attorney kept needling me. Hardly a week passed without my sitting before one of Joab Banton's assistants answering questions about bank accounts that didn't exist, stock deals I never heard of. I wanted to sign a waiver of immunity and testify before the grand jury about my finances, but there were no takers. They didn't want me before the grand jury.

One day I received a subpoena and arrived at the D.A.'s office to find that the rest of the commissioner's confidential squad had been subpoenaed. There were Yost and Coonan and McMahon and the others. We sat in the outer office on a row of chairs and talked together in whispers, fearing a planted mike. From time to time a door to an inner office would open and a pair of eyes would stare at us, then the door would softly close.

After this had happened a couple of times, Yost whispered to me, "You catch that door?"

"Yes," I whispered back. "I've been wondering."

"Something funny about this whole thing, Bob. Let's you and me switch seats. Quick now."

We switched seats just before the door opened wide and an assistant district attorney entered the room with a well-dressed stranger. The assistant district attorney said, "We have a complainant here who wants to identify one of you men."

The stranger walked over to the seat I had just vacated, placed his hand on Yost's shoulder and said, "This looks like the man who extorted five hundred dollars from me."

"What's your name?" snapped the assistant district attorney.

"Patrolman Yost."

There was a moment of dead silence while the assistant district attorney and the stranger dropped their jaws in amazement. The silence was broken by McMahon's low, bitter voice. "You dirty, framing bastards."

We all stood up and marched out of the office, and that bright young assistant district attorney never called us back.

Once on the street, I thanked Yost for being a real pal and headed at once for Bill Fallon's office. This thing was giving me the jitters, and I needed the reassurance a talk with him always gave me.

Fallon was in conference when I arrived, but he soon came out of his office with a man and a woman. Even before he introduced them, I recognized Fanny Brice and Nicky Arnstein.

Nicky Arnstein, a notorious Broadway gambler and confidence man, had recently been indicted in a bond-swindle case, and Fallon was his lawyer. He was a tall, slender man with a dark complexion and hooked nose above a carefully trimmed mustache. He was dressed in the height of fashion —complete with pearl homburg, spats, and cane.

Fanny Brice's love for this man was already a legend on Broadway. He disgraced her by his shady deals, lived on her earnings, and pursued other women—but he was her man, and she sacrificed everything for him. And as she came out of that office holding his arm, I could see that she thought he was the finest man alive. It occurred to me that the gambler Arnstein and the cop McAllister had one blessing in common—the love of a good woman to help him through trouble.

When the others left and I was finally alone with Fallon, I told him what had happened at the D.A.'s office. He reached for the phone, and his voice was cutting when he told the D.A. that he was ready to surrender me on a bench warrant if they had new evidence of extortion, but they had better stop bothering me with subpoenas. He slammed the receiver down before the D.A. could disconnect.

"Bob, I think we've got them off our neck on any new counts, and believe me, we'll get that perjury charge laughed right out of court when it comes to trial."

"When?" I moaned.

He looked at me soberly and said, "Need a job?"

"Bill, you've done enough for me. I'm not going to burden you with my nonlegal problems."

He didn't seem to hear and began writing a note. He

put it in an envelope, addressed it, and handed it to me and said, "Go see him. He should be able to do something for you."

When I got home I showed the note to Mabel. She read the address, "James J. Hines—but Bob, isn't he a Tammany leader?"

"He sure is, a sachem on the upper West Side. He's head of the Monongahela Club."

"But it's Tammany that's been causing us all the trouble. Why would Mr. Fallon send us . . ."

"Honey, this fellow Hines has split with Tom Foley and with Grand Sachem Charley Murphy. Why, Fallon told me that his partner was Hines' campaign manager, and Murphy's men beat him up and shot him."

She shook her head. "I don't understand it all."

I threw my arms around her and kissed her and said, "Hon, I don't either. But if Bill Fallon tells us to see Jimmy Hines, don't you think we should do it?"

"Oh, of course . . . of course."

I telephoned him that evening at the Monongahela Club, and he was extremely cordial and insisted that Mabel and I come to his house for dinner the following evening. We dressed up in our Sunday best and presented ourselves at his brownstone house on 116th Street. Hines himself opened the door. He was a big, bluff, handsome man with a ruddy, Irish face.

"Bob McAllister," he boomed, without waiting for me to introduce myself. "And this is your missus, eh? Come in, folks . . . come on in, and welcome to ya."

His wife came forward, plump and motherly, and then his two boys, ages ten and twelve. Hines said to them, "This is the 'flying cop' I was tellin' ya about. He's one of the greatest runners of our time." The boys looked at me, wide-eyed. Hines said, "And if ya don't bother the man until he's had his supper, maybe he'll tell ya a couple of stories about his runnin' career."

"I sure will," I said. I was being treated like a celebrity and a hero, rather than a down-and-outer come to beg a job.

We had a fine supper and I told the boys some stories about my career. About ten o'clock, Hines took me into his study for a private conversation. He said, "Lad, you've had a bum deal."

"You don't have to tell me that, Mr. Hines," I said. "I want you to know I'm innocent."

He waved his hand. "Don't even mention it. You've been caught up in some dirty politics, that's all there is of it. And it's a shame, too." He thought a minute, then said, "Can ya drive a bus?"

"I've driven trucks, so I guess I could drive a bus all right."

He pulled a piece of paper in front of him and began to write rapidly on it. "I'll give ya a letter to Freddy Richter. He's in charge of the city buses in the department of plants and structures under Commissioner Whalen. He should be able to find a spot for ya. Now, don't try to thank me. Ya just keep yer chin up, lad . . . and good luck to ya."

Mabel and I left the Hines house in great spirits. There was about Hines an aura of quiet power and authority. It was a good feeling to have him in your corner. With Hines and Bill Fallon with me, I felt eager to face my enemies in a showdown. And in the meantime . . . I'd even have a job!

And so I became a bus driver. And I headed again for some of the most lurid headlines the tabloids could compose.

My route was the 79th Street crosstown that ran from the East River west to Fifth Avenue, then through the Central Park transverse to Central Park West, then on to Broadway, the end of the run. There I'd join the feed line, headed back east again. It was a monotonous job, but at this stage I was glad to have a little monotony in my life.

Several weeks slid by, then one Saturday evening I saw a familiar figure standing at the corner of 79th Street and Broadway. It was Billy Quaine, a detective from East Harlem, and he was waiting for me. As I swung down from the bus for a quick smoke, he hurried up, visibly excited.

"Tell me, Bob," he said, "is there any special reason why the Bronx mob might be out for you?"

"The Bronx mob? That's Dutch Schultz."

"Yeah, and Joey Rao."

"I flattened Dutch once when I was a rookie."

"You . . . what?"

"Flattened him. Draped him over the hood of his car. He vowed to get even with me, but I'd pretty much forgotten about it."

"Well, apparently he hasn't forgotten. I got a tip from a stoolie of mine. Some of the Bronx mob and a couple of Rao's boys have instructions to kill you tonight on one of your late runs. It's supposed to look like a holdup."

I looked at him blankly, feeling the cold dampness of fear gather between my shoulder blades. Driving through the night in a brightly lit bus, without even a weapon to defend myself . . . yes, I was scared. I was no longer a cop, prepared to shoot it out. I was a sitting duck, a patsy. I might have shrugged this off if anybody but Billy Quaine had brought it to me. He was a square cop, and his information sources were the best. It had to be true.

"My God, Billy," I said, "what can I do?"

"Go see your old boss, Inspector Bolan, at the Third. I'm sure he'll give you a cover when he hears the story."

"Yeah, maybe he will." I started to climb back into the bus, but then turned to grab Billy's sleeve as he walked away. "Billy," I started to say, but he wouldn't let me finish the sentence.

"Don't thank me, Bob. Any guy on the force would have done it for you. We all know you got a bum rap and we're behind you, all the way."

My bus was the third one back in the feed line, and I left it to go up to the starter and tell him I had to see a doctor because my stomach was acting up. He pulled my bus out of the line, and I grabbed a cab to 67th Street and Tenth Avenue. Then I went a devious route the rest of the way, through a basement and over a back fence to the 68th Street station house. If the gunmen were tailing me, I didn't want to tip them off about any police protection I might have.

Inspector Bolan saw me at once and listened to my story. He said, "If Quaine got that from one of his stoolies, you can bet on it. Now, Bob, go back to your job as if nothing has happened. We'll cover you."

My trip to the station house hadn't taken long, and by the time I got back to the feed line only two buses had left and I could keep my regular schedule. The trip east was uneventful, and at the end of the line my bus was boarded by two plain-clothes men, Timothy Keating and Frank Roewer. They took seats in the rear, and since we were as yet alone on the bus, they told me that Jake Saylor, one of the best shots in the department, was riding a sector car behind, along with Tom Sheehan, Andy McLaughlin, and Tom Weppler. I put the bus in gear and we lumbered back toward Central Park.

Six men to protect me, still, the cold sweat trickled down my spine. Each car that drew alongside made me all but freeze the wheel; each passenger that boarded made my heart pound. One small bullet was all that was needed . . . and it could travel so fast!

The first round trip was completed with nothing happening. The second was equally uneventful. When I came to the feed line for the third time, Saylor poked his head in the door and said, "Bob, we think this tip is a lot of crap. We're gonna pull out."

"Jake, for God's sake . . . !" I cried.

"It's Saturday night, and you know how that is in the Third Division. There's a lot happening, and I can't tie up all these men on a stoolie's tip that may be phony."

"At least leave Roewer and Keating with me for another run. If nothing happens by then, I'll lay up the bus."

"Okay," he agreed. "Roewer and Keating stay, but we gotta roll." Through the rear-view mirror, I saw the sector car make a U-turn and disappear into the night.

I put the bus in gear and started another run, feeling quite deserted and vulnerable, even though two plain-clothes men were still with me.

It was close to ten o'clock when I approached 79th Street and East End Avenue, the eastern end of the run. I pulled over to the curb and let out my last passengers and, as they stepped down, I saw two men move out of the shadow of a warehouse and make for the bus. I knew at once that this was it.

Before I could cry a word of warning, a squat man with a scar on his left cheek stood on the bus steps, his hand in his pocket pointing directly at my stomach. The second man, taller, stood right behind him and in his hand was an automatic pointing at my head.

I was facing death, yet a most leisurely thought took possession of my brain. It occurred to me that they were both well dressed, Shorty was wearing a light-brown suit and a gray fedora; the other one a gray suit, gray topcoat, and pearl-gray hat. They were the best-dressed passengers I'd had all evening. I thought how strange it was.

The next instant I was snapped out of my reverie. The short one snarled, "Up with your hands, McAllister."

This was the first that Keating and Roewer knew something was happening, but as they moved for their guns, the tall one trained his automatic on them. "Get your hands up, you bastards," he snarled. The two plain-clothes men reluctantly raised their hands.

The short one had taken a step into the bus, and I rose slowly from my seat, pleading as I came. "Gimme a break . . . don't kill me," I begged. My hands were out, in a gesture of supplication, coming closer to him, closer. Then I lunged, grabbed at the pocket of the little guy, and slammed him against the taller man behind. The second thug's automatic spat viciously close to my ear, but the shot passed over me and through the window. Keating ran up now, blasting as he came. The second thug fired back, but now he was excited, and he jerked his shots. I was struggling with the shorter one, holding his gun hand downward while I groped on the floor for a tire wrench. I found it and brought it across the side of his head. He closed his eyes and sank to the floor. I looked up just as the taller one was backing out of the bus, and a shot from Keating's gun ripped a gash across his mouth. I saw the enamel of his teeth spatter. He screamed and fired blindly, the shot only shattering another window.

The thugs had a cover man who now began to fire out of the shadows of the warehouse. Roewer went into action against him, pumping bullets into the blackness at the spot where we'd seen the spurts of flame. Keating's gun was empty, but Roewer kept pumping away as the wounded gangster and his cover made a run for it. We saw them climb into a black sedan standing on East End Avenue, facing south. The car roared away and was lost. All we had captured was the short one, unconscious at my feet.

The sound of shots had brought people from all directions, and now their white faces peered into the bus and at the unconscious man on the floor. Roewer and Keating pushed their way back through the crowd. "Get the station house," Keating called. "There's blood all over the street, so one of them must be shot bad. Send out an alarm."

Detective Barney Clark was on duty when we arrived at the 67th Street station house, and he questioned our short prisoner. He said his name was Thomas Kleint, an undertaker's assistant, one previous arrest for felonious assault. Captain Johnny Lyons, commanding officer, arrived to take over the questioning, but Kleint remained true to the gangster code of silence. He didn't know who his partners were, and this was a simple holdup that went sour. McAllister? He never heard of him.

The interrogation was interrupted by a bulletin from the East 22d Street precinct. They'd found a dead man lying in the gutter, and he had two slugs in him. We figured it might be the gunman Keating had shot. Captain Lyons, Detective Clark, Keating, Roewer, and I piled into a sector car and headed for 20th Street and the East River.

The body was in the gutter, face down. Clark turned him over and there was no mistaking him. The broken teeth made identification easy. The fatal shot had been a neck wound that severed the jugular vein. The mob had kept his hat and coat to prevent quick identification, then dumped him.

The press descended on East 67th Street station house and backed me into a corner. I refused to make any comments except to insist that they get the story from Keating and Roewer, the cops who had saved my life. The October 15, 1923, edition of the *New York American* handled the story as follows:

> What man wished to hush forever the mouth of Bob McAllister—and why?
>
> This man is being searched for by police following the mysterious attempted holdup Saturday night of the city bus which McAllister, champion police sprinter and suspended detective, was driving. One man with a police record, Charles Murdock, twenty-four, of 125 Milton Street, Brooklyn, was killed by a detective guarding McAllister. Thomas Kleint, of 179 East 119th Street, was captured.
>
> Saturday night's affair was just another small link in the chain of bad luck which has nipped McAllister in the last year. . . .
>
> [Here came a factual account of the shooting.]
>
> These are the facts on the surface of the case. Police do not for a minute believe the affair was

merely an attempted holdup on a city bus which McAllister by chance happened to be driving. The prospective take was too low for a gang of at least four men, counting the driver.

A feud? Yes, it may have been that. McAllister long has been the nemesis of certain gangs, which may attack him with less fear, now that he is under police suspension. But McAllister is known to have much information regarding the devious ways of certain men, who possibly would wish to hush his mouth forever. Did one of these seek to put McAllister away for all time, so that certain secrets would never be divulged?

I suppose the newspapers couldn't be blamed for implying that I knew a lot of dark secrets. Who would believe the truth? Who would believe that a cop could be hounded in this way merely because he had done his job?

Up in Harlem, three of the best detectives on the force, Quaine, Shields, and Begley, went to work on the case, determined to pin this attack on the Bronx mob, and particularly on Schultz and Rao. But after a week they came to a dead end. Their source of information, Quaine's stoolie, was found dead in a lot near the East River. He had been shot, garroted, soaked in gasoline, and burned.

All we were left with was Kleint. At least he would be sent to prison for the attack, and maybe he'd talk. But no, neither happened. Right to the end, Kleint refused to admit that it was anything but a holdup. And he was smart in protecting his real bosses, for they in turn protected him. He was never brought to trial. Even after all I'd been through, I found this terribly shocking. I could only conclude that Dutch Schultz now had such influence in the city government and the courts that he could protect one of his men actually caught in the commission of a crime.

If this seems farfetched now, what other conclusion was possible? It certainly looked ominous for me. My enemies were growing in strength month by month, and they seemed to be closing in from all sides.

The newspapers had remarked about my "chain of bad luck." Well, they helped add another link to that chain. I was fired as a bus driver from the department of plants and structures, headed by Commissioner Grover Whalen. Whalen, too, had chosen sides in the Tammany quarrel. He was later to become Jimmy Walker's police commissioner.

Another job lost! But if I had powerful enemies, I also had a lot of good friends. This time it was Al Copeland who came through. He said that a friend of his, the novelist Robert W. Chambers, was looking for a chauffeur, and the job was mine if I wanted it. Did I want it! Mr. Chambers hired me and thus performed a great act of kindness and courage. Nobody knew when the gangsters would open fire on me again; it might well happen while I was driving him, and he might be caught in the rain of bullets. But he didn't give a thought for his own safety. He knew I needed a break and he gave it to me. God bless him.

The job was not only easy, but also gave me a chance to get back to a regular training schedule for the indoor track meets. Jake and I concentrated on getting me into condition, our eyes upon the Olympics that were scheduled to be held the following year. My body responded marvelously to Jake's careful handling, and at the Fordham Games on January 19, I hit 11⅗ seconds for 120 yards, equaling my own world's record. A few days later, in the

Brooklyn College Meet, I set a new world's indoor record for 100 meters. The time was 11 seconds flat.

When Jake was rubbing me down after that race, he said, "Bobby, I never before said you were *ready* for Olympic trials. I always said you had it in you, but never before did I say *now* is the time. Today I say it. You're ready, Bobby, now!"

"You really think so, Jake?" I asked.

"Would I be saying it?"

"When are the trials?"

"In June, at the Harvard Stadium. We got five more months. You'll be at your peak in June. There's just one thing, Bobby. . . ."

I looked up at his suddenly sober face. "You mean the indictment?"

He nodded. The Olympic Committee had very strict rules about eligibility, and no man or woman convicted of a crime, or even under indictment, could become a member of the team. Jake said, "When's your case coming to trial?"

"Any day now," I said. "And don't worry, Jake, Bill Fallon says the whole thing will be thrown right out of court."

But my case didn't come to trial during the rest of January, nor during February, nor during March. It was nine months since my indictment, and I began to haunt the district attorney's office, pleading for an interview with Joab Banton. At last it was granted.

He was the only man empowered to bring my case to trial, and I humbled myself before him, begging for a break. I told him how faithfully I had trained for this chance at the Olympic team. I was now twenty-four, at the peak of my ability, and it was now or never.

"Look, Mr. Banton," I said, "I'm not asking you to squash the indictment or anything like that. I'm only asking that you put me on trial . . . soon. Don't leave this indictment hanging over me. If I'm guilty, let the jury say so . . . but at least let them hear the evidence."

He said, "I'll give your case my deepest consideration."

Jake stepped up my training schedule, and every hour I could sneak away from my duties as chauffeur I was in sweat clothes and pounding the track. The days fell by, and I watched the calendar with increasing apprehension. Every waking hour was consumed with my driving ambition to wear my country's colors in the Olympics. It seemed to me that the Olympic shield on my chest would somehow wipe out the disappointments and frustrations on the police force. Except for Charley Paddock, whom I had never raced, I had beaten every top sprinter in America. I was good . . . I knew I was good. I only wanted a chance to prove it.

But there was no compassion in Joab Banton's heart. The Olympic boat was to sail the first week of June; he set my trial for the last week of June. When I heard the news I was beyond shame, beyond pride; I dropped my head and cried.

When my case came to trial, Bill Fallon was tied up with the Fuller and McGee bucket-shop hearings, and his partner, Joe Shalleck, took over my defense. The presiding judge was the Honorable Cornelius F. Collins, the prosecutor was Assistant District Attorney Mullins. A jury was impaneled and the D.A. presented the facts of the case, as he saw them. He told how I allegedly kicked in the door of the Zittel basement storeroom, and stated that the superintendents of the building had observed me in this illegal act. He read my statement denying kicking in the door, and therefore charged me with perjury.

The moment the D.A. had finished his opening presentation, Shalleck sprang to his feet to denounce it all as "wholly immaterial, irrelevant, and incompetent." He went on to explain that my search of Zittel's storage room was illegal in the first place because it had been made without a warrant, and the manner in which I made entry was entirely beside the point. He concluded with: "Your Honor, I move that the charge of perjury be dismissed."

Judge Collins thought a moment and then said, "Counsel, I agree with you." He turned to the jury box and instructed the foreman that the perjury charge was to be dropped. The jury retired and a few minutes later filed back into the courtroom and the foreman said, "We find the defendant, Robert McAllister, to be not guilty."

How long I had waited for those three words! And now that I had heard them, what bitterness remained in me for a man named Joab Banton! As an experienced lawyer, he must have known the indictment could not stand up in court, yet the trial was delayed for almost a full year. He had deprived me of my job, disgraced me, made me a setup for Dutch Schultz's gunmen. I might have forgiven all that, but one thing I will never forget or forgive is the fact that he withheld my inevitable vindication just long enough to disqualify me for the Olympics.

Chapter Ten

CHORUS

IN THE TOMBS

On July 17, 1924, Commissioner Enright reinstated me in the police department. I was assigned as foot patrolman in the busy 14th Precinct in Harlem. I had been on my way up, a vice cop, a member of the commissioner's confidential squad, a detective . . . now I was back down again to the lowest rank, a foot patrolman. But I was again a cop, that was the important thing. I had my badge back, I had my self-respect back. The headquarters assignments had brought me nothing but trouble and notoriety. Now that I was again an obscure patrolman, maybe I'd be left alone to do my job, a job I loved. No man ever pounded a beat with greater satisfaction.

For about three weeks little happened except the routine work—traffic accidents, an occasional street fight, a knifing, a purse snatching. When my late tours began at 11:45 on a clear summer night in the fourth week, the outgoing platoon was called before Captain Wall for instructions. He said, "There's been six auto thefts in the 14th Precinct so far this month. This ring of thieves has been operating mostly on Manhattan Avenue. Be on the alert for them."

My patrol post ran from 110th Street to 116th Street on Manhattan Avenue, so the Captain's words were directed particularly to me. I made a mental note of them and reported to my post at midnight.

All was quiet. At about 3:20 A.M., I ran into Jimmy Hines and Morris Friedman as they left the Monongahela Democratic Club. I felt deeply grateful to Hines for getting me that bus-driving job, even if it hadn't turned out too well, and I fell into step with him to escort him home. I said good night to him at his home on 116th Street, then began to walk with Friedman toward his apartment at 312 Manhattan Avenue. As we came to the corner of 115th Street, I glanced down the block and felt instinctively that something was wrong. A good cop develops the ability to sense something before he actually sees it.

I paused, then saw two men in the middle of the block. One was bent over the open hood of a car, the other stood beside him and was looking up at the dark windows of the apartment house.

"Keep walking, Morris, and don't turn your head," I said. "I think I've got a couple of auto thieves."

As I was speaking to Friedman, I saw the lookout nudge his partner, who immediately closed the hood of the car. Both of them started to walk slowly down the street, apparently thinking I hadn't seen them. I pretended I hadn't and walked on a few steps, then I whirled and started after them. I slipped my gun from its holster and held it pointing downward behind my right thigh. My nightstick was in my left hand, the end of it nestling under my left armpit.

I caught the two men just before they reached the corner. "Do you own that car?" I demanded.

"What car you talkin' about?" one of them said. "I don't see no car." He whispered something in Italian to the man on the outside. They were dressed alike in light summer suits and panama hats.

"Put your hands over your head," I said.

The man on the inside paused for an instant, then lightning-quick grabbed my club and pulled it from underneath my arm. At the same instant, he reached his right hand back toward his hip pocket. Thinking he was going for his gun, I whipped up my revolver and shot for his right arm, intending to disable him, at the same time jumping behind them to force them to turn if they started shooting. Unfortunately there was a strand of wire protecting a hedge around the building and I tripped over it, falling down and losing sight of them for about ten seconds.

When I regained my feet, both men were on the ground, one lying motionless between the hedge and curb, the other crawling on his belly along the hedge. I grabbed him and found a knife. When I turned to the other man, I found he was unconscious and seriously wounded. Two more shots in the air brought Patrolman Stanley Fisher from his post on Eighth Avenue, and I sent a cab driver to call the station house. Detectives Howard Hagan and Charles Carey came on the run and took the wounded man to St. Luke's Hospital.

Detective Hagan looked over the car and found the thugs had made a jump by changing the wires so that they could start the car without a key. J. Morton Mayer of 350 Manhattan Avenue, the owner, was hustled down to examine his automobile; he had not left the wires in that condition when he parked his car. The prisoner stood sullenly by as the detective put the pieces of the case together.

The lieutenant on desk duty notified the telegraph bureau of the shooting, and Inspector John D. Coughlin, chief of the detective bureau, arrived at the station house to conduct the investigation. This is standard procedure when a member of the department is involved in a shooting.

Fingerprints disclosed that the wounded man was Vincent Fighera, a notorious pickpocket with a criminal record of fifteen arrests and seven convictions, an alumnus of Sing Sing, where he had served several terms. The other prisoner gave his name as Joseph Dandio, alias Joe Barry, Joe Barrie, Joseph Dentico, and Joseph Dantis. I quote from his record: "Rogue's Gallery Picture Number B. 45977, convicted for selling narcotics and possession of a loaded gun, served 18 months in Elmira State Reformatory for same and later arrested for burglary and grand larceny."

Both men were booked for attempted grand larceny. A twenty-four-hour guard was assigned to the prisoner in St. Luke's Hospital pending his removal to Bellevue Hospital prison ward. Everything about the case was routine, and I had a clear conscience and an easy mind. But I had forgotten that anything Bob McAllister did was hot copy. Within an hour, the station house was besieged by reporters. I referred all questions to my superiors.

Inspector Coughlin, aware of the press interest, made a very thorough investigation and finally issued the following statement to the reporters:

"I have investigated the case completely. The prisoner McAllister shot has a long criminal record and his companion has a record. Both men could give no explanation as to where they were going or what they were doing in the neighborhood, miles away from their own at that hour in the morning. Both gave conflicting stories. It is evident they are lying. Captain James Wall in command of the precinct informed me he had given explicit instructions to the outgoing platoon at midnight to be on the alert for automobile thieves operating in the vicinity of Manhattan Avenue. From the actions of these men, their failure to obey the officer's command (they couldn't fail to recognize him as he was in full uniform), one man wresting the night-stick from under his arm, making a hostile feint as if to draw a gun, I find the officer had reasonable apprehension that his life was in danger and under the circumstances acted properly and in the performance of his duty."

Before he left the precinct, Inspector Coughlin told me I was a good cop. Captain Wall congratulated me and gave me a day off for a good arrest.

I was ordered to take Joseph Dandio to the lineup at police headquarters and then to court for arraignment on the charge of attempted grand larceny. As I led him from the detention pen, he said, "See this, you ruined my good suit. That shot missed me." I was dumbfounded. I grabbed his coat for a closer look. There was a powder burn and bullet hole on the inside. The bullet had passed through the lapel, missing his arm and striking Fighera in the chest. This was a strange trick of fate. Until that moment I had believed Fighera, whom I had shot, was the man on the inside, the man who had grabbed my club and pretended to reach for a gun. The man who did nothing to resist arrest lay in the hospital with a bullet wound meant for Dandio.

Although I had gone twenty hours without sleep, I

hastened back to the precinct after the arraignment and told desk lieutenant Baxter I had made an error. It was Dandio, not Fighera, who had made a move as if to draw a gun. Lieutenant Baxter, an old-timer, corrected the error in the records. My guardian angel was watching over me when he guided my footsteps back to the station house.

For the next few days my name was all over the newspapers, and it made good reading for Mabel and me. It was fun to again be a hero instead of a goat, though the newspaper accounts were often full of imagery that made good reading, but had only a distant relationship with the truth.

The *New York World* reported that there were *three* men, and that one of them had beaten me over the head with my own club before I subdued them all. The *American* had me making like a private eye as I knelt in a "darkened doorway" to fire a single shot that dropped Fighera who then moaned, "I am dying." The account went on that I then pursued Dandio with "the speed of wind." The *Post* said that I "fired from the hip" to drop Fighera, and "with his own weapon acting as a starter's shot, McAllister was out after them. In a little over 100 yards he overhauled the fugitives."

I wasn't going to argue with the reporters over the accuracy of their stories. They had the essentials down: I had apprehended two criminals in the performance of a crime. That was my job.

Forty-eight hours later I was notified that the prisoner at St. Luke's Hospital had died. That morning I was sent to Bellevue Morgue to identify the body of Fighera. As I looked down at the corpse and realized that here was a human life I had taken, I dropped to my knees and said a prayer for Fighera's soul and for my own forgiveness.

Surely God knew that sometimes His Commandments were violated by accident, sometimes by necessity. Surely He knew that a New York cop had a duty not only to Him, but also to the 7 million people he was sworn to protect. I prayed for His mercy upon Fighera and McAllister alike.

I left the slab room and in the corridor was met by a man dressed in black. His thin face carried a look of deepest hate. It was Fighera's brother.

"You cop bastard," he hissed at me, "you're gonna die for this."

"Fighera," I said, trying to put a comforting hand on his arm, but he broke away from me. "Fighera, I'm sorry about your brother, believe me. You've got to realize that Dandio is the guy responsible for his death. Dandio's got a long criminal record and he got your brother into this car-stealing racket."

But Fighera wasn't even listening to me. He said, "We'll kill you! I swear it on my brother's blood!" Then he put the second knuckle of his right index finger in his mouth and bit it—the Sicilian death sign. There was no point in trying to talk to him, to reason with him. I turned and walked away.

I knew I had acted in a proper manner, I knew I had done my duty as a police officer, yet the killing of a man is a heavy weight on the conscience. I went to confession the next morning and told the priest about it, and I guess he saw that I was pretty upset. I said, "Father, I don't believe I have sinned. It is a grievous matter to kill a man, but there was not sufficient reflection, nor full consent of the will. He was a criminal, Father, and I'm a cop, and I did my duty. Tell me, Father, was it a mortal sin I committed? Should I ask absolution?"

He assured me that I had not committed a mortal sin, and I left the church feeling strong again.

Death is a shocking thing, but if you can't face it, you have no business being a cop. I resolutely put the case out of my mind and went about my job. Again the routine of police work set in. During the time I was not on beat, Mabel and I worked on our apartment, painting and decorating it. We had a piano, of course, and she'd often accompany me while I sang. She was both encouraging and critical, and worked hard to teach me about breath control and voice projection. And, too, we talked about having a child. The future looked bright.

Four days passed. On the fifth, I came home to find Mabel looking very grim. She had a copy of *The New York Times*, dated August 17, 1924, in her hand. "Have you seen the paper?" she asked.

"No, why?"

"Bob," she came and put her hand on my arm, "they're after you again."

I tried to strike a light note. "Honey, lots of people are after me, but they gotta run mighty fast to catch the flying cop." I kissed her. "Who's breathing down my neck this time?"

She handed me the *Times*, and there was a story about me and the Fighera shooting, only this time I wasn't the hero. It was a long story, but the important part was contained in the lead paragraph:

> Patrolman Robert McAllister, who on last Wednesday morning fatally wounded one of two alleged automobile thieves, will face a charge of homicide Monday morning, according to the announcement

by Acting District Attorney George N. Brothers. . . . His Captain, in the West 123rd Street Police Station, will be directed to produce him in the Homicide Court before Magistrate House on Monday morning.

I read the story through twice, then put the paper down and looked at Mabel. My mind was confused, I had difficulty understanding the significance of those words. It all seemed unreal to me.

"Bob . . . ," Mabel started to speak, but her voice broke.

She was afraid, and suddenly I was afraid too. Now the full impact of the words hit me. I was being hunted again.

"Bob . . . what does it mean?"

"I don't know, honey. I . . . don't know."

"But your captain said you did the right thing. And so did Inspector Coughlin. Didn't they . . . Bob?"

"Yes, they did."

"Then . . . I don't understand."

Slowly, I was beginning to understand. This was the same district attorney's office that had tried to convict me for perjury and for extortion. I had licked them twice, but they hadn't given up. They had been biding their time, waiting for another chance at me. The Fighera killing had given them that chance.

I stared at the cup of coffee before me—it was cold and bitter. I felt so small beside my enemies, so defenseless before their power. And the charge was no longer perjury or extortion—but homicide! Yet, deep inside me, below the layers of fear and apprehension and anger, was a core of conviction that they'd never get away with it. Despite what had happened to me, I still believed there was justice in

America. They'd never send me to prison for doing my duty. I was certain of that. I tried hard to bring that conviction to the surface where Mabel could see it.

"Don't you worry, honey," I smiled. "We'll lick them. This is a more obvious frame-up than the other two, and we licked them on those, didn't we?"

"We sure did." Mabel grinned, grasping eagerly at the encouragement I offered. "But just the same, I think you ought to talk to Mr. Fallon."

"I suppose you're right. And to Jimmy Hines, too. We've got some powerful friends on our side, thank God."

I couldn't get Fallon on the phone that afternoon; he was out of town, and it gave me an uneasy feeling. I felt better after seeing Jimmy Hines, however, for he was both cordial and reassuring. He said to me, "Sure I saw the papers, Bob. They're after you again, and it's a shame. But don't you worry about it."

"I try not to, but. . . ."

"Bob, I've talked to Morris Friedman and he saw the whole thing. He said he thought those guys were gonna shoot you, and he ducked. He said it was justifiable homicide, and if there's ever any trouble about it, he'll tell the truth. You've got nothing to worry about."

I felt considerably better when I left him. And when I got to the station house, all the guys there laughed at my fears, too. One detective said, "What are they gonna do, lock you up for being a cop? Look at the records of those two bums you took. Nobody expects you to wait to shoot until the hoods start blasting you. It's just newspaper talk, Bob. Forget it."

Mabel and I couldn't forget it, of course. We spent the entire weekend talking about it, examining the situation from every angle, trying to encourage each other with brave words. And half a dozen times I called Fallon's office only to receive the information that he was out of town. We would have felt better if we'd been able to talk to him. Still, it was with good heart that we faced Monday when it arrived.

I had a morning tour and kissed Mabel good-by at seven o'clock and started out for the station house. When I arrived, the desk lieutenant called me. The captain wanted to see me. When I entered his office, he said, "Son, I've received orders from Assistant District Attorney George Brothers to arrest you on the charge of homicide."

Here it was, the thing Mabel and I had spent the week-end preparing for. But now that it was here, all the courage I had stored up for this moment seemed to melt away. "Captain," I cried, "they're trying to frame me!"

"Now don't worry about it. You have nothing to fear. This is just a technical arrest for the record."

I looked at the white-haired, kindly Captain Wall and I wanted so desperately to believe his words. He was a much older and more experienced man than I, but already I knew a lot more about the rottenness of this city than he did.

With a sinking heart, I said, "Captain, can I call my wife to bring over a suit of civilian clothes so I won't have to be booked in uniform? The photographers are sure to be there and. . . ."

He shook his head. "There isn't time. We have to go right down to court where Magistrate House is waiting to hear the case."

When Captain Wall and I appeared in court, the place was jammed with photographers and spectators. I felt a deep shame to have to be brought before a judge in my uniform, but I held my head high and defiant. I was full of hot words to be used when I got the chance . . . but I never got that chance.

Assistant District Attorney Brothers made a very short speech charging me with homicide and before I could say a word in self-defense, I heard the magistrate intone: ". . . and he is remanded to the Tombs prison without bail."

I was being sent to prison! Nobody had bothered to hear a word in my defense, and I was being sent to prison . . . without bail!

The photographers swarmed about me, climbed on chairs and tables to get a picture of me . . . the picture of a cop in disgrace, a cop being sent to prison!

They handcuffed me to another prisoner and bundled us off into a department of correction patrol wagon for the trip to the Tombs. There must have been a half dozen of us in the dark and airless vehicle as it bounced and jolted its way downtown. One of the other passengers leaned close to peer at me and said, "Hey, ain't that a cop's uniform?"

I said, "Yes."

"What ya in for?" he said.

I said, "Murder."

They put me in cell 1116 and I slumped down on the bare iron cot suspended from the wall on chains. I was numb from what had happened, and I couldn't think very clearly. Surging, choking waves of rage swept over me, leaving me exhausted.

A sound like a gathering thunderstorm came to my ears

and then penetrated to my consciousness. It was a chant from the other prisoners—hundreds of them on the fifth, sixth, seventh, and eighth tiers were battering their tin food pans on the bars and yelling. They were yelling at me! The grapevine had passed the word that McAllister the cop was here, and they screamed their hatred of me. The ancient prison seemed literally to rock with the sound.

"Fry the cop bastard . . . fry the cop bastard . . . fry the cop bastard," came the rhythmic chant. I put my hands over my ears to shut out the sound. But there were other ugly sounds inside me I couldn't shut out. Sometime far into the night I fell asleep.

I was awakened the next morning by a piercing yell from a cell near mine. It was my name. "McAllister, you dirty sonofabitch, I hope you get the chair!"

The yell awoke the entire prison and again the chant was taken up, the banging of the tin food pans. It went on for an hour, until the prisoners had exhausted themselves.

Along about noon I was told I could see my wife in the visitors' pen. As I was led out of the cell blocks and through the corridors, I heard distant echoing shouts which sounded like the reverberations in a swimming pool. I had the momentary, ridiculous thought that prison might not be so bad if I could work out in a pool and keep myself in condition. The next moment I was ushered into the visitors' pen, a great, high-ceilinged, tiled room—and here was what I thought had been the swimming pool. The ear-splitting clamor was being made by the prisoners and their visitors trying to make each other heard through the heavy wire-mesh partition that divided them. I was ushered into cage number 32 and there, just barely visible through the dirty screen, was Mabel. She looked so small and frightened and so precious. And I couldn't even touch her. We had to yell, like the rest, to make ourselves heard.

"Did you see Bill Fallon, honey?" I yelled at her.

"He's gone," she yelled back.

"Gone? But where? When will he be back?"

"He's a fugitive from the law!"

I thought I wasn't hearing her correctly. The din in the room was terrible, and her words were distorted. I asked her again where he was and she repeated the same information.

"He's disappeared, Bob. Nobody knows where he is. There's a warrant out for his arrest. He's a fugitive . . . charged with jury tampering."

"Oh, my God," I moaned. Then I said, "What about his partner, Joe Shalleck? Go see him."

"I did. He wants five hundred dollars to handle the case, and. . . ."

She didn't have to finish the sentence. I knew that all she had in the world was my last pay check of eighty-seven dollars. I couldn't really blame Joe Shalleck for wanting a big fee. After all, his firm had done plenty for me on the muscle. But oh, how I needed that big, handsome, brilliant man named William Fallon at this moment.

"I finally found a lawyer who will take the case and let us owe him the money," Mabel said. "His name is Sidney Lash and he's coming to see you this afternoon."

We talked on, or rather yelled on, trying to cheer each other up, to communicate courage and hope through the thick, dirty screen. When our visiting time ended and I saw her walk away, so small and defenseless, the life I had given her so ugly, I hated myself.

That afternoon I had two more visitors. The first one

was my lawyer, Sidney Lash. I suppose after knowing Bill Fallon any other lawyer would have seemed colorless and ineffectual, but I felt a great letdown when I saw Lash. He was the opposite of Fallon in almost every respect; he was short and thin and rather crabbed, like an overworked school teacher. On a beak of a nose he wore a pince-nez, and from it dangled a wide, black ribbon. He wore his hair long, preacherlike. He regarded me critically with his pale blue eyes, and I realized he wasn't at all certain I was innocent. He didn't slap me on the back, the way Fallon would have; he didn't boom out his confidence that we'd lick the enemy; he merely asked me questions in a thin, nasal voice. I thought to myself, if *he* has to save me . . . I'm lost.

As it turned out, I underestimated Sidney Lash. He was a smart and hard-working lawyer and he gave unsparingly of himself to my case. But he did not inspire me the way Bill Fallon always had. And at this moment I needed inspiration.

However, I did receive one break that afternoon. Just before Lash arrived, I was taken down to block 32 to see my old pal Detective Billy Quaine. He was still working tirelessly in my behalf and had collected information from a stoolie that he hoped would be of great help to me. He had discovered that Vincent Fighera and Dandio worked as strong-arm men for the Monongahela Democratic Club during the elections. On the night of the shooting, they planned to steal a car and take out a couple of prostitutes who worked in Sadie Chink's house on 113th Street near Manhattan Avenue. The same stoolie said that Dandio had a gun when I stopped them, but had ditched it in the thick hedge that moment when I fell.

"Didn't you search the hedge, Bob?" Billy asked.

"No, but I think Hagen looked it over when he arrived."

"Well, the stoolie says Dandio wedged it in the thick branches and sent a friend later to recover it. That gun must be hot if Dandio was so careful to keep it out of sight."

"Thanks, Billy," I said. "I can't say any more in words, but you know what's in my heart."

When Billy left, I returned to my cell. A few minutes later Lash arrived, and I told him about the gun. "If we can prove that Dandio had a gun, doesn't that strengthen my case?"

"Of course it does," Lash said, "but we won't have that proof in time for tomorrow's arraignment."

"What exactly is going to happen tomorrow, Mr. Lash?"

"The magistrate will formally hear the case against you and decide whether to hold you for the grand jury or to dismiss you."

"He *could* dismiss me, then?"

"He could."

I clung to that thought, that hope, all during the next twenty-four hours. Magistrate House *could* end this nightmare.

The next afternoon I was led across the Bridge of Sighs that connected the Tombs with the court building, to meet Sidney Lash. When we entered Magistrate House's court, it was jammed with reporters, photographers, the morbidly curious. Mabel was waiting for me at the door, and we were able to embrace briefly before I was led inside the railing to sit at the defendant's table.

There were a lot of legalistic arguments between the lawyers, and I didn't try to follow them; I kept my eyes on Judge House, trying to read my fate in his expressions. What kind of man are you? I wondered. Is there courage and justice in you? Is there compassion? I soon learned.

The judge rapped his gavel to cut off further arguments, cleared his throat and spoke in a resonant tone so the reporters would not miss a word. He began to excoriate me. He said, "Assuming that this officer did suspect these men, that gave him no right to shoot them down in cold blood. Even if one of them made a pass at him with his fists, that would not justify killing the man. There is not the slightest evidence in this case that the defendant was justified in shooting the deceased. I order him held for the grand jury, without bail. I further order that the charge of homicide be stricken out, and a charge of murder in the first degree be substituted."

A great wave of buzzing swept over the courtroom, and I felt as if I were about to be drowned in the sound. I started to stand, but my knees were weak and I only lurched forward in my chair. The judge gaveled the room to silence. Now he looked directly at me for the first time. Ever since I had entered the room, I had tried to get his eyes, his attention, and now it was too late. His eyes were savage and his voice was filled with scorn when he spoke to me. He said, "You'll be lucky if you don't go to the electric chair!"

I felt Lash's hand under my arm, urging me up. It was time to leave the court, to walk back through the long aisle of exploding flash bulbs. I was still a cop! I stood erect, thanking God that my knees now worked, squared my shoulders, and started forward. Lash was leading me; I hardly knew where I was going. I heard their voices call to me, demanding a statement; the flash lights blinded me; this was a kind of purgatory. At least, let their pictures show that McAllister was not broken.

Then suddenly, out of this inferno, a tiny figure came toward me. It was Mabel. I took her in my arms and then, unbidden, unwanted, the tears came to my eyes and ran down my cheeks. The photographers knelt in a circle about us, bathing us in their hellish lights, recording for all the city to see . . . that a cop cried. Let them.

I was torn from Mabel's arms and led back across the Bridge of Sighs, back to the Tombs. I was greeted by a chorus of abuse from the prisoners, but I hardly heard it. I grasped the bars of my cell and prayed God for His help and His mercy.

Chapter Eleven

WHO DARES

SAY "FRIEND"?

In the days of my freedom, I had looked at the Tombs from the outside and thought that any man who entered this somber, gray stone fortress would surely hate and fear it so that he'd go straight. The ugly monster squatted on the site of a pre-Revolutionary gibbet, its towers and spires dwarfed by the skyscrapers of lower Manhattan. Remote, ominous, I wondered how the sunlight could ever penetrate the narrow, barred windows.

I didn't wonder any more. We lived in a twilight world —tier upon tier of men waiting trial. My cell was 1116 and was on the fifth of eight tiers. There was no window; my only view of the outer world was through a narrow slit on the opposite wall 50 feet from my cell door. Through that window I could glimpse the hand-hewn stone wall that surrounded the prison yard.

Cell 1116 had quite a history. Its alumni included Harry K. Thaw, who killed Stanford White in the same Madison Square Garden where I graduated as a cop; Chapin, editor of the *New York World*, who killed his wife; Police Lieutenant Charley Becker, a grafting cop who killed his partner, gambler Herman Rosenthal; Owney Madden, the organizer of that bout of mine up in Sing Sing; and behind these notables, a long, faceless parade of felons and murderers.

It was seldom quiet in the Tombs; every waking hour was filled with a growl of voices, a clatter of pans, a sudden snarling argument or a snatch of song. Sometimes the prisoners would be caught up in a common emotion, and they'd bang and curse and scream until exhausted. Often, at mealtime they'd roar their hatred and disgust at the gray swill fed them, hurling the slop out of their cells. Heavy wire mesh, hung between the fifth and sixth tiers, caught the refuse.

We had company in the Tombs, although I didn't realize it until the first mealtime. The prisoners on the tiers above me yelled their disgust at the food, and I saw the swill come hurtling down into the fifth-tier screen. Then I saw them—the army of gray rats that moved out to gorge themselves. They jibbered as they came, their sharp white teeth flashing, their red eyes rolling greedily. They were sleek and fat from offal, and we prisoners were safe from attack. Still, I always came shudderingly awake when one of them crawled over me at night.

I learned to live with them, just as I learned to live with the stench of sweat and garbage and excrement rising above the acrid smell of Lysol.

The prisoners had no recreation, no work, no diversions of any kind, only the gray monotony of one day following another. Small wonder they turned upon me, a symbol of the restraint they hated. I became the focus of their anger, their diversion, their pastime. Each day new obscenities were created just for me.

Some of the toughest gangsters in New York were my tiermates on the fifth; men like Joe "Kid Cabbage" Lavin from Hell's Kitchen, alleged killer of Clicker Holmes in a bootleg war; Harlem's Yellow Charleston, who murdered the cabaret owner Baron Wilkens when he refused to pay protection money; and Kid Weiss, the California bank bandit. During exercise period these men would stroll together along the tier. I walked alone.

The thing that sustained me during those first days in the Tombs was the knowledge that I had not yet been indicted by the grand jury. Magistrate House had been so obviously prejudiced against me in his remarks that it was not surprising he held me for murder. But the grand jury was something else again. Twenty-three men would not be as subject to the pressures and mood of the times as a single magistrate who owed his position to politicians. The grand jury would surely vindicate me and turn me loose.

While I waited for the grand jury session, I had a visitor who cheered me up a great deal—my commanding officer, Captain Wall. I was taken down to block 32, where he was waiting in full uniform.

"Bob," he said, "this has been a terrible shock to me."

"To me too, Captain," I said with a wry smile.

"When I brought you down here that first day, I was convinced that it was only a token arrest, something for the record. But now. . . ." He shook his head.

"There's still the grand jury, sir. They're to hear my case later this week and I'm sure they'll throw it out."

"I pray so, Bob. And so do all the men back in the precinct. And . . . well, we took up a little collection." He fumbled inside his jacket and brought out an envelope stuffed with bills. It contained more than $200. He said, "This is a token of our esteem and respect for you, and a way of telling you we're behind you 100 per cent."

I choked up and couldn't find any words for a minute, but I grabbed his hand and held it. Finally, I said, "Would you give this to my wife, sir? She'll be needing it."

"Of course, Bob."

"And tell them what it means to me . . . them being behind me. Tell them I'll be back just as soon as the grand jury turns me free."

Optimistic words! Maybe that's the way God helps a man, by always giving him hope. No matter how black things are, there's always hope. Well, almost always. There came a time when I was without it, when I thought God had forgotten me. But not yet. There was still the grand jury and they could refuse to indict me.

The day came for the hearing, and again I made the trip across the Bridge of Sighs. My lawyer met me, and we waited in the witness room outside the grand jury hearing chambers. Lash had requested that I be heard, and I had signed a waiver of immunity so that my appearance and testimony would not bar me from prosecution. While we sat there, I saw a dark-haired, slender man pass the open door and go into the grand jury room. It was Joseph Dandio. I had almost an overpowering urge to run after him and grab him by the throat and force the truth out of him.

Minutes later Dandio came out of the grand jury room and hurried away without looking at me. I didn't wonder why he wanted to avoid my eyes, with what he had on his conscience. Lash left the room to confer briefly with an assistant district attorney and, when he returned, his face was long.

"Bob," he said, "the grand jury is not going to hear your testimony."

"What?" I cried. "They refuse to hear my side of the story? But they can't do that!"

"Yes, they can. As the law now stands it's optional whether they hear any defendant. They are only required to listen to the evidence *against* a man."

"But they listened to Dandio's lies," I cried. "Why won't they listen to me?"

He shrugged his shoulders. "It's up to the grand jury. There's nothing we can do about it. Apparently the district attorney's office advised them not to listen to your testimony . . . that's the only thing I can conclude."

"Of course the D.A. doesn't want them to hear the truth," I burst out bitterly. "He's out to railroad me!"

"Shhh, Bob. Take it easy. They'll hear you. Don't jeopardize your case by this kind of outburst. Maybe the grand jury has decided *not* to indict and just doesn't want to bother with your testimony."

Again . . . hope. But it was short-lived. The grand jury deliberated less than thirty minutes, and then the D.A. came out into the corridor to announce to the waiting newspapermen that I had been indicted for murder in the first degree.

I heard the fateful words above the clamorous voices of the reporters. I felt as if a giant hand was squeezing me between thumb and forefinger. A cold, tingling sensation ran up my spine, followed by a hot sickness that made the lights blur and spin in an arc above my head. But the sickness passed in a moment. I would continue to suffer but I would not faint.

Indicted for murder! And on the testimony of a dope pusher! I had always talked about justice . . . worked for it . . . defended it with my life! Where was it now?

As the reporters waited eagerly with poised pencils for my words, I could find none. I felt only a great lassitude. I wanted to go to bed. I was led back to my cell.

When I awoke from a long sleep, I thought for a moment I was home and I reached over to touch my wife, but felt instead the cold iron bars and I smelled the stench and I heard the growl of voices, the never-ending chorus of hate and cruelty. The nightmare of prison life began again.

Nor would I escape it for a long time to come. As this realization went through me, I began to pant, as if I was being suffocated. Hysteria began to build up and it took all my will power now not to beat on the bars and scream. I literally clung to the cot with every ounce of my strength, fighting a force that was trying to rip me loose and fling me against the walls of my cage. At that moment I was in danger of going stir-crazy. But it passed. I was soaked with perspiration and exhausted, but I had won. I didn't scream, I didn't beat the bars.

In the days that followed I began to observe prison life, if not with interest, at least with a sort of morbid curiosity. I wondered to what depths of degradation men would sink when caged by cruel and cynical keepers.

The keepers were in this for money, and everything was available at a price. The slop that was served for food was so bad that it made most men sick, so the most lively trade was in outside food. A dry but edible sandwich was smuggled in for a dollar plus its cost, and I spent what money I could spare on this sort of a diet. A letter from Mabel cost me a dollar and clean clothes sent by her cost me a dollar. I had to pay five dollars for blankets for my cot and then an additional dollar for a can of disinfectant to free them of lice. Those were the minimum needs of a man and about all I could afford, but all sorts of other delicacies were available. Wine came at five dollars a bottle plus cost, whiskey at ten dollars a bottle plus cost. Books, with a few of the pages impregnated with cocaine so they could be chewed, were fifty dollars a book. A card or crap game with three men in a cell cost five dollars. A crap game with ten men in a cell was ten dollars plus a cut of the pot. An all-night game was twenty-five dollars.

Disguises were for rent for prisoners who faced a damaging identification at the police lineup. Wigs and mustaches and even cleverly arranged false teeth were available at prices up to one hundred dollars.

Sex was for sale, too. The homosexuals were all isolated in one tier, but could be ordered by the other prisoners at ten dollars for a quick visit and twenty-five dollars for all night. There was a special grapevine for sex which would buzz excitedly whenever a new fag came into the prison. There would be lively bidding for his services if he was handsome. The keepers allowed the fags to use perfume and to peddle themselves during the exercise periods.

If a new prisoner was handsome and young, he was often compelled to enter the sex traffic even if he wasn't a homosexual. I saw such a boy forced into the cell of a brutal degenerate on my tier. First came his pitiful cries of fright and pain while the other prisoners yelled out obscene advice. And after it was over, his muffled sobs filled the night to shame the men who had done this to him. But there was no shame here.

One day after I had left Mabel in the visitors' room and was being led back to my cell, a keeper said in a low voice, "How'd you like to have your wife in a lower tier cell for an hour? Only twenty-five dollars."

I had a sudden vision of Mabel, so clean and wonderful and courageous, stepping into the middle of this filth. I turned away, sickened.

During exercise periods, I, of the whole prison population, walked alone. I didn't mind; I preferred not to associate with the rest of them. I was a cop in my heart and mind and I had nothing in common with the hoods around me. But I wasn't to be left alone.

After the first few days, I became accustomed to the murderous looks, the snarled obscenities whenever I passed a group of prisoners. What startled me, therefore, was a group of four men on my tier who suddenly stopped spitting out their hatred but fell silent whenever I came near. They were planning something, I knew.

It occurred when I had been there about a month. I had completed two laps jogging around the fifth tier and was slowing for a turn when I came to this particular group. They were leaning casually against the shower cells but came together and moved toward me as I approached. I stopped, but there was no escaping them. They came in a rush, and a stiletto flashed dully in the gray prison light.

It was a fight in silence, just out of sight of the keepers. The sight of the knife drove me to a frenzy and I lashed out with my fists, careful to keep my back against the wall. I saw the knife flash downwards at me and I threw up my hand to protect my face. I felt nothing but suddenly my hand was dripping blood. Then came another flash of steel and a sickening jar as the blade ripped across my chin, lay-ing it open. Then I heard the keepers rush up with clubs, heard them yell, "Into your cells!"

I was led back to my cell, weak and nauseated, but alive. The palm of my left hand had been cut to the bone from the base of my little finger to my wrist. Blood poured from my chin from the thrust meant for my jugular vein. A doctor from Bellevue arrived and put five stitches in my hand and four in my chin. Mabel wept when she saw me, the only time she ever broke down.

She had a job now and every cent, beyond barest living costs, was going for legal fees. Yet, we had to have money for the keepers. She saw my brother, and he sent the very last of his savings so we could bribe the keepers to let me exercise alone in the mornings while the rest of the prisoners were locked up.

Now I was free of my tormentors, I thought. Let them yell at me, I had gotten used to that, but at least they couldn't harm me physically. But I was wrong.

The new campaign against me began about a week later. It was the afternoon exercise period for all the prisoners except me. I was locked safely in my cell. Safely? A prisoner walked slowly by, looked up and down for a guard, then quickly opened his pants and began to urinate through the bars. I screamed a curse and lunged for him, but he backed off beyond my reach and now urinated on me. Then he buttoned his pants and went on down the tier as if nothing had happened.

It was useless to appeal to a keeper, of course, and all I could do was change my clothes and clean up my cell floor as best I could. I had made a mental note of that guy's face and vowed to settle with him some day. But it wasn't just one guy, it turned out to be an organized campaign by the entire tier. That evening a half dozen at a time stopped to urinate into my cell while I jumped about and cursed them like a crazed animal.

Two days later they stepped up their harassment. They saved their excrement and threw it by the bucketful into my cell as they passed. I was immediately sick, which only meant I had my own vomit to clean up with the rest of the filth. Now I buried some of my pride and begged a keeper to put an end to this.

He said, "What you expect me to do? Put a special guard in front of your cell twenty-four hours a day? There aren't enough men."

"But it's your job to keep order," I said.

"Oh, so now yer tellin' me how to run my job, eh, McAllister? That's your trouble here—that's why they hate you . . . you think you're so goddamn much better than anybody else."

"I'm not a crook like the rest of them—I'm a cop!"

"A cop my ass," he sneered. "Get wise to yourself, McAllister. You're a prisoner here just like everybody else."

Just like everybody else . . . he said. But it wasn't true. I was a prisoner set apart from everybody else . . . scorned and tormented. And it continued day after day, night after night, the urine and the excrement thrown into my cell . . . and my own vomit on top of it. And now a new horror was added . . . a choking fear that I might lose my mind.

The district attorney's office, I was convinced, knew what was going on in the Tombs and hoped to break me by keeping me there. At least once a week an assistant D.A. would come to see me, always with the same message:

"Stop being stubborn, McAllister. The D.A. will take a manslaughter charge. Better accept it. You'll get the chair otherwise."

My answer was always the same. "No! By God, no! Try me for murder or for nothing. I'll rot in jail before I make a confession to any charge."

And I *was* rotting in jail. And each week my defiance of Tammany became weaker. My nerves were so shot that I knew they might go at any moment, and I'd be reduced to a sniveling, broken man. The politicians waited.

After two-and-a-half months of this living hell, it came— that small and final burden that can crush a man. I had been down to counsel's room to again be offered a deal of manslaughter by an assistant district attorney and upon returning to my cell found that my tormentors had been at work again. On the middle of my bunk was a decayed and scabrous thing oozing a putrid, green fluid that was making a wide, wet stain on the blankets. It was one of the enormous rats that had been slaughtered, kept in a bucket until decayed, and then thrown into my cell.

The sight and the stench made me gag, and I turned away to lean my head against the bars while the rest of the prisoners began to hoot and jeer. I felt no resentment, I had no fight left. At that moment I only wanted to be free of the torment of living.

"Hey, McAllister," one of them cried, "how'd you like your brother, you rat bastard?"

"He smells better than you do, McAllister!" another shouted.

"They're gonna cook your ass in Sing Sing," a nasal voice chanted from a tier above. "They're gonna cook your ass . . . and I wanna see it sizzle."

Suddenly, from far down at the end of tier five, a voice boomed out above all others. "All right . . . lay off that cop. He's a right guy . . . and he's a friend of mine."

There was a moment of stunned silence. Who dared call McAllister a friend? Then a bedlam of catcalls and hoots and foul cries filled the air. My "friend" topped it all with his booming voice. He shouted. "I'm Baldy Dealey and I'm takin' over this stir. I say to leave that cop alone."

The nasal voice whined, "I'll piss in his cell tomorrow!"

"You do," Dealey said, "and you'll learn who's running things here."

Baldy Dealey! His name haunted me through the rest of the night. Toward morning I remembered. He was the "United Cigar Store Bandit," a two-gun desperado who had escaped from Sing Sing over a year ago. He had been captured two days before by Detectives Dwyer and Barrett of the West 100th Street station. He and I had both attended Holy Name Parochial School and we had a mutual friend in Bobby Gleason, the welterweight fighter, another Holy Name boy. Baldy Dealey, from my old neighborhood. A boy who had gone wrong but who had the guts to call me "friend."

At two o'clock the next afternoon the men moved past my locked cell during their exercise period, and suddenly a thin Italian who had been one of my chief tormentors paused to urinate into my cell. At once a short, powerful man stepped up, pulled a piece of iron pipe out of his shirt and hit the Italian a terrible blow on the back of the head. The hoodlum let out a soft moan, then sank down, unconscious. Baldy Dealey calmly put the pipe back in his shirt and continued his leisurely walk. The guards appeared and hauled away the unconscious figure.

After that demonstration, no prisoner threw excrement into my cell, or dead rats, or even cursed me. It was an amazing thing to see a man openly boast that he was taking over a prison that housed some of the toughest killers and felons in the world—it was even more amazing to see him do it.

When Baldy Dealey called me "friend," he saved my sanity. He was a crook, but he was a human being who may well have been God's instrument, the answer to my constant prayers.

After Baldy arrived in the Tombs, I recovered my courage and knew I'd never make a deal with the politicians, I'd defy them right to the end.

They must have understood this because now they stopped waiting for me to break. They brought me to trial for murder.

Chapter Twelve

ARISE AND

FACE THE JURORS

By Armistice Day, 1924, twelve men had been selected for the jury. They sat in the jury box and stared at me. I stared back at them. They were: Martin Freeman, accountant, foreman; William Dann, salesman; Charles Strahley, clerk; Lyman Bartlett, treasurer; Murray Whiteleaf, manager; Byron J. Weaton, insurance; Louis R. Wendell, insurance; William Graf, manager; John R. Ninrock, assistant purchasing agent; Alfred E. Broddell, sales agent; Paul W. Eller, salesman; and Albert Moyer, manager.

Put down on paper, they are only names. Sitting in a jury box, they were transformed into something more than mere men, for they held in their hands the most awful power—that of life or death. And each of them had assured Assistant District Attorney James A. McDonald that, if the evidence warranted it, he had no qualms about sentencing a man to the electric chair.

Mr. McDonald's opening address to the jury impressed

them, I thought. His quiet manner gave the impression of great sincerity tinged with reluctance, as if he had an unpleasant but necessary job to do. He was a handsome man as he paced back and forth before the jury, taking the twelve men into his confidence, trusting them to see that it was their duty, too, to electrocute Robert McAllister.

When he had finished, my attorney stood up to give his opening remarks. Mr. Lash said, "This is a simple case of the word of a vicious criminal against that of a young patrolman, in full uniform, performing his sworn duty on the city's street at four o'clock in the morning. You shall hear how Chief of Detectives John Coughlin exonerated this patrolman after an investigation. You will hear from Captain Wall, his commanding officer, that he gave McAllister explicit instructions at the outgoing roll call to watch for automobile thieves in that neighborhood. I shall produce witnesses who will tell you how they found the regular wiring of the automobile in question tampered with, and a wire attached from the switch to the coil so that the automobile could be started without a key. Gentlemen, when you hear the defense, you will wonder why no police officers were called before the grand jury and why such ruthless tyrannical methods were used to throw the weight, power and influence of the district attorney's office against this unfortunate young patrolman. The defense knows the reasons. McAllister is hated by someone in power, but unfortunately we will be unable to prove this as a matter of law. Gentlemen, when you draw your own conclusions after hearing the evidence, your consciences will cry out for a verdict of Not Guilty."

There was a buzz of voices in the court as Mr. Lash sat down. His references to my powerful enemies had the re-

porters scribbling madly on their pads. He hadn't mentioned Tom Foley or Murphy or any of the Jimmy Walker
crowd by name, but the reporters knew what he was talking about.

Mr. McDonald presented his first witness, Dr. Benjamin
J. Vance, assistant medical examiner, who testified that the
bullet fired from my gun caused Fighera's death. Lash had
no questions and Dr. Vance stepped down.

McDonald stood up at the prosecutor's table and said,
"Will Mr. Morris Friedman please take the stand?"

From the back of the room came Mr. Friedman, a short,
gray-haired man walking with precise steps. As he moved
toward the witness chair, I remembered what Jimmy Hines
had said to me the last time I saw him: "I've talked to
Morris Friedman and he saw the whole thing. He said he
thought those guys were gonna shoot you and he ducked.
He said it was justifiable homicide, and if there's ever any
trouble about it, he'll tell the truth. You've got nothing to
worry about."

I nudged Lash excitedly and said, "Wait until the D.A.
hears *this* testimony. He'll be rocked on his heels."

Friedman was sworn in and took the witness chair.
McDonald walked toward him and said, "Mr. Friedman, in
your own words, will you please tell the jury what you saw
the night of the shooting."

"A short time before the shooting," Morris Friedman
said, "I met McAllister in front of the Monongahela Club,
and he offered to accompany me home after leaving Tammany leader James J. Hines at the latter's home nearby. We
were walking south on Manhattan Avenue when McAllister
called my attention to two youths standing beside a parked
automobile a short distance from Manhattan Avenue. Mc-

Allister said, 'Morris, those two fellows look suspicious to me.'

"Then McAllister turned east as we reached the opposite corner. He said, 'I'll be back in a minute; wait.' I said I wanted to get home and continued walking. I had gone about 30 feet further south when I heard the shot. I quickly turned around and went back. I saw two men lying on the sidewalk. McAllister was standing over them with a revolver in his hand. I walked up to him as McAllister was sounding his club on the pavement, and then he fired two shots in the air.

"McAllister said to me, 'These men made a pass at me.' Dandio kept shouting, 'What did I do? What did I do?' Then McAllister said, 'The next time I tell you to stick your hands up, you stick them up.' The other fellow, Fighera, moaned, 'Look, cousin, what he did to us.' And turning to McAllister, he said, 'Why did you shoot me? I did nothing to you.'

"McAllister asked them what they were doing around the car in that neighborhood at four o'clock in the morning, and they replied that they were on their way to visit a cousin.

"Two other policemen arrived and they were all talking. They put the wounded man into a taxicab and the other officers took him away. Dandio had risen from the sidewalk and started to walk away when McAllister shouted, 'Don't you go away, you're under arrest.' There was a large crowd present by now. A short time later Dandio was placed in an automobile and taken away."

That was the end of his testimony! That was all! The district attorney asked him a couple of questions, but only things concerning minor details. I sat there stunned. Jimmy

Hines had told me that Morris *saw* the shooting . . . that he thought I was going to be killed . . . that it was justifiable homicide . . . that I had nothing to worry about because Morris would tell the truth. What had happened to change this?

Had Jimmy Hines lied to me? Or had Morris suddenly decided to change his attitude toward me? If he had, why? A dozen questions raced through my mind and I could find answers to none of them. I couldn't seem to figure anything out. I only knew that the man I had pinned my hopes on had failed to help me.

"No question," I heard Lash say, and Friedman began to climb down from the witness chair.

I grabbed Lash's arm and whispered hoarsely, "My God, aren't you going to cross-examine him?"

Lash said, "His story confirms the facts in the essential details. He might damage us if we cross-examine him."

It seemed to me that Friedman had "damaged" us already. But when you're on trial for your life, you have to follow your lawyer's advice.

The final witness of the day was a ballistics expert of the police department, who testified that the bullet fired from my gun was the same as that removed from the body of the deceased. Court of General Sessions Judge Otto A. Rosalsky adjourned court until the following day.

Friday morning Mr. McDonald put the State's star witness, Joseph Dandio, on the stand. Here was the mainstay of the prosecution's entire case. Unless Mr. Lash could discredit him in the jury's eyes, my chances were slim. How I hated that man as he rose to take the stand. He was dressed in a dark blue suit, and on his face was a sanctimonious expression. He carried a rosary in his hands. That my church's prayer beads could be used as a stage prop in such a vile plot . . . it made me rage. Mr. Lash put his hand on my arm to calm me, for the jury was glancing in my direction.

Dandio answered Mr. McDonald's direct examination in a calm voice, sitting relaxed in the witness chair, the rosary dangling from his hand for all to see. He swore that he and Fighera had never stopped to tamper with any car, that they were merely walking down 115th Street when I raced up to them, and, without a word, pulled my gun and killed Fighera. As he told it, tears ran down his cheeks. Judge Rosalsky granted a short recess so the witness might regain his composure. The performance was decidedly hammy in my eyes, but I wasn't at all sure how the jury saw it. He was a good actor, no doubt about that, and perhaps the jury had been taken in.

Court reconvened and Mr. Lash rose for cross-examination. There was a hushed expectancy throughout the vast, paneled room. I saw my dear wife lean forward in her seat, twisting her handkerchief in a small, hard knot. What torture for her! Mr. Lash now had to prove that Dandio was a liar, a thief, a drug peddler devoid of human decency, scum whose word could not be accepted. Mr. Lash opened the cross examination bluntly:

Q. (By Mr. Lash.) How many times have you been convicted of crime?

A. Twice, I think.

Q. On December 21, 1916, were you convicted for selling narcotics?

A. (Turning to the judge.) Do I have to answer that, Your Honor?

Judge: Answer the question.

A. Well, it was for possession, not selling narcotics.

Q. The charge was possession with intent to sell, wasn't it?

A. That's right.

Q. Did you have in your possession a half ounce of un-adulterated heroin when you were arrested?

A. I can't remember how much it was.

Q. Did you plead guilty to the charge?

A. Only to possession of drugs.

Q. Tell me, did you have the half ounce of heroin for your own use?

A. No.

Q. You haven't got the monkey on your back, have you?

A. I'm not a user, if that's what you mean.

Q. Will you explain to the court and the jury how you came into possession of the heroin?

A. Well, it was like this. (His composure crumbled slightly.) On the night the bulls grabbed me, I did a friend a favor. I accepted ten dollars to deliver a package to a fellow named Squint. I stood on the corner of 107th Street and First Avenue waiting for him to show up. All of a sudden, I was it.

Q. Did they tell you they had been trailing you and suspected you of being a dope peddler?

A. They never told me anything.

Q. Were you surprised when they arrested you?

A. Very much so. I didn't know what the score was.

Q. You never suspected that there was heroin in the package?

A. I didn't know a thing.

Q. Did you tell the detectives who the friend was who gave you the package to deliver?

A. I told them I would never be able to recognize him, only met him once and was just doing a favor.

Q. A favor for ten dollars? You got paid, didn't you?

A. (Squirming.) Yeah, I got paid in advance.

Q. Look here, Dandio, isn't it a fact that you are employed by the Mafia to peddle drugs? (Lash shouts.) And isn't it a fact you're a member of that organization?

A. I never heard of the Mafia.

Q. I'll spell it out! M-a-f-i-a. Does that ring a bell?

A. That's all news to me.

Q. Don't you know the Mafia dominates and controls the illicit drug trade in East Harlem?

A. (He shuffles his feet.) That's the craziest thing I ever heard.

Q. Mr. Dandio, were you born in this country?

A. No, I came over from Sicily.

Q. Are you a citizen?

A. No.

Q. How old are you?

A. Twenty-eight years.

Q. Are you employed gainfully?

A. I don't get you.

Q. Do you work for a living?

A. Not at the present.

Q. Were you employed on August 13?

A. No steady job, a little job here and there.

Q. On the night of the shooting you said you were out taking a walk. Can you tell me where you were going at 4 A.M.?

A. Just walking, getting a little fresh air.

Q. Did you hear Mr. Friedman of the Monongahela Democratic Club testify for the People?

A. Yes.

Q. Then you will recall what he said—and I now read from the record: "McAllister then asked them what they were doing around the car in that neighborhood at four o'clock in the morning, and they" (meaning you and Fighera) "replied they were on their way to visit a cousin." Did you say that?

A. I don't remember saying that.

Q. Did Vince say that?

A. I don't remember.

Q. Was your mind clear on the night of the shooting?

A. Yes, very clear.

Q. Was that a truthful statement?

A. I don't remember saying that. All I can tell you, we were going to call on a friend.

Q. What was the name and address of this friend?

A. Vince knew it.

Q. Was your friend's name Sadie Chink?

A. I don't know any Sadie Chink.

Q. Maybe I can refresh your memory; Sadie Chink runs a disorderly house on 113th Street off Manhattan Avenue.

A. I'm not acquainted with any prostitutes.

Q. Isn't it a fact that you and your friend Vince were going to meet two prostitutes after Sadie Chink's place closed and take them for a drive?

A. Absolutely not. Where did you get that bunk?

Q. You had no intention of stealing a car and taking anyone for a drive?

A. Absolutely not. There was no parked car to steal when McAllister shot us.

Q. Didn't McAllister catch you and your friend in the act of stealing a car?

A. How could he? There was no car there to steal.

Q. You testified before Magistrate House and the grand jury that there was no parked car near the scene of the shooting. Is that correct?

A. Yes, I testified to that.

(Mr. Lash hands the witness a photograph taken after the shooting by Detective John Barry, official police photographer. The photo of 115th Street looking east from Manhattan to Eighth Avenue shows five cars parked in the block, with Mr. Mayer's car a few feet from the shooting.)

Q. This is a picture of the street, taken less than ninety minutes after the shooting. Is that the way it looked?

A. No, I can't say that's the way it looked. I didn't see any cars.

I began to feel pretty discouraged because of Lash's inability to break through Dandio's lies. It was becoming apparent that Dandio was a clever, chronic perjurer, who would stick to his story, come hell or high water.

Q. (By Mr. Lash.) You testified that on the night of the shooting, McAllister walked right up to you and shot you at point blank range, without saying a word?

A. Yes, that's right.

Q. You never did a thing to provoke the shooting?

A. No, we were walking arm in arm on the sidewalk, minding our own business.

Q. Did you grab McAllister's club from under his left armpit?

A. I did nothing.

Q. Did you draw your right hand back as if reaching for a gun?

A. No, I never carry a gun.

Q. After McAllister shot at your right arm and missed, he tripped over a wire fence surrounding the hedge. Did you slip a gun into the hedge?

A. I told you I didn't have a gun.

Q. Can you give me any reason why McAllister, in full uniform, would want to kill you or your friend?

A. (Shouting.) Everything I testified to is the truth. He just walked up to us and tried to kill us.

Q. Dandio, you were convicted on a loaded gun charge in 1917?

A. Yes, that's right.

Q. You were arrested by Patrolman Noar, 39th Precinct.

A. I don't remember his name.

Q. You pleaded guilty to that charge.

A. Yes.

Q. There's no mistake about that, is there?

A. No.

Q. You were arraigned in this very courtroom before the Honorable Judge Malone?

A. Yes.

Q. Did you hear the arresting officer testify you were going to shoot him, lost your nerve, and slipped the gun into an ash can?

A. I don't remember that.

Q. (Reads from the trial testimony in which Dandio admitted possession of a gun with intent to kill Patrolman Noar.) Is that statement correct?

A. I was only bluffing.

Q. So you were bluffing with a loaded gun?

A. I said I was only bluffing.

Q. So on the night you were accosted by Patrolman Noar, you had a loaded gun but had no intention of shooting because you were only bluffing?

A. (Rolls his eyes toward the ceiling, then clasps his hands together.) Like I told you before, I wasn't going to shoot anybody. I was only bluffing.

Q. On the night of August 13, when Patrolman McAllister ordered you to stick up your hands, didn't you have a gun on you and didn't you try to bluff him?

A. I told you I didn't have a gun.

Q. Dandio, you had a gun and tried to shoot McAllister, but he was too fast for you. Isn't that the truth?

A. I didn't have a gun. All he found on me was a knife.

Q. What sentence did you receive from Judge Malone on your plea of guilty?

A. I got an indefinite term in Elmira Reformatory.

Q. How about those arrests for the crimes of burglary and grand larceny after you got out of prison?

McDonald: Objection! Don't answer that question. Counsel knows that's an improper question.

Judge (to Mr. Lash): Counsel, ask the witness about his previous convictions only. Not arrests. (Instructs the jury and stenographer to disregard the last question.)

Q. (By Mr. Lash.) Dandio, did you know your friend Vince Fighera had a criminal record?

A. No, I didn't know a thing about it.

Q. Did you know he was several times convicted of crimes?

A. Nope.

Q. (Incredulous.) You didn't know he served time in Sing Sing prison for peddling drugs?

A. Absolutely not.

Q. Was Vince your cousin?

A. Well, we called each other cousin, kind of related like, way back.

Q. You surely knew your cousin from way back was known as the Yap and was the best pickpocket in Harlem?

A. No.

Q. (With rising temper.) Do you mean to sit there and tell me you didn't know your cousin was arrested fifteen times and convicted seven times for picking pockets and selling drugs.

McDonald: I object to the question.

Judge: Sustained; disregard. (Waves toward the jury.) We'll take an adjournment for lunch; that should allow tempers to cool off.

As the court broke up, I watched Dandio step down from the witness chair and walked arrogantly toward the exit. Unthinking, I began moving toward him when I felt a strong hand on my arm. It was Lash who whispered urgently, "What in hell are you trying to do?"

"I . . . I don't know. I guess I just wanted to come face to face with Dandio."

"Sure, you come face to face, and next you take a poke at him, and that will fix things just fine. Now watch yourself, Bob. You're on trial for your life."

I couldn't help but look at Dandio longingly . . . longing to get my hands on him. Mabel came to my side and took hold of my arm. She smiled up at me and said, "Everything is going all right, Bob."

I kissed her and said, "But did you hear Friedman? I don't understand it, honey. I don't understand it at all."

"Don't try to. Just think about the rest of the trial, what's yet to be done."

"But Jimmy Hines told me. . . ."

"Bob, forget about it. His testimony is over, and it really wasn't too bad."

"All right, baby," I sighed. "All right."

I was led back to the Tombs for my lunch, but I didn't have any appetite. I sat on my cot, staring at the tray of gray food and wondering what the jury was doing now, what it was thinking. Dandio had obviously lied on the witness stand, at least it seemed obvious to me. But how had those twelve men in the jury seen it? How I wished I could search their minds at this moment.

I sat lost in thought for what seemed to be a matter of minutes, but suddenly the keeper was opening the door of my cell, and it was a quarter to two and time to go back to court. As I followed him down the tier, the other prisoners began to call out to me. I heard: "Good luck, Mac." "You'll make it, Mac." "Give 'em hell, Mac."

How different from the way they had yelled at me before! The change wasn't only because Baldy Dealey had taken over the prison and was my protector. It was because I was on trial for my life, and their natural sympathies were with me. I was no longer a cop; I was a man faced with the electric chair. They knew what that meant. I waved back at them, feeling warm and grateful toward them. What strange things a prison can do to a man!

Back in the courtroom, I searched the crowds for Mabel, but apparently she hadn't returned from lunch. Reporters, spectators and court officials were standing about, but nobody came near me as I sat alone at the defense table. I saw

Lash pushing his way through the crowd, and his face was flushed with excitement.

"My God," he exclaimed, when he got to me, "the most amazing thing has just happened! Do you know a cop named George D. Maher from the East 126th Street station house?"

"No, I don't think I do. Why?"

"Out there in the hall, just now, he tried to arrest Dandio. He recognized him as the man who shot and crippled him on the nineteenth of April."

My heart began to pound. "You talked to him?"

"I sure did. Maher tells me he was on post last April when a car came through a play street closed to traffic. He attempted to pull the car over to the curb, but as it swept by him, Dandio, who was sitting next to the driver, leaned out the window and shot him. It sounds incredible, but that cop swears he never forgot Dandio's face. There was a big fuss in the corridor, and I got hold of the district attorney; we've just been to see Judge Rosalsky with the story. He won't talk to Maher, said he'll have to appear in open court this afternoon. Because of legal technicalities, Maher can't arrest Dandio until after the trial. Frankly, Bob, I don't know what's going to happen. I never heard of a case like this before."

At this moment the full significance of this development hit me. I grabbed Lash's arm and almost shook him in my excitement. "Don't you see? That was the same gun he ditched in the hedge. He didn't want to be caught with a gun on him in the first place, but *this* gun was hot. If we'd ever caught him with this gun, ballistics would have had him dead to rights on the Maher shooting."

"You're right," Lash cried excitedly.

"This proves what I said was right . . . he *was* going for a gun when I shot. Everything dovetails together."

"It does . . . it does. It's perfect, Bob. Now, the question is how to get Maher's story to the jury."

"My God, just put him on the stand."

Lash shook his head. "There's rules of evidence, Bob. I'm not sure they'll let Maher tell his story. The court may hold it immaterial to the charge against you."

"Don't they want the truth? Why must everything get so legal? The jury has *got* to hear this . . . somehow they've got to."

At this moment the judge came in and we all rose. The trial of Bob McAllister resumed.

Lash strode out to resume his cross-examination of Dandio. He bore in relentlessly. Did I imagine it, or had Dandio's complacency given way to apprehension? He no longer lounged in the witness chair, but sat on the edge and shuffled his feet nervously.

Q. (By Mr. Lash.) Dandio, did you ever shoot a cop?
A. Who, me? Certainly not.
Q. Did you shoot a uniformed policeman on the evening of April 19 last, when the officer tried to stop a stolen car in which you were riding?
McDonald: (Shouting.) I object. The witness is not on trial.
Lash: I'll connect this question, Your Honor.
Judge: At this time I'll allow it.
  (The question is reread by the stenographer.)
Dandio: (Screaming.) No! What is this, a frame-up?
Judge: Sit down and answer the questions. Stop the dramatics.
Q. (By Mr. Lash, who asks Patrolman Maher to stand.) Did you ever see this officer before?
A. (Hesitates a split second.) Up to this afternoon, I never seen him before in my life.
Q. That's all.

Lash walked slowly back to our table and sat down. McDonald rose at his table and said, "The State rests." The State's case against me was finished. It consisted of one man —Joseph Dandio. Did the jury believe his story? I searched the faces of the twelve men, but could find no clues.

Lash stood up beside me and said in his clear, earnest voice, "Your Honor, I submit that the State has failed to prove the charge of premeditated murder by competent evidence. I petition the court to dismiss the indictment."

My throat tightened as I watched the judge. He could dismiss me at this moment; in the next thirty seconds the nightmare could end. Judge Rosalsky cleared his throat and said, "Motion denied. Proceed with the defense." I slumped in my seat. I hadn't expected a dismissal, Lash had warned me not to expect it, but it *could* have happened. At this moment I could have walked out of the courtroom, a free man, my wife on my arm. . . .

Lash sat down and began arranging the papers that pertained to my defense. The courtroom was hushed and expectant. I felt the mounting tension within myself as well. The electric chair was potentially one step closer.

All eyes were upon Lash as he stood up and said in a calm voice, "Will Patrolman George D. Maher please take the stand." A burst of excited talk swept the courtroom, and spectators stood up to get the first glimpse of the new witness. I stood with the rest, my heart pounding.

A young, uniformed cop made his way slowly through the crowd. He was walking with a pronounced limp. I felt sure he could save me if only he got a chance to tell his story. As he came closer, I waited for someone, the judge or the D.A., to stand up and say, "No! You can't take the stand. You can't tell about Dandio being a cop shooter!" But no one did.

Maher stood calmly before the bailiff, his hand raised, and listened to the familiar words: "Do you solemnly swear that the testimony you are about to give in the case of the State versus Robert McAllister is the truth, the whole truth, and nothing but the truth, so help you God?" Patrolman Maher said, "I do." He took the stand.

Lash walked slowly toward the witness, taking his time, letting the tension in the courtroom mount. And when he began his questioning, he spoke so quietly that everyone had to strain to hear his words.

Q. (By Mr. Lash.) Officer Maher, were you attached to the East 126th Street station house on April 19, 1924?

A. Yes, I was.

Q. Will you tell the jury what happened to you on the evening of April 19 at 122d Street and Pleasant Avenue?

A. I was on patrol at 122d Street and Pleasant Avenue when I observed a black touring car northbound, heading in my direction, run through a play street closed to traffic and set aside for children. I ran out into the street and raised my hand to the driver, intending to pull him over to the curb and serve a summons on him. Instead of stopping, the driver stepped on the gas and steered the car directly at me. As I backed out of the path of the machine, the passenger sitting next to the driver leaned out over the front door and shot me through my hip.

Q. Is the man who shot you present in this courtroom?

A. Yes, he is sitting right there (points toward Dandio).

Judge: Please step down and make the identification.

Maher: (Limps over and places his hand on Dandio's shoulder.) There is the man who shot me; I'll never forget his face.

Dandio: (Jumps to his feet, screams.) It's a lie, it's a lie!

Judge: (To Patrolman Maher.) Step back on the stand, officer, and resume your story.

Maher: Despite my wound, I fired at the car as it gathered speed, then commandeered another car and gave chase. We pursued them through the crowded streets of East Harlem. I fired at the car every chance I got, when it had to slow down momentarily at the intersections, until my gun was empty. My shots attracted the attention of Sergeant Butler, who took up the chase. Then I blacked out from loss of blood and came to in Harlem Hospital. I was confined for six weeks, and when they discharged me, my right leg was a quarter of an inch shorter than the other.

Q. (By Mr. Lash.) Did Sergeant Butler apprehend the occupants of the car?

A. No, sir. We got the license number of the car and it was later found abandoned at 110th Street near First Avenue. It proved to be a stolen car.

Q. Officer Maher, are you positive the man who shot you and escaped is Dandio?

A. Positive. His face is indelibly printed on my mind.

Q. Your witness (to McDonald).

Mr. McDonald went into a huddled debate with his aides. When he rose, he looked slightly bewildered, but he could still think fast on his feet. He argued that all the testimony of Patrolman Maher was immaterial and asked that it be stricken from the record. Mr. Lash fought back, arguing that the information was pertinent.

"Recess for fifteen minutes," said Judge Rosalsky.

I turned around, smiled and blew a kiss to my wife. The saints were on my side.

When court resumed, Judge Rosalsky looked down from the bench and addressed the jury: "The motion made by the district attorney is granted. The evidence is clearly immaterial, and it is ordered stricken from the record. And,

Gentlemen of the Jury, you are instructed to disregard it. Court adjourned until Monday morning at ten o'clock."

I swung in my chair toward Lash, and at once he put a restraining hand on my arm. "Not here, Bob. Don't make a scene in front of the jury. Wait until they've gone, and we'll discuss it." Mabel came up to the table to join us and Lash said to her, "Keep him quiet, in the name of heaven. I don't want any fuss while the jury is present."

Mabel sat beside me and took my hand in hers and held it hard. Contact with her was like a lightning rod: it drew some of the sparks out of me. The three of us sat there while the courtroom cleared of everyone except the bailiff, who was waiting to return me to the Tombs. At last Lash said to me, "Bob, we got a break this afternoon."

"A break!" I said bitterly. "You heard the judge tell the jury to disregard Maher's testimony!"

"Of course, but they're human beings, Bob. They won't be able to forget his story no matter how hard they try. When they're considering your fate, they'll always remember that Dandio tried to kill Patrolman Maher, no matter what the judge tells them."

"I'm not a lawyer," I said, "but it does seem strange. . . ."

"Now look, Bob, I told you right at the beginning that Maher's testimony was probably immaterial, yet what happened? The district attorney and the judge let it all be put before the jury before ruling against it. They could have stopped his story right at the beginning, but they didn't. Don't you see what a break we got?"

I was beginning to. "But why?" I asked.

"If you want my opinion, I don't think McDonald likes this case. He had to take it. He was pressured into it by

Tammany, but he's basically a decent guy and he hates the job he's got to do. He'll do his best to convict you, make no mistake about that, but he's got a sense of fair play that just wouldn't let him silence Maher before the full story was told."

"Maybe you're right, at that," I said.

"I'm sure I'm right. Things are breaking so well for us, Bob, that I don't think I'll put you on the stand at all."

"What!" I exploded.

"It isn't necessary and it might run some risk. If McDonald gets a crack at you in cross-examination and makes you look bad in any respect, we'll lose the advantage we now have."

"Mr. Lash," I said, "nothing under God's heaven can stop me from taking that stand. I've been rotting away in prison for three months, waiting to tell my side of the story. The grand jury wouldn't listen to me, but this one has to listen. I've got a right to my day in court; I'm going to take it."

Lash looked at Mabel. She said, "I know how Bob feels. I think he should always follow your advice, Mr. Lash, but in this case, I think he's right."

Lash shrugged his shoulders in resignation. The bailiff came up to lead me back to the Tombs, where for three nights and two days I waited and dreamed of my moment on the witness stand.

During the weekend, Chief of Detectives Coughlin came to see me. He told me that Dandio was going to be arrested for the shooting of Maher as soon as my trial ended. He said, "When Maher identified Dandio yesterday as the man who shot him, I remembered that the detectives in the case had lifted a perfect single print from the stolen car. Last night a comparison showed the print belongs to Dandio."

It made me feel good to know that Maher was going to be square with Dandio. But I wasn't square with him, not yet. Everything hinged upon what happened Monday, when I took the stand in my own defense.

When I arrived in court Monday morning, I found it more crowded than ever. The weekend newspapers had been full of the case, and as a result, hundreds of people came who couldn't even get into the courtroom. I wondered vaguely at their eagerness to see the spectacle of a man fighting for his life. How I wished I had a choice of coming here or not!

Mabel sat with me until the judge arrived. She squeezed my arm and said, "This is our day, darling."

I nodded. "This is our day . . . one way or the other."

The judge appeared, and the opening ceremonies were disposed of. Sidney Lash arose, and I heard the words I'd waited and prayed for: "Will Robert McAllister please take the stand."

I was sworn in. Lash said to me, "In your own words, please tell the jury exactly what happened the night of the shooting."

Slowly, carefully, I told the whole story. I spoke directly to the twelve men in the jury box, ignoring the rest of the courtroom. In that moment, neither judge, lawyers, nor spectators existed for me. One by one, I looked at the twelve jurymen as I talked, and they looked back at me, their faces attentive but otherwise expressionless. How can one man know the truth in another? There was no answer that I could find, no key to unlock their hearts and their minds to me. I could only tell my story as it actually happened and pray that they had heard the truth in my words.

After I had completed my story, Mr. Lash asked a few

questions to bring out various aspects of the case, then said to McDonald, "Your witness." I braced myself as McDonald sprang from his table like an eager fighter hearing the bell. He tore into me, doing everything he could to make my testimony appear inconsistent, to trap me in a lie. At one stage he became so exasperated with my careful answers that he told me to take my left hand away from my chin when I was mulling over a question.

The New York Times of November 19 published the salient details of Mr. McDonald's efforts to break me down:

> McAllister had been subjected to a gruelling cross-examination by Assistant District Attorney McDonald, who dwelt at length on a report which the policeman, known as the "flying cop" because of his having been a champion runner, wrote in his police memorandum book the day of the shooting. The entry contained the statement that immediately before he shot Fighera, the latter grabbed his club and made a movement with his right hand towards his hip pocket, indicating he was about to draw a pistol.
>
> In his direct testimony on Monday, McAllister swore that it was Joseph Dandio, companion of Fighera, who had grabbed his club and made the move as if to shoot him.
>
> "Why didn't you write in your memorandum book that Dandio was the man who grabbed your club and made a motion towards his hip pocket?" pursued Mr. McDonald.
>
> McAllister hesitated before he answered and then said, "Well, when I made that report at the station house it was just an honest mistake in the names."
>
> "At any rate, one of the two men took your club away?" interjected Judge Rosalsky.
>
> "Yes, sir," the policeman replied. He added that "Things happened so rapidly at the time of the shoot-

ing that I could not be certain of everything that took place."

The policeman illustrated to the jury the manner in which he alleged Dandio had taken the club from him and made the movement with his hand toward his hip pocket. He added that he was one or two feet away and that he then jumped to Dandio's left when he fired at his arm.

McDonald returned to the memorandum book again and again. Finally he pointed his finger at me. "Tell the jury why you did not change the entry in your memorandum book. You had six days to do it before we seized it as evidence. Why?"

"I didn't think it was necessary to change it."

"So that's your best answer!" McDonald scoffed. "No further questions."

Mr. Lash then put Captain Wall on the stand. He was a veteran of a quarter century of service, white-haired and full of dignity, and I saw the jurymen look at him respectfully. He lectured the jury as if they were rookie cops, explaining to them how the police department works. He lauded my work, called me a good cop, and said I had reason to fear for my life when Dandio reached for a gun. He concluded with, "Inspector John D. Coughlin, commanding officer of the detective division, made a full investigation of the shooting, questioned and took statements from the witnesses, and exonerated the patrolman. His findings were that the shooting was justifiable and in the performance of duty."

Mr. Lash said, "Did you concur in the findings of Chief Coughlin?"

"I did."

McDonald went after Captain Wall in the cross-examination but couldn't make a dent in his testimony. Wall explained patiently the difference between felonious homicide and justifiable homicide, and the D.A. couldn't twist his words or his meaning. The captain concluded his testimony with this significant point: "There could be no mistaking Patrolman McAllister for someone other than a police officer; he was in full uniform."

McDonald said grimly, "No further questions."

Lieutenant Baxter, the next witness, testified that he had almost thirty years' service in the department. He explained, under the questioning of Mr. Lash, about changing the records. "McAllister came into the station house about 4:40 P.M. the day of the shooting and stated he had made a mistake in the names of the men and asked that I substitute the name Dandio for Fighera where it was necessary. Under the regulations of the police department, when a member makes an error or mistake in a department record, he will, as soon as possible, report his mistake to the desk officer, who will draw a line through the erroneous matter and enter the correction above and initial same."

"At this point," said Lash, "I wish to introduce the Arrest Record and Blotter and ask that they be marked as exhibits. They will show a change was made as soon as the defendant discovered his error."

Picking up the heavy Blotter, Lieutenant Baxter explained, "This is the chronological record of the command. Here, on the thirteenth of August, it showed the following entry: '4:30 P.M. Patrolman McAllister present at this command and reports the following.' As you can see, gentlemen, the changes I have testified to are duly recorded in the Blotter with reference to the Blotter entry of the shooting and changes in the Arrest Record. The Blotter remains on the desk under the supervision of the desk officer, who in his own handwriting enters, in the order of time, all police happenings affecting the command. For instance, there is the entry following McAllister's report: '4:45 P.M., Patrolman Katz present from 125th Street and Eighth Avenue with the following property removed from a D.O.A.,' a person dead on arrival of the ambulance. All the facts relating to the property were entered in the Blotter. Upon completion of the entry, the desk officer draws a line from the margin across the page in the center of the line below the last word."

Lash was quick to take advantage of the lieutenant's testimony. He said, "Let me ask you, Lieutenant Baxter, which record is more important, the Blotter or the memorandum book, and please explain why."

"The Blotter is more important; the reason is obvious. The Blotter never leaves the desk or the record room of the station house except under certain conditions, mostly under due process of law. A memorandum book is in the control of a patrolman or sergeant at all times. He must have all his books ready for inspection when called upon to produce them. It would be a simple matter for a dishonest officer to say he lost his book or to rewrite a new one. This would be impossible to do with a Blotter. It leaves no room for contradiction."

Mr. Lash said, "The defendant has admitted that he failed to change the error in his memorandum book, which the district attorney has offered in evidence against him. Much has been made of this omission. Now, will you tell the jury if this was a very serious violation of the rules of the department."

"In my opinion, it is not a serious violation because the defendant rectified his mistake in the most important record in the police department as soon as he discovered it."

"Then the defendant acted properly in reporting his mistake to you?"

"Absolutely, sir."

"Thank you, Lieutenant, that's all."

McDonald walked over toward the witness chair. He was about to ask a question when he suddenly changed his mind. "No cross-examination."

It was a very smart move on McDonald's part. He was satisfied to let well enough alone. No district attorney could contradict the documentary evidence offered in my behalf. Thank God I had gone to the precinct that day!

In quick succession, Mr. Lash called the owner of the automobile in question, who testified that the wires of the ignition had been tampered with.

Following that, Detective John Barry, a police photographer, testified he had taken the picture of the scene which had been previously introduced by Mr. Lash. Lash passed the picture to the jury. This mute piece of evidence was worth a thousand words of testimony. On it hinged an important question: whether the witness Dandio was telling the truth when he testified three times under oath that there was no automobile to steal at the scene of the shooting. I wished it were possible to read the jurors' minds as they passed the picture among them.

At this point Mr. Lash said, "The defense rests."

Judge Rosalsky apologetically notified McDonald, Lash, and the jury that the pressure of another case on the calendar was forcing him to hold a night session. "Counsel for the defense and the district attorney will sum up after a two-hour dinner recess. I will charge the jury tomorrow morning."

At 7:00 P.M. on Tuesday evening, November 18, the fight for life went into its final stages. Mr. Lash was eloquent in his summation of the evidence; he talked for almost three hours. He finished by branding Dandio a drug peddler and a member of the Mafia—"a despicable cur who bartered in human souls, wrecking lives, homes, and health, driving addicts to crime, degradation, and despair. I don't have to point out the comparison between him and the defendant, a war veteran, athlete, and cop. I know he's innocent of committing murder. It is for you, gentlemen of the jury, to make a choice. Whom do you believe?"

McDonald, in his summation, stressed the unfortunate upbringing of his principal witness, Dandio, "underprivileged from birth, a product of the East Side slums." He told the jury the district attorney couldn't pick all his witnesses from Park Avenue, and decried the fact that there were no other witnesses who had seen "a brutal murderer on the loose in a police uniform, a man who would kill without compunction, and did, when Dandio and his unfortunate friend met up with him in the early hours of the morning."

McDonald told the jury that the prosecution of a police officer for murder was a most unpleasant duty, but a duty that could not be shirked. He concluded with: "I charge the defendant killed without provocation. He is guilty of a wanton killing."

As he sat down, the bells of a nearby church tolled the hour of midnight, and the melancholy sound echoed through the hushed courtroom. Did those bells toll for me, I wondered?

The next morning at 10:30, Judge Rosalsky began his

charge to the jury. At 12:17, he completed the charge, and the jury retired to deliberate its verdict. I was led back to the detention cells, exhausted in mind and spirit. The fight for my life was over, whatever the verdict.

I flopped down on my cot and stared at the ceiling, wondering in a vague way how long the jury might be out. An hour? Two hours? Two days? I seemed withdrawn from it all, like a spectator who idly wondered, but didn't really care. At the next moment, however, I cared very much.

A court attendant stopped by my cell and whispered, "The jury reached a verdict on the first ballot. Just got it through the grapevine."

My throat contracted and I could hardly get the words out. "What's the verdict?"

"Not guilty," he whispered.

It was 12:40 by the clock in the courtroom when I was led back to my seat beside Mr. Lash, and the jury began to file into their box. The judge asked me to stand and face my jurors. I heard the words intoned, "We find the defendant not guilty." The next moment Mabel was in my arms, weeping uncontrollably.

There was a bright winter's sun flooding the streets of New York when Mabel and I stepped out of the Criminal Courts building. The air was crisp and clean, and for a moment I simply stood on the steps and breathed deep of the good air of freedom. Then I took Mabel's small hand in mine and started off uptown.

"We can take a taxi, darling," she said.

I smiled and shook my head. I wanted to walk. It was a privilege I had never before appreciated.

Chapter Thirteen

ONE ORDER OF HAM

I had been in the Tombs three months, not long in the measurement of a man's life, but the time was spent in such isolation that the city actually seemed changed when I reentered it.

As Mabel and I walked slowly uptown, I took in the sights and the sounds. Women's skirts had grown shorter, or hadn't I noticed before? Now almost every woman I saw had a shingle haircut.

The black model-T Fords still dominated Broadway, but there was a surprisingly large number of Chevrolets, with gear shifts instead of friction pedals, and some even painted blue! Mabel told me that the newspapers were full of stories about Henry Ford building a new car to be called "model A," and people were in a dither of excitement to see it.

The Presidential campaign had taken place during my imprisonment. The Democrats had nominated John W. Davis, but he had been licked by Calvin Coolidge. Out in

Chicago, Leopold and Loeb had been arrested for the murder of young Bobby Franks. The Prince of Wales had just completed a visit to Long Island, where he danced with thrilled society debutantes. Movie star Gloria Swanson had married a title, and a long one—the Marquis de la Falaise de la Coudray. And in the back pages of the newspapers there appeared a black and white diagram that was to take the place of mah-jongg as the national craze . . . the crossword puzzle.

Mabel and I stopped off at an Automat where we had a beef pie. It was one of the most wonderful meals of my life. Around us the Broadway marquees blazed forth the names of Peggy Hopkins Joyce and Joe Cook in *The Vanities*, Frank Fay in *Artists and Models*, and W. C. Fields in *Poppy*.

While I was in prison, Mabel had moved to a furnished room on West 105th Street. It was small; the two windows looked out on the brick wall of an air shaft, but after three months in the Tombs it was luxury. And there was my wife with me, to hold and to love. Only a man who's been in prison can appreciate how I felt!

A Frenchman named Emile Coué had brought to America a slogan that was on everybody's lips: "Day by day in every way I am getting better and better." That suited me fine. I was ready for big things.

The day after my acquittal I went down to headquarters to see Commissioner Enright and find out about my job. As I had feared, there was a lot of departmental red tape to be gone through before I'd be back pounding a beat. Every policeman who is indicted for a crime has to stand a departmental trial, no matter what happens to him in the courts.

"Don't be impatient," the commissioner said. "Deputy Commissioner Leach will conduct the hearing, but it will only be routine, and you'll be exonerated."

It was only a formality, but still it would be a few months before it was completed, and in the meantime I had to pay rent and buy groceries. I was not quite so buoyant when I returned home to Mabel that afternoon. The next morning a telegram arrived that changed everything. It read:

> HAVE INTERESTING OFFER TO MAKE
> CONCERNING STAGE APPEARANCES. IF
> INTERESTED TELEPHONE ME AT
> CENTRAL PARK CASINO FOR
> APPOINTMENT.
> > CHARLES ZITTEL

I handed the telegram to Mabel, and her eyes widened when she saw the name of the sender. "Isn't that the man who . . . ?"

I nodded. "The man whose liquor I confiscated. The man who was the complainant in my perjury trial.

"And now he's offering you a job?"

"Seems that way."

"But why, Bob? What's behind it?"

"One way of finding out, hon. I'll go down to the corner drugstore and call him for an appointment."

When Mabel and I arrived at the Casino the next day, Mr. Zittel greeted us warmly and led us into his private office. There he introduced us to his brother-in-law, Bert Jonas. He said, "Bert's one of the best theatrical agents in town, Bob, and has a good idea for you." Mabel and I looked at Bert.

"McAllister," he said, "you're a hot piece of property and we might as well skim some gravy while the gas is burning."

I looked at Mabel to see if she understood what he was saying. I didn't.

"What Bert means," Zittel put in, "is that you're famous, Bob. You're a celebrity."

Jonas nodded vigorously. "You been in the newspaper headlines for almost a solid year now. What with your athletic career and all your trouble in the police department, everybody in town knows who Bob McAllister is. And everybody is eager to look at you firsthand. So, let's charge them for the privilege. Now I've contacted some of the neighborhood theaters about an act starring the flying cop, and they're hot for it. I think you can pack them in, McAllister, but we gotta do it fast while they still remember the headlines. What do you say—like to take a whirl in vaudeville?"

I didn't know what to say. It seemed ridiculous that anybody would pay money to see me. But while I hesitated, Mabel said, "Bob's got a bit of ham in him. He'd love it."

We all laughed, and that settled the matter.

Jonas hitched his chair forward and got down to details. "We gotta build an act for you. Now here's how I see it. We'll build it around your athletic career, of course. You come out in your running clothes and do a short workout on a treadmill. Then we give you a bit of dialogue on running and a couple of jokes. I'll get a writer working on it right away. I'd like to open you in the Bronx in about a week."

"I'm sorry, Mr. Jonas," I said, "but I can't do it."

The three of them looked at me. "I don't get you," Jonas said.

"I can't capitalize on my athletic career. I can't make money out of it, or I'd no longer be an amateur and wouldn't be eligible for the Olympic games."

Mabel touched my arm and said gently, "Bob, the Olympic games are over."

"There's more coming."

"But, darling, not for another four years. By then. . . ." She stopped and bit her lip.

"Go on and say it. I'll be twenty-nine when the next games come around. I'll be an old man competing against eighteen- and nineteen-year-olds. Okay, but I'll lick them just the same. They won't have spent four solid years preparing for that race . . . they won't *need* to win it the way I will. The D.A. kept me out of the last Olympics, but nobody on God's earth is going to keep me out of the next one."

Jonas broke in. "McAllister, let me ask you a couple of questions. You working now?"

"No, sir."

"You got any money?"

"I'm broke."

"You can make more money in vaudeville in a month than you made in a year as a cop."

"I'm sorry but. . . ."

"Maybe you oughta think of your wife. Seems to me she deserves a break."

Mabel spoke firmly. "If Bob says he can make the 1928 Olympics, I'm sure he can. In the meantime we can't do anything to jeopardize his amateur standing. There's no point in discussing it further."

There was a heavy silence for a few moments. I was about to stand up and say good-by when Mabel spoke again.

"Bob has a fine singing voice. Why don't you build an act around that?"

"Yeah?" Jonas said. "What do you sing?"

"Irish songs," I said. "What else?"

"I'll send for a piano player," he said.

"I'll accompany him," Mabel said.

There was a piano in Zittel's office. Mabel played a few opening chords, and I gave a lusty rendition of "My Wild Irish Rose." When we'd finished, Jonas slapped his knee and said, "By God, that's it. We'll book you as a straight singer, and that terrific piano player you married will be your accompanist and do a piano solo break and catch the customers you miss!"

We signed the contracts, and Jonas said he would have songwriter Jimmy McHugh make some arrangements for me. It was arranged for me to open at the Willis Avenue Theater in the Bronx at the end of the month. As the conference ended, and we started to leave, I stopped to have a few words with Zittel.

"I want to thank you for this break, Mr. Zittel," I said. "But I'm sure surprised. I thought you were sore at me."

"Not at all, Bob. You're my kind of guy even if we did meet under unpleasant circumstances. You were only carrying out orders."

"Yes, sir, that's right."

"After that hearing before Judge Corrigan, I realized you were jobbed."

"I sure was," I said with feeling. "And not only that time."

"The same politicians were out after us both, Bob. But

let's forget about the past. You've got a whole new career ahead of you. I wish you the best of luck."

Bert Jonas provided rehearsal space, and during the next week Mabel and I rehearsed to the point of exhaustion. The act finally boiled down to me singing "Somewhere," followed by "Marquita." Then Mabel played a Rachmaninoff prelude. I closed with "Ah, Sweet Mystery of Life." My encore was "My Wild Irish Rose."

The Willis Avenue Theater was a combination movie and vaudeville house. I was to be the closing act of vaudeville, not because I was the best, but because I was the most notorious. When Mabel and I arrived at the theater about noon, there it was up in lights—"The Flying Cop . . . in person."

Now, I'd had buck fever when I was a rookie cop. I'd had a bad case of nerves before an important race. But they were nothing compared to the galloping stage fright that seized me now. Seeing people line up at the box office to pay money to watch me perform, I felt sick at my stomach! Mabel led me backstage to our dressing room, a pale and shaken man. I was certain I would never make it to the stage, and if I did, I would be able only to stare bug-eyed at the audience, my throat swollen shut with terror.

The next hour was a nightmare that only vaguely penetrated the mist of my fears. I remember standing in the wings to watch an acrobatic act, and getting my first sickening look at the sea of faces out in the black cavern of the theater. Suddenly I felt Mabel tug at my sleeve, trying to get me to move, for we were on!

The footlights mercifully blinded me, blotting out the faces of my tormentors. I heard Mabel's piano introduction, and then I was singing. I was amazed that any sound came from me. I didn't know whether I was singing well or poorly, but at least I was singing. Just as suddenly as the act had begun, it was over. This blessed relief cleared my ears, and I was able to hear the applause. It rolled over us as we took our bows, and an enormous basket of flowers was handed up over the footlights. It was from the cops of the 3rd Division!

Limp and exhausted, but almost hysterical with relief that it was over, we returned to our dressing room where the theater manager and Bert Jonas both announced we were a smash hit. The *Bronx Home News* appeared the following day with praise for my "rich, dramatic, tenor voice." Most important of all, bookings began to roll in. My status as an alumnus of the Tombs certainly helped, but I think we gave the customers their money's worth in entertainment.

During the next months, we performed not only in the Bronx, but in neighborhood houses in Manhattan, Brooklyn, Queens, and the Westchester hinterlands. I was a guest on Nils T. Granlund's program over radio station WHN. And the money rolled in. Mabel and I moved to a more comfortable room, rented a piano, and when we passed furniture stores, we stopped to window-shop with something more solid than hope.

Bert Jonas said to me one day, "Bob, I think you're ready for the road. I've talked to Reid Albee and. . . ."

"Hey, wait a minute," I interrupted. "I can't leave town. I've got a police department trial coming up."

"Don't tell me you haven't resigned from the police department!" he exclaimed.

"Of course not. I'm going to be reinstated."

"And when you're vindicated, you expect to go back pounding a beat?" His voice was incredulous.

"I'm a cop," I said.

"My God, man!" he cried. "You're making big money, and it's going to get bigger. You can't throw this over. Think of the future."

"Mr. Jonas, I am thinking of the future. And I can't imagine not being a cop. I'm sorry, and I appreciate all you've done for me, but that's how I feel."

"Okay, okay, we won't argue about it now. We'll see how you feel when the time comes."

"But you understand why I have to stay in New York?"

"Sure, I understand. Well, how about cabaret work?"

"Why not?" I said.

Cabarets, clubs, speak-easies—I performed in all of them during 1925. In cabarets the management served only setups, and the customers brought their own liquor in flasks; in clubs and speaks the liquor was supplied by the house. Aside from that difference, they were all pretty much the same. They were small and dark and choked with people. The air was so dense with smoke as to water one's eyes. They were an inferno of noise, punctuated by the shrill, drunken laughter of women. The sexes were drinking together in public for the first time, and they weren't holding it well. They were making love in public, and it wasn't pretty. They gulped down whiskey, gin, and worse, seeking drunkenness and a release from the morals and manners and the responsibilities handed down to them by society.

These clubs were not pleasant places for an entertainer to work. The noise was such that few people beyond those at the ringside tables heard the performer, and those who could hear were often too drunk to know what was being offered, or too busy petting to care. Still, it was a living, and there were even times, if you got to the audience before it was drunk, when you were enthusiastically applauded. I loved the applause. Mabel had been right about the ham in me.

My first booking was in the Ebony Club in Harlem. I got it through my old friend, Bill "Bojangles" Robinson. We played the same bill up there; Bojangles tap-dancing up and down stairs, and I singing Irish songs to a mixed audience of whites and Negroes.

After that engagement, Jonas booked us into the Club Danbil, then into Tommy Guinan's club. "Texas Tommy" didn't use his famous sister's greeting of "Hello, suckers," but his philosophy was about the same.

One morning at about 3:30, after Mabel and I had done our last show and were in our dressing room taking off the make-up, Tommy came in and said, "There's a table of five out there that doesn't want to go home. They're a little rough, but I don't think they're gonna cause trouble. They want to hear some old-time songs, Bob. How about a little private concert for them?"

I looked at Mabel and she shrugged her shoulders. It was a part of our job.

We went back to the floor to find the chairs stacked on most of the tables, but in a far corner was a party of five men engulfed in a cloud of cigar smoke. A couple of waiters pushed a small upright piano over to them, and Mabel sat down to run her fingers over the keys. I stepped up to them and said, "Well, gentlemen, what would you like to hear?"

The smoke cleared, and I looked straight into the eyes of Dutch Schultz. They were soft with gin but as they came to focus on me they cleared and hardened. "McAllister!" he said and everyone at the table turned to stare at me. Schultz reached under his armpit and removed an automatic which he rested on the edge of the table, its barrel pointing at my stomach. There was silence in the deserted cabaret. Mabel had stopped playing the piano.

"This is the cop bastard who hung one on me a couple years ago," Schultz snarled. "I been waitin' a long time for this moment."

He was crazy with both gin and hate, and I knew he was apt to do anything. I gripped the edge of the table and leaned over until our faces were inches apart, then I whispered, "You're too smart to shoot me here in front of witnesses. And remember, I'm hot copy and it will be spread all over the papers."

He glared back at me, giving no sign he'd heard a word. The gun elevated an inch, pointing directly at my chest. All I could do was take a desperate chance.

"All right, shoot me in the back," I said, and turned on my heels to walk slowly toward the piano and Mabel's white face. With each step I expected to hear the shot, feel the tearing crunch of a bullet in my back. I was almost to the piano. Was he going to let me get away?

There was an explosion of laughter behind me, then Schultz yelled, "Ya crazy sonofabitch, you got more guts than brains. Come on back here, I was only kiddin'."

I turned and walked back to the table as he holstered his gun. Now that the boss had laughed, there were grins on the faces of all his henchmen. Schultz waved me to a chair.

"Have a drink, McAllister," he said.

"No thanks, I don't drink," I said. "I'm in training."

This annoyed him for a moment, but he smiled again and clapped me on the back. "Ya know something? I could use a man like you. You'd make a good bodyguard. How about going to work for me?"

"No thanks, Dutch."

He snorted and said. "How much you make in this joint?"

"Two hundred and tips. I do okay."

"I'll pay you five skins a week. You can work with my boy Danny, here."

He was referring to Danny Amascia, who later tried to shoot it out with Detectives Julius Salke and Stephen de Rose and died full of slugs from their service revolvers. I grinned at him and said, "No thanks, Dutch. It's not my type of work."

He leaned close to me. "Get smart, McAllister. I'm gonna run this town. Every sonofabitch and his brother is gonna want to work for me, and I'm lettin' *you* in because you got guts. How about it?"

"I'm a cop, Dutch."

"The hell you are. They reamed you plenty. You're on the hump. I know all about it."

"I'll be a cop again soon."

He shook his head. "You must be nuts."

"Maybe," I said, rising, "but I'll sing some songs for you. What'd you like to hear?"

He slumped down in his chair and growled, "Sing me 'Sweet Mystery of Life.'"

Mabel struck up a chord and we went into "Sweet Mystery." I felt that we were singing and playing for our lives. Dutch kept me singing old sentimental tunes while he got drunk and maudlin, finally weeping visible tears. At last he stood up to indicate the party was at an end. He handed me a tip—a hundred-dollar bill.

"If you change your mind," he said, "I'll be around."

He turned and walked out of the club, his bodyguards closing protectively about him. The Dutchman's death mark against me had been erased by the song, "Sweet Mystery of Life."

Chapter Fourteen

LET 'EM EAT CROW

My police department hearing opened in September, 1925. The evidence and the witnesses were the same, but what a different setting and atmosphere! Instead of a courtroom jammed with spectators, reporters, and photographers, there was a simple hearing room with a long table, and chairs sufficient only for Deputy Commissioner Leach, his staff, and the witnesses. There was no Roman carnival atmosphere this time, only the lean, hard, sober business of clearing the name of a police officer.

The very first morning of the hearing, as I walked through the long corridors of Centre Street headquarters, I felt a touch on my arm and turned to look into the eyes of a young cop who was a stranger to me. He said, rather diffidently, "You McAllister?"

"That's right."

"I just wanted to wish you luck, that's all."

He stuck out his hand. I took it gratefully, "Thanks an awful lot," I said.

243

"Every man in the department is pulling for you. But I guess you know that."

"I guess I do," I said, "but it's awful good to hear you say it, just the same."

Then I walked into the hearing room, feeling strong and good and among friends.

The hearing followed the pattern of my criminal trial— it was Dandio versus myself, the word of a cop against the word of a criminal. But this time Dandio faced a completely hostile room. Every man here was a cop, and every man knew that Dandio had shot a brother cop. Dandio knew how we all felt about him and was quiet and subdued, abandoning his phony theatrics with rosary and tears. Still, he clung to his story, retold the old lies. I hated that man.

The formal hearing ended in two days. I went back to my night club work until the commissioner would make the findings public and I would again put on the blue uniform and go back to my regular job. There was less money in it, sure. Harder work, more dangerous work, of course. But first, last, and always, I was a cop. I would never be happy doing anything else. I waited with painful impatience for the commissioner's decision.

The decision on my case came October 21, 1925. The first I knew of it was a headline in the *Brooklyn Eagle*. It read:

"FLYING COP" OUSTED FROM POLICE DEPARTMENT: REASON A MYSTERY

* * *

Enright Order Fails to Reveal Charges
Against McAllister Although Trial is Cited

Patrolman Robert McAllister, better known in the
Police Department as the "Flying Cop" because of
his prowess as a runner, was dismissed by an order
of Police Commissioner Enright which stated that Mc-
Allister had been tried on charges before a Deputy
Commissioner and found guilty. Commissioner Enright refused to state what the charges consisted of.

The commissioner had turned against me! The man I
had always admired and served with all the loyalty my
heart possessed—he had failed me. Why?

I rushed down to headquarters, but the commissioner's
door was no longer open to me. Nor could I see Deputy
Commissioner Leach. I suppose I became noisy. Detective
Barney Ruditsky took me by the arm and led me out into
the hall to calm me down. Barney was an old friend of
mine and he tried to talk sense into me.

"Mac . . . Mac, for God's sake, take it easy."

"Take it easy?" I stormed. "My career in the department
is gone and I can't find out why . . . and you tell me to
take it easy!"

"Well, acting like you were gonna punch the commissioner in the nose isn't going to help anything."

Suddenly all the fight left me. I felt weak and had to
lean against the wall. I grasped Barney by the arm and
said, "Why'd he do it to me, Barney? I would have walked
through fire for the commissioner."

Barney shook his head sadly. "The old man is not what
he used to be, Bob. They're after him, cutting him down
from all sides."

"But *I* wasn't after him. Why did he . . . ?"

"Somebody got to him, sold him a bill of goods on you.
You've been seen hanging out with reporters and there

were rumors you were gonna write an exposé of the department, write about the graft and corruption in it."

"I'm a cop! I'd never foul my own nest like that. Sure I hang out with reporters, but they're sports writers. I never had any idea of writing anything about the department or the commissioner."

"As I say, somebody got to him and sold him that story. And, Bob"—he looked at me straight and sober—"you gotta face the fact that you're trouble. You been in the headlines ever since you put on a uniform. You got a lot of enemies, and the minute the Old Man puts you back on the force, all the hounds of hell would be after him again. I don't say he did right by dropping you, and I don't say you haven't got a burn coming to you. All I'm saying is, there's only so much the Old Man can take. After all, he's a human . . . and he's awful tired."

That was all the satisfaction I could get at headquarters. Dandio had won at last.

It was days before I became calm enough to make any sense out of what had happened. One day I called Jimmy Hines to ask him what he thought. I had intended to call before, especially since Morris Friedman had given such odd testimony, but having won my criminal trial, it didn't seem necessary or advisable. But now, well, maybe Jimmy could help me. It would help if he could only explain things to me and make some sense out of what had happened.

At the Monongahela Club they asked for my name, then said he wasn't in. I called his home, and he wasn't there either, and they didn't know when he was expected. I called the club or his house several times a day for three days;

it took that long for it to sink into my thick skull that Jimmy Hines was ducking me.

I made my last call one evening between acts in a speakeasy supper club. I hung up the phone and went back to our dressing room and slumped down in front of a table littered with make-up. I thought of myself covered with make-up, rouge and eye shadow, and lipstick! Me, a cop, performing in front of drunks for the rest of his life!

"What is it, honey?" Mabel asked from her dressing table next to mine.

"I just tried Hines again. He wasn't in."

"Bob, I don't think he's ever going to be in when you call."

"I'm beginning to get the idea." Then I turned to her and cried, "What's wrong with me? Am I a leper or something?"

"Bob. . . ."

"Damn it all, I don't intend to feel sorry for myself but. . . ."

"I know . . . it seems like the whole world's against you."

"Not even that. I know I've got good friends, and thank God I've got you. But when I'm found innocent by the courts, and then to have the commissioner do this to me. I can't even find out what's behind it all. . . ." I spread my hands helplessly.

"Darling, I've been thinking about this, and maybe the answer is right before our eyes."

"I must be blind, then."

"Now look. There was a split in Tammany, with one side out to get the mayor and you, the other side out to defend the mayor and you. Right?"

"Sure."

"Well, look what's happened now! The split is over. The mayor has lost, and nobody wants to defend you any more."

I thought about what she said, and it began to make sense. It was the end of October, 1925, and Mayor Hylan had lost his fight for the Democratic nomination to Jimmy Walker. This meant that Tom Foley and Murphy were now in full control. Hines, and the other Tammany leaders who had supported Hylan, had come to heel, and there was party unity for the election in November. Commissioner Enright fired me because my old enemy Tom Foley was now undisputed boss. It was as simple as that.

I could only speculate on this, of course. Perhaps Foley hadn't called the commissioner and said, "Dump McAllister," but politically, the handwriting was on the wall. Tammany's grip on New York was such that Jimmy Walker's nomination meant his election. Enright was probably trying to prepare himself and his department for the new administration. But if he thought dumping me would placate the Tom Foley crowd, he was mistaken.

Two months later, Jimmy Walker took the oath as mayor and Police Commissioner Enright was immediately fired. When I read about it, my bitterness against the commissioner had largely drained away, and I felt only sadness and compassion for him. He had had a long and honorable career in the department, but crooked politics had gotten him, too.

Under Jimmy Walker, the town was *really* wide open. The link between Tammany politicians and the underworld became so close as to be a partnership in many cases.

It became common knowledge about town that gambler George McManus operated his game in City Clerk Michael J. Cruise's political club at 226 East 32d Street; that Johnny Baker's "play" was being steered to the club of Harry C. Perry, Chief Clerk of the City Court at 4th Street and the Bowery; and that Baldy Froelich and Gus Mayo were operating their games in Sheriff Thomas M. Farley's clubhouse at 369 East 62d Street.

Okay, so what! I was no longer a cop, and as far as I was concerned, they could keep their city as rotten as they wanted. I had done my level best to honor the uniform I had worn, but a dope pusher named Dandio had been able to break me. To hell with them all!

That's what I told myself. But that's not how I felt deep in my heart. And when there appeared a possibility of getting back on the force, I jumped at it. Oddly enough, it was my singing which presented that chance.

At Mabel's insistence, I had been taking voice lessons from Professor Franz Erdody. No Irish melodies for Herr Professor, he made me learn arias from grand opera. When he thought I was ready, he gave a private musicale for me at his studio. The audience was a group of his personal friends. My voice was good that day, and with full confidence I burst into "E Lucevan le Stelle" from *Tosca*, followed by "Vesti la Giubba" from *Pagliacci*. An Irish cop singing in Italian . . . the saints be blessed!

When I had finished, Professor Erdody put his arm across my shoulders and said, "Ladies and gentlemen, it's hard to believe this young man is a former member of the police department and has not studied professionally all his life. What do you think of him?"

The rising crescendo of applause left no doubt. Ahead of me lay not just vaudeville, but perhaps a career in serious music.

Tea followed the concert, and Mrs. Erdody introduced me to Alexander Konta, the state parole commissioner. He guided me to one corner of the vast studio and said, "McAllister, there's a lot of people who don't like what happened to you in the department."

"I don't like it myself, Mr. Konta."

"You ought to fight back."

"I fought every way I knew how, sir."

"Well, there are some people who are ready to pitch in and help." He handed me a card. "I wish you'd go see this man as soon as possible." On the card was printed the name and address of Frank C. Laughlin. I thanked Mr. Konta and pocketed the card, not sure I'd do anything about it. I didn't see how anybody could help me.

But that card began to burn a hole in my pocket. Who was this Frank C. Laughlin? How could he possibly help me? Finally I called my lawyer about it.

When Lash heard the name, he exploded, "Good Lord, how'd you ever get an introduction to Laughlin?"

"From Mr. Konta. I met him at my concert."

"Don't you know who Laughlin is, Bob?"

"Haven't the faintest idea."

"He's one of the most distinguished and gifted men in the legal profession. Before his retirement from the bench, he spent twenty-eight years in the Appellate Division of the Supreme Court. Never once did the court of appeals reverse one of his opinions. I suppose only another lawyer would appreciate what a magnificent record that is. Go see him, Bob, by all means."

Mabel's advice was the same as Lash's. "Darling, if there's only the slightest chance of getting back on the force, you've got to see him. We both know you'll never be really happy until you put that uniform back on."

The next day Mabel and I entered the offices of Laughlin, Gerard, Bowers, and Halpin, and were awed by its air of massive dignity. The reception room was a vast hall, with heavy carpeting on the floor and beautiful wood-paneled walls. A crystal chandelier hung from the high ceiling, casting a soft light over the entire room. Mabel and I automatically spoke in whispers, as if afraid of offending the official hush of the place. Had we known the full history of this firm of lawyers, we would have been so awed we might not have entered at all. Take, for example, one partner—James Watson Gerard. He had been American Ambassador to Germany for the four years just before our entry into the war, and his diplomatic reports helped President Wilson formulate American policy in that crucial period.

We were almost immediately ushered into the private office of the senior partner. Judge Laughlin bore a marked resemblance to pictures I'd seen of Mark Twain, with long snow-white hair curling above his ears and over his neck, framing a kind and gentle face. He listened attentively but without comment, jotting down notes from time to time as I gave him the details of my case.

When I finished, he said, "Have you the minutes of your trial before Commissioner Leach?"

"Yes, Your Honor," I said, handing them to him.

He read them, then looked up with a puzzled expression on his face. "There must be some mistake. It appears that only part of the record is here."

"That's the complete record, sir."

"But this is incredible. You were dismissed from the department upon *this* evidence?"

"Yes, sir."

"But it's only the unsupported word of a convicted felon and trafficker in drugs . . . a man who admitted under cross-examination that he is under indictment for shooting and maiming a policeman! On *his* testimony the department dismisses you for negligently discharging a firearm? Preposterous!"

"Your Honor, I feel like the old con whose lawyer visited him in jail and said, 'They can't do this to you.' The con replied, 'Maybe they can't, but I been here two years now.'"

Judge Laughlin's eyes twinkled. "Son, I heard that chestnut forty years ago but it does seem to apply to you, I must say. Now tell me what's happened to this Dandio."

"It's a long record, Your Honor. Here's the part of it that occurred just *since* he testified against me at my trial." I handed him the list which revealed:

December 1, 1924: N.Y.C. Felonious assault on police officer. (gun)

July 31, 1925: N.Y.C. Robbery.

January 29, 1926: N.Y.C. Assault and robbery. (gun)

February 11, 1926: N.Y.C. Burglary. Pleaded guilty to attempted robbery, third degree, Judge Mancusa, General Sessions Court. Plea covers five indictments, including shooting of Patrolman Maher. Sentenced to Sing Sing Prison five to ten years.

Judge Laughlin read it all through carefully, then sat deep in thought for a few moments. He reached for the phone and instructed his secretary to connect him with the

police commissioner. There had been a change of regime
at headquarters, of course, but Jimmy Walker's police
commissioner, George V. McLaughlin, knew very well
who Judge Laughlin was and was quick to agree to a conference.

When he hung up the phone, Judge Laughlin said, "This
case is one of the gravest miscarriages of justice I have
ever encountered. I will be most happy to represent you
and see that the travesty is righted."

Mabel and I tried to thank him, but the judge waved
aside our words, making it clear he was doing it not only
for a lowly cop, but also for the abstract cause of justice.
At the door of his office he took me by the hand and said
soberly, "Young man, you can forget all your worries about
your job in the department. I assure you that this case will
be impossible to lose."

Mabel took my hand and held it hard as we left the
judge's office. We were so overjoyed, we could hardly
maintain the necessary decorum as we walked across the
enormous reception room. The minute we were in the hall
I let out a yell, grabbed Mabel, and waltzed her about.
An elevator stopped and the door slid open to reveal a
dozen people staring at us as if we were insane. We didn't
care. We laughed and stepped into the elevator. They all
crowded back to give us plenty of room. We needed plenty
of room that day.

Judge Laughlin's negotiations with the police department
came to nothing. They refused to take me back on the
force. But I wasn't discouraged as long as I had somebody
like Laughlin fighting for me. He said we'd have to take
it to court, to the Appellate Division of the Supreme Court,
and thus force the department to take me back. So be it.

In March of 1927, the case was about to come to court, and Judge Laughlin called me with some advice. "Bob, you've got to be very careful during the next few months about bad publicity."

"Yes, sir," I said, not quite knowing how I could control what the newspapers might say about me.

"It would be bad publicity," he said, "if you were to take any more singing engagements in clubs that violate Prohibition."

"I understand, Judge," I said. "From now on it's nothing but vaudeville or private parties."

The rest of March slid by, then April, and then May. It lacked only one month of being three full years since the day I was suspended from the force and sent to the Tombs because of the lies of Joseph Dandio. On June 3, 1927, the call came from Judge Laughlin's office. I was reinstated in the police department. I was delirious with joy. Mabel, I, my brother George, and all our friends—most of them cops—had a big celebration party that night at the Tip-Toe Inn on Broadway and 86th Street.

The next day Mabel was busy with her scrapbook, and there was plenty to paste in it. The following is a typical example:

> The Appellate Division of the Supreme Court to-day reversed the determination of the police department in removing from the force Robert F. McAllister, the "flying cop" and athlete, for his connection with the death of Vincent Fighera, an ex-convict. The court restored McAllister to service.
>
> The Appellate Division in reviewing the testimony said in a per curiam decision that the evidence taken by Deputy Commissioner Leach was insufficient and unsatisfactory evidence and that the determination of

the police commissioner was contrary to and against the weight of credible testimony given upon the hearing.

Today's ruling by the Appellate Division will not only restore him to the force but will entitle him to back pay accrued since his suspension and dismissal.

Two weeks later I received an official notification to appear at the office of Deputy Commissioner Leach. He had been my police trial judge, the man who had dismissed me on (in the words of the court) "insufficient and unsatisfactory evidence." I guessed the new police commissioner had decided to let Leach eat his own crow.

When I entered headquarters on Centre Street, I was welcomed as a conquering hero by my old friends. Hands were extended all along the corridors, and my ears rang with good wishes. The atmosphere was radically different when I entered Leach's office.

He looked up from his desk with a stony face and grunted one word: "Congratulations."

"Thank you," I said, unsmiling.

As we faced each other in this chilly atmosphere, Chief Clerk Vincent Finn burst in, his face beaming. "Good to see you back, Bob," he boomed. Then he handed me my old shield, No. 10252.

Leach said in a dead voice, "Pick up your service revolver in the property clerk's office. You are assigned to the Police Academy for a refresher course on laws and procedures. After that you will be assigned to the 22d Precinct in the Bronx. Good luck."

I walked out of headquarters not only with my badge and my gun, but a back pay check that amounted to $10,042.35.

Again, I was a cop.

Tammany Hall didn't want me to be a cop.

The mayor didn't want me to be a cop.

Some of the top police brass didn't want me to be a cop.

The gangsters didn't want me to be a cop.

But I wanted to be a cop more than anything in the world, and I had licked them all. There was justice to be had in this city if you had the guts to fight for it . . . and good friends to help you.

I was reinstated in the police department in June, 1927. My first assignment after putting on the blues was to join nearly every man on the force in holding back 7 million people on the streets as they hysterically cheered a young aviator who had just flown the Atlantic—Charles Lindbergh.

Chapter Fifteen

THE WORLD'S
A CINDER PATH

It always seemed to me a paradox that the decade after World War I was an outstanding one for sports. In a period of widespread lawlessness and dissipation, a generation of great athletes was produced. Gertrude Ederle became the first woman to swim the English Channel; Bill Tilden's blazing service was displayed at Forest Hills; Babe Ruth blasted home runs at Yankee Stadium; Gene Tunney took Dempsey twice; Knute Rockne at Notre Dame and Red Grange at Illinois made football history.

The average American man, no longer content with spectator sports, took golf away from the eastern society blue-bloods and made it his own. Country clubs sprang up in every town from coast to coast, and the raw new fairways and tender greens were thronged by men in baggy plus fours with tassels at the knees, and checkered stockings. Each time they sliced a drive or topped an approach, they scratched their heads and wondered how that shot would have been played by Bobby Jones or Walter Hagen.

It was sprint racing that preoccupied me. Whether in prison or free, whether in uniform on a beat or wearing a tuxedo while I sang in a night club, I thought constantly of the 1928 Olympics. According to some of my friends, it was an obsession. Maybe it was. The district attorney had robbed me of a chance at the 1924 team; no man living would stand between me and the 1928 team.

Jake shared my confidence. He knew I would be considered an old man (twenty-nine years) for those sprint trials, but he also knew my determination.

Along about August, 1926, Jake laid down a training routine and a schedule of meets that was to carry me right up to the Olympic tryouts in 1928. I bought myself an airedale dog which I named Lucky Briar (remembering old Fighting Briar and my Uncle George), and the two of us became familiar figures to the residents overlooking Riverside Drive, where I jogged 10 miles each morning. Every afternoon I'd have a two-hour workout at the Fordham University gym. September, October, November, the grind continued without letup. Each day Jake worked over my leg muscles, beaming his confidence. "Just wait, Bobbie boy," he purred, "you'll show them doubters and scoffers."

Jake entered me in my first race in December. He warned me, "I expect you to run close, to run a good race, but whatever happens, Bobbie, don't get discouraged. Remember, we're shooting for the big race, the Olympic tryouts at Cambridge. This race is just part of your training. Look at it that way."

The story of that race was told by Jesse Abramson in the *Herald Tribune:*

A crowd of more than 4,000 filling the old 23rd
Regiment Armory to capacity, saw the new indoor
track and field season ushered in with huge fields
in almost every race. They saw, too, a successful comeback attempt by Bob McAllister, the former "flying cop," who came back to the races after two years
of retirement and stepped the 100 yards twice in
10 1/5 seconds to win his heats . . . His brilliant
sprinting brought a big hand from the crowd.

More weeks of hard training followed. Then on January
22, Jake entered me in the Brooklyn College meet to be
held in the 13th Regiment Armory. What memories I had
of that place! Five years before, as a rookie cop, I had
set the world's record for 150 yards in this armory, a
record that still stood. Tonight I would race 100 meters.
How would I compare with my former self? Here was the
test that would determine whether I could come back, or
whether I was an old man who would have to content
himself with his scrapbook.

Jake led me to the starting line, whispering comfortingly
in my ear, but I hardly heard him. My nerves were drawn
so tight that nothing penetrated my mind. The race . . .
I had to win the race! That one thought occupied my
whole being. Automatically I ground resin into my shoes,
and crouched in position and waited for the starting gun.
The explosion uncoiled nerves and muscles and sent me
hurtling down the track. I felt a heart-convulsing burst of
elation as the tape broke across my chest. Helping hands
restrained me from going through the armory wall behind
the finish line. I had won the race, but in what time? That
would be the measure of my career. With pounding heart,
I waited for the announcer's voice.

It came crackling over the loudspeaker: ". . . the time,

10 4/5 seconds, establishes a new indoor world's record for 100 meters."

Two days later H. V. Valentine did an article about me and my comeback in the *New York Telegram:*

> Is Bob McAllister, who made the grade in record time . . . at the Brooklyn College sports meet last Saturday night, sprinting's man of destiny?
>
> The former Flying Cop has pulled the unexpected on the track sharps twice now. Back in 1922 Mac— then just an ordinarily good young sprinter—announced, with verbal flourishes aplenty, that he was going to win the senior national Amateur Athletic Union 100 yard championship at Newark a few weeks later. "Yes, Bob will do just that," chimed in Jake Weber, who was preparing McAllister for the national meet. "He's the greatest hundred yarder that I have seen in years."
>
> The track sharps admired McAllister's enthusiasm —also Jake's—but the betting was something like 10 to 1 against Bob when he took the mark against Alf Le Coney of Lafayette, Loren Murchison of the Illinois A.C., Eddie Farrell of the N.Y.A.C., and Billy Hayes of the Boston A.A., for the national century test.
>
> McAllister got away none too well, but halfway down the straight he came with a rush to nip the flying Le Coney right on the tape. The experts could hardly believe their eyes, but there was Mac—the national hundred champion, just as he had predicted.
>
> Four and a half years later we find McAllister pulling his destiny stuff again. It was but a month ago that the news that Bob was comeback bent got about in athletic circles. "Yep, and Bob is going to make 'em all run," offered the optimistic Weber. "He'll be doing 10 seconds within a month."

The athletic regulars doubted again. "He's as fat
as a washerwoman," was one comment heard when
McAllister went out on the track to warm up for
the handicap "100" at the Columbus Council K.C.
meet on January 8. But heavy as he was, Bob won heat
and semi-final in 10 1/5 seconds, in flat shoes, and
was nosed out by half a foot in the final in the same
time.

Another second off scratch, in the Fordham games
a week later, made us comment that McAllister needed
a lot more work, but Bob rang the old comeback bell
with three smashing victories and a new world's indoor record for 100 meters last Saturday night to
knock this theory into a cocked hat.

Pointing for Olympics

And now McAllister, after taking three firsts and
two seconds in the first three meets of his comeback campaign, announces that his ultimate goal is
nothing short of a place on the American Olympic
team that will go to Amsterdam, Holland, next year
to show the world that Uncle Sam is still "cock of
the walk" in track and field. This time no one is
going to give Bob the "ha ha" in spite of the fact
that he must make the grade in the 1928 national tryouts against men like Hank Russell, Rollie Locke,
Charley Borah, George Sharkey, Claude Bracey,
Frank Wykoff, Charley Paddock, George Simpson,
Chet Bowman, Loren Murchison, Jackson Scholz,
Francis Hussey, and "Truck" Miller.

"Nothing to it," is Jake Weber's view. Jake is
going to handle the former "Flying Cop" across the
stretch of sixteen months of preparation for the crucial
Olympic tryout race. "Bob is going great now,"
further commented the Fordham track coach, "but
watch him later on."

It was not one continuous parade of triumphs from that night to the Olympic tryouts. I began to lose quite a few races. My training problems became acute after I was re-instated in the police department.

"This job of yours," Jake muttered, shaking his head. "I don't like it."

"I'm a cop, Jake. That's something we've just got to face."

"Yeah, I know. You're standing out there on a post dur-ing freezing nights, eating irregular hours, while all the college boys you gotta beat are snug in their beds. It's gonna be tough, Bobbie."

"There's nothing I can do about that, Jake."

"Being a cop and a sprint champion is two different things. You oughta choose."

"I can't choose. I want to be both. I've got to be both."

And that was that.

April, May, and June were consumed with intensive training and a variety of races, some of which I won and some I lost. On July 2, Mabel and Jake and I motored up to Harvard's Soldiers Field in Cambridge for the Olympic tryouts.

The tryouts started on the Fourth of July. The huge, ivy-covered horseshoe stadium was humming with ac-tivity. Instead of firecrackers, there were flash bulbs pop-ping all over the place. The cameramen ground out miles of movie film, and the reporters buttonholed all the leading contenders. They ignored me. I suppose my erratic show-ing in recent meets had eliminated me from their minds as a serious contender.

Jake told me to warm up, jog a half mile, stride through

three 150's, and swing a 300, all on the grass. He wouldn't let me take any starts. When I had showered, he gave me a good rub, then told me to spend a day relaxing.

Friday, July 6, the sun rose on a perfect day for dash men—very hot. Jake patted me on the back as I went out on the field. "Wait for the gun," he said. "Don't try to beat it."

Each time I returned to the dressing room for a rub signified that I had been successful in the heats. I didn't win either race but I was second each time, which qualified me for the next round.

The semifinals were tremendous contests. Nine men qualified; the semi's would be run in two heats, with the first three in each race to qualify for the final. In the first race four sprinters lined up, dug their holes, pulled off their sweat clothes, and were ready to go. They were Charley Paddock, Jimmy Quinn, Claude Bracey, and Jackson Scholz. I tried to control my excitement as I watched those famous runners fly out of their holes. As the tape snapped, the announcer read the results: "Quinn first, Scholz second, and Bracey third. Time, 10 3/5 seconds, equals the Olympic record."

Now it was my turn. Next to me stood Frank Wykoff, who had equalled the record in his heats. Frank Hussey, George Simpson, and Hank Russell completed the field. Once more the gun sounded, and almost before the echo died, it was over. It's funny, but in a closely contested race, no man knows where he finishes. I remember vividly the scream of agony George Simpson let out as he tried to overtake me near the finish. It was so terrifying it drove me to greater efforts. Simpson, who had the lane on my right, was rolling on the ground still screaming when I trotted back to the starting line for my clothes. He had pulled a muscle.

I was jittery until I heard the results: Wykoff first, Russell second, McAllister third. Time, 10 3/5 seconds, equals the Olympic record.

Only when Jake cut my shoelaces, was I aware that my feet were hurting. My toes, nails, and insteps were black and blue. "Come on, move," said Jake. "The final will be run at seven o'clock; that gives us a little over a half hour." Jake got the blood circulating and pepped me up with a douse of alcohol and a whiff of ammonia. Then he spread a blanket on the crowded dressing-room floor and made me lie down.

A few minutes later I saw a strangely familiar figure enter. I got to my feet. "Judge Rosalsky," I said incredulously. It was the same magistrate who had presided at my murder trial.

"No, lie down, Bob," he said. "Don't let me disturb you. I just wanted to wish you luck."

"But, Judge, I didn't know you were a track fan."

"Not a track fan—perhaps, but a Bob McAllister fan. You know, Bob, I got to know you pretty well a few years ago. If anyone deserves a berth on that Olympic boat, you do."

I hadn't seen the judge since the termination of my trial; his visit was a great lift.

When the call for the final of the 100 meters came, Jake handed me two lumps of sugar. "Slip 'em under your tongue and let 'em melt slowly. You'll need a little extra energy for this one."

Just before I toed the mark, Jake inspected my shoes,

laced down tight. He pulled out a roll of adhesive tape and strapped double strips around each instep. "Just in case," he said. "Insurance."

I was ready.

"Now just remember," Jake said, "Amsterdam is at the other side of the tape, but you have to get there first. Good luck and God bless you."

With the bark of the gun, I was conscious of Wykoff on my right, tearing away from me. I put every ounce of strength into the effort to catch him. I found myself moving up on him. Get him! Get him! It was over in seconds, and as we hit the tape in a blur of motion, I could almost swear I nipped him. But that was Wykoff, I thought; where was the rest of the field?

Cheers rolled across the field. Then came the hush as the announcer bellowed: "The results of the final 100 meters: Wykoff first, McAllister second, Russell third, Bracey fourth. Time, 10 3/5 seconds, equals the Olympic record."

Jake went crazy with joy as he cut the shoes from my feet. I didn't even feel the pain of my bruised and blackened toenails. Reporters mobbed me.

When I finally got to Mabel, she laughed and cried as I held her close to me. "Darling," she said, when she was finally coherent, "do you know what the crowd in the grandstand called you? The hero of the Olympics."

Of that race, Jesse Abramson wrote in the *New York Herald Tribune*:

> McAllister's notable performance in finishing second to Frank Wykoff, the sensational nineteen-year-old California schoolboy, was the talk of all Boston after the games, for none could be found anywhere

who gave the veteran a chance even to reach the semi-finals. And it was the general opinion that no sprinter ever flashed a finishing spurt to equal the phenomenal burst that brought McAllister from last place to second in the final, a whisper back of Wykoff. In the last thirty yards McAllister gave the vivid impression of shooting through a standing field with the blinding force of a comet.

The ninth American Olympic team, headed by General Douglas MacArthur, sailed from New York for Amsterdam July 11. The decks of the S.S. *President Roosevelt* resembled an outdoor stadium. A boxing ring appeared, then came special canvas tanks for the swimmers, and finally one large enough for the sculling teams. The sprint team ran twice a day and took calisthenics to keep in shape.

When our ship dropped anchor in the famed Amstel Canal, directly off Amsterdam, we joined liners from Germany, Italy, and Finland. Athletes from rival countries scouted us closely, making notes and talking excitedly. We were equally as interested in their techniques.

A few days before the opening of the games, after two solid days of rain, we exercised in the big new Olympic Stadium. After Coach Robertson examined the new track, he said that in the few days remaining nothing could be done to get it into shape for record-breaking performances.

Jake came over to me, shaking his head. "We're 24 feet below sea level and it's cold and damp. We've had two days of rain and we'll have more before the games are over. It's going to play hell with the sprinters."

At last the big day, Saturday, July 28, arrived. Outside the huge stadium, 75,000 people from all nations, finding it impossible to obtain tickets at any price, jammed the streets and plazas so tight that the athletes had a tough time getting in for the parade. A crowd of more than 40,000 packed the stands. When the Finns found all entrances blocked, they scaled the walls to join in the parade of athletes being assembled to march.

We Americans gathered together at one end of the field. We were all dressed alike in blue coats, white trousers, white shoes, and straw hats with red, white, and blue bands; the girls wore white skirts. Usually there was a lot of joking and horseplay when we got together, but not this time. We were solemn, awed. I felt my throat tighten as we formed ranks, and General MacArthur took his position before us. Beside him stood Dr. Clarence "Bud" Hauser, discus thrower from Los Angeles, who carried the Stars and Stripes.

Suddenly a clear, shimmering trumpet note blared from the top of the Marathon Tower. A cannon boomed, and we came to attention as Queen Wilhelmina and Prince Consort Hendrik entered the royal box. The Olympic emblem was run to the top of the flagpole, where it tripped a mechanism that released a thousand pigeons. They soared about the stadium and then streaked into the heavens.

A massed band struck into a march, and the parade was on; 3,000 athletes representing 46 nations marched in review. I was prejudiced, of course, but it seemed to me that the Americans marched more smartly than the others. With our eyes on General MacArthur's proud back, we followed his crisp marching beat down the track while the band played. Opposite the reviewing stand, General MacArthur barked, "Eyes right!" We snapped our heads to the right, not to admire the Queen, but to be admired. We were America!

The track-and-field competition began on Sunday. The call came for the world's 100-meter championship. Instructions were translated into the languages of the contestants. Only two would qualify in each heat, eliminating four men every time. To the competitors, this meant that every race would be a final, and Lord help him who faltered in this fast company.

A heavy-set six-footer, sporting a droopy handle-bar mustache, informed the sprinters he would give the international start: *"Auf der Platz . . . fertig . . . bang!"* In any language, the sound of the gun meant "get going."

Frank Wykoff won the third heat, Claude Bracey won the fourteenth, Hank Russell won the fifteenth, and the sixteenth and last heat was mine all the way in 10 4/5 seconds.

In the second trials, the U.S.A. came through with flying colors. Russell, Bracey, Wykoff, and I made it a clean sweep, ending the first day's racing. Back on the ship that evening, everything looked rosy for the 100-meter men. All the forebodings about the poor track had proved nonsense. The old Olympic record of 10 4/5 seconds had been equalled ten times that day on the heavy track.

Jake told me my form had never been better. "Run like that tomorrow," he said, "and you'll be the first Yank to equal or break the Olympic record of ten three. I expect great things of you."

On Monday afternoon, July 30, we were on the starting line once more, this time for the semifinals. Three men would qualify out of six starters in each semi, leaving six for the final. Arrayed against me were Williams, Houben, Pina, Legg, and Bracey. After digging my holes and making a few warm-up starts, I thrilled to hear the Yankee section cheer:

Ray . . . Ray . . . Ray . . . U . . . S . . . A . . .
A . . . M . . . E . . . R . . I . . C . . . A . . .
Bracey . . . McAllister!

It split the air and ended in a volcano of sound from the throats of thousands of Americans.

In that race I broke the tape a foot ahead of Williams, equaling the Olympic record of 10 3/5 seconds. Legg was third. It was the greatest race I had ever run in my life. I felt like yelling with joy, except for one thing—a peculiar pain in my right thigh. As I trotted back to the starting line, my eyes searched for Jake among the crowd of well-wishers.

Jake gave me a stout clap on the back, then a bear hug. "Bobby, you're going to win, I know it. I never saw you race better."

"Wait a minute, Jake, I have a little pain in my right leg. I think you'd better bake it right away."

"Nonsense, boy, your legs are all right."

"Honest, Jake, I feel a twinge and I'm worried. Bake it just to make sure?"

"How can I bake it? There's no electricity in the stadium."

"Let's go down to the boat and use the Swiss baking machine."

Jake was becoming impatient. "Don't be a prima donna, Bob. Now do as I say, lie down and rest your legs. You're all right."

I went to the dressing room to rest. I should have been the happiest guy in the room, but that nagging pain bothered me. I had never had any trouble with my legs, even after the toughest of late police tours. When Jake came into the dressing room, I tried once more. This time

I pleaded with him to strap my leg as only he could. Jake waved my suggestion aside with an impatient gesture; I never knew him to be so stubborn.

"I'll rub you and get you rested up," he said. "The only race that counts is the last one. Stop worrying, kid."

Jake rubbed me, and I drifted into a sound sleep, only to be awakened for a final rub. Jake finished off with oil of capsicum on my legs.

As the call for the 100-meter final echoed through the corridor, I was ready to go. Maybe the old fox, Uncle Jake, was right; there wasn't a trace of pain now. It was dusk as we warmed up. There was a real chill in the air and the grandstands were more than half empty. As we lined up, Wykoff was in lane one, I came next, London had the third, Williams the fourth, Lammers the fifth, and Legg the sixth.

As we took our positions, there flashed through my mind the stunning thought that here was the climax of my career.

"*Auf der Platz!*"

All the years of training, all the races I had run were but for this moment.

"*Fertig!*"

A lifetime of hopes, of prayers, would be distilled in the next ten seconds.

Bang!

Six of us shot from our holes like one man. I had never made a better start, and with no one ahead of me, I started to generate a terrific explosion of energy with every ounce of strength I had—that extra burst that would get me there first. Then, like a rifle shot, it happened—a sharp, agonizing, crippling pain searing through my right thigh! I screamed and staggered, and the rest of them thundered past me. I didn't fall, I kept going on momentum and with the dim hope that I could place.

What a grim joke! As I limped to the finish line, I saw Wykoff with tears running down his cheeks. He had finished fourth. The twenty-year-old Canadian, Percy Williams, was first to the tape in 10 4/5 seconds. For the first time in the history of the Olympics, Uncle Sam's sprinters had finished out of the money.

Back in the dressing room, Jake unpinned my Olympic number, 550, with trembling hands. "We'll save them for souvenirs, Bobby. Now let's take care of that leg." When his fingers pressed the knotted tendon, I cried out in agony —but the pain was mostly in my heart.

"My last chance, my last chance," was all I could say.

"Bob," Jake said miserably, "if you think you feel bad, just think of what I'm going through. All I keep asking myself is why didn't I listen to you? Why? I'll never forgive myself."

When we sailed for home at the end of the meet, General MacArthur presented each member of the team with a solid gold ball bearing our name, the Olympic insignia, and the engraving: "Ninth Olympiad, Amsterdam, Holland, 1928." Wasn't this honor and glory enough—just to be a member of the American team? But I had wanted to win. How I had wanted to win!

And the chance would never come again. Those ten seconds out of a lifetime were gone.

Chapter Sixteen

THE LUNATIC FRINGE

For months after the Olympic Games I was seized by hideous nightmares in which I ran that final race over and over again. Each night I'd wake up wringing wet, struggling to reach the tape but never making it.

But a man can nurse his wounds only so long. I was twenty-nine years old and my career as an athlete was over. I had to face it. I hadn't won the Olympic sprint but I had set a couple of world records that might stand for a while. In the meantime, there was the rest of my life to be lived. I had a lot to be thankful for: I was a cop; I was married to a wonderful woman; and on September 24, 1929, Robert McAllister, Jr., was born.

One month and five days after my son was born I was on my beat in the Bronx, walking slowly past the towering apartment buildings on the Grand Concourse, when something hurtled downward eighteen stories and landed at my feet with a sickening sound. From a broken mass there projected a pair of shoes that revealed this had been a man.

Five miles south was Wall Street, where the stock market had just crashed. This man had crashed with it, taking his life with a wild leap from his penthouse into space.

As I covered up the remains of this human being, I couldn't help but think about his life and mine. A stock market could never steal the things that were precious to me.

The events of my life forced an entirely new attitude toward my job—I now became fiercely ambitious for promotion. Competitive civil-service exams could lead to sergeant, lieutenant, and finally captain, all ranks above being appointed by the police commissioner. So I enrolled in the civil-service schools. There were several reasons for my new ambition. I had a son and was determined he should receive a college education, and therefore I needed more money. Also, I was out to show the police brass that I was a good cop. Grover Whalen, the man who had once fired me from my bus-driver job, was now commissioner, and I was determined to show him, along with the rest of the Tammany Hall crowd, that they couldn't keep me down. They hadn't wanted me to be a cop at all, it was the courts who had forced them to take me back, and now I wanted to show them how wrong they had been about me. I wanted to be an officer, and a good officer. I wanted to shame them.

And, too, there was the question of Joseph Dandio, the man who had been the instrument for framing me on the murder charge. Dandio had finished his short sentence in prison for the shooting of Patrolman Maher and was now back in the Harlem rackets. I had a score to settle with him. There was something I wanted that only he could give me

—the truth about my frame-up. Tammany influence was there, I was sure, but I wanted actual names. And I wanted to send Dandio back to prison for perjury. Being an officer would be considerable help in this undertaking. The higher the rank I achieved, the more power I'd have.

During the long, grinding months of civil-service study, I fought off fatigue and discouragement by remembering the face of Joseph Dandio.

In the fall of 1932, the Civil Service Commission listed the results of its examination for sergeant's rank. Eight thousand men had taken the examination, only seven hundred passed it. Of the seven hundred graduates, I stood fifty-sixth. I had many athletic trophies, loving cups, and medals set with precious jewels, but none was so wonderful as the gold sergeant's shield No. 1177.

During the 1930s, the New York Police Department faced a whole new set of problems in law enforcement. Nothing in the civil-service studies had prepared us for the particular kind of violence that was to stalk the streets— political violence. Under President Roosevelt, America began to recover from the depression; men on breadlines went to work for the WPA, "Hoovervilles" in the vacant lots gave way to slum-clearance projects, the ordinary working man was no longer hungry and therefore no longer a potential thief. On the surface, it looked to us cops as if things were settling down. But there was a lot beneath the surface that was to erupt during the 1930s.

The depression had been world-wide and it had set up political forces in Europe that were to have their echoes in New York. Suddenly the New York Police Department found itself in a bitter struggle with the political extremes of right and left—with the Nazi Christian Fronters, and with the Communists.

To try and cope with this new development, the department created the undercover squad commanded by Captain Jim Donnelly. Members of this squad joined the German-American Bund, the Christian Front, and the Communist Party, then fed intelligence reports to the department. This was necessary and helpful, but in the final analysis the question of peace in the streets had to be solved by the local precinct commanders and their staffs. And it soon became clear to me that the only way to keep these fanatics from terrorizing the city was by liberal use of the nightstick.

LaGuardia was mayor of New York during most of this period, and it seemed to some of us cops that he spent most of his time conducting official investigations into alleged "police brutality." We knew that every time we had a fight with Communists, some left-wing politician would cry "Cossack!" and the "Little Flower" would launch another investigation. It wasn't that LaGuardia was sympathetic to any political lunatic fringe, I think that he just didn't like cops very much. Certainly, he didn't understand the problem we had on the streets.

As always seemed to be my destiny, I was in the thick of the fight. I was attached to the 40th Precinct in the Bronx, and my commanding officer was Captain Johnny Collins. A sergeant's first loyalty is to his captain, but it didn't take the rule book to make me loyal to Johnny. He was one of the best police officers I ever served under, and he was my kind of person. When we took on street bullies, we moved as a team, each knowing exactly what the other man would do, trusting him completely.

Typical of our trouble with the Communists was the long and bitter strike at the National Urn Bag Company, 139th Street and Southern Boulevard. We had received word from Captain Donnelly's undercover squad that this strike was to be led by the Communist Party and was considered extremely important. Even without the undercover report, we would have soon known what was behind it all because the plant only employed 200 workers, only a small part of whom went out on strike, yet the picket line was 300 to 400 strong. After the first week, the pickets openly sang the "Internationale," the Communist Party anthem. A police photographer mugged the pickets with a high-speed camera, and we discovered that most of them were Communist bully boys imported from Detroit and Chicago, along with a fair sprinkling of New York longshoremen and seamen.

When the strike started, Captain Collins and I conferred and laid out a basic pattern. We would allow two pickets on the sidewalk in front of the factory entrance. The rest of the mob would be held across the street. We figured that about three mounted men and thirty foot patrolmen should do the trick. And they did, for a time.

As the strike dragged on for week after week, enough employees reported for work to keep the plant in operation, and the Communist *Daily Worker* became shrill in its abuse of the police. We were "Fascist troops at the command of Wall Street imperialists"; we were "labor-haters who want to turn the nation into a concentration camp."

Then came a tip from the undercover squad that on a Monday the picket line was to be reinforced even more, and that it was going to charge the plant and wreck the machinery. Captain Collins and I laid our counterplans.

Principally, we added more police and established a shoulder-to-shoulder line with instructions to let no picket break through and enter the plant. Captain Collins was there in person to take charge; I was his second in command.

Monday morning the picket line swelled in size and took on an ugly mood. It was kept across the street by a great semicircle of blue uniforms. In the middle of the semicircle, right in front of the plant entrance, were Captain Collins, myself, and about a dozen men in reserve. The demonstrators hooted and jeered and sang the "Internationale" and marched back and forth. They were being whipped up by a couple of ringleaders, who shouted obscenities about the cops which the mob echoed shrilly. I watched the two ringleaders closely, guessing that one of them would give the signal for the charge, and wanting to brace my men for it.

It came about noon. A squat, ugly man wearing a seaman's watch cap threw up his arm for attention, yelled hoarsely, and pointed toward the plant entrance. With chilling animal cries they came at us. Long staves that had held the picket signs now became clubs and the blue line of patrolmen wavered, and here and there a man went down with a bloody gash in his head. Rioters poured through the breach. Mounted patrolmen charged into the secondary defense; the horses screamed and reared as long pins were stuck into their sides.

I rallied my reserves for a last-ditch stand in front of the entrance. Then they were upon us . . . led by the man in the seaman's cap. The entire street was a wild melee of fighting men, but this particular Communist was deadly calm and purposeful. He made directly for my captain and, before Johnny Collins quite knew what was happening, he raked him with a vicious left hook on the temple. Collins staggered backward, fell to one knee, then came raging back to drive the Communists into the wall with a flurry of blows. At this point, a *Daily Worker* photographer appeared out of nowhere to snap a picture of a uniformed police captain slugging a "helpless and innocent worker."

I lunged forward and brought my nightstick down on the camera, knocking it to the ground. It was immediately trampled and destroyed by the mob. Then I rallied my remaining men, and inch by bloody inch we drove the rioters back across the street and reformed our line to hold them there. We captured about ten of the leaders.

Captain Collins, his face streaked with blood, was directing the care of the wounded, both Communist and cop, until the ambulances arrived. I said, "Captain, you'd better report to the hospital."

He touched the wound on the side of his head and said, "It's nothing, Bob."

"It's plenty," I insisted. "This was a plot to get a picture of you hitting a picket. I destroyed one camera, but maybe some other Commie got a picture."

"Let 'em take all the pictures they want to," he growled.

"Captain, listen to sense," I insisted, taking him by the sleeve and pulling him to one side. "They're gonna scream police brutality, and the mayor is gonna have another investigation. If you report to the hospital, then it's on record that you were attacked and wounded in the performance of your duty. If you don't report, they'll have you over a barrel."

He shook his head and muttered, "Maybe you're right. Okay, I'll report. You take charge here. Book them on disorderly conduct." Then he marched off to a sector car and was driven away.

It all turned out the way I predicted. The *Daily Worker*, and even some of the non-Communist press, complained about police brutality and demanded an investigation. The mayor promptly gave it to them. But there was no photograph. And there was the hospital record of Captain Collins reporting for wounds received by "felonious attack." The police were at least partially vindicated, and the Commies lost one battle.

For a month or so afterwards there were some editorial mutterings about a police officer smashing a camera and thus interfering with the freedom of the press. Nobody quite seemed to know who the cop was. I didn't enlighten them.

At the other end of the political spectrum were native Fascists, and if their avowed goal was different from the Communists', their methods were much the same. When the time came for us to take on the Fascists, I faced one of the most difficult jobs of my life. Many of these Fascist fanatics were of my own ancestry and religion (Irish Catholic), and I was mightily ashamed of them. Ashamed is a mild word for what I felt—I was outraged.

The Bronx was a hotbed of Fascist agitation under a variety of labels. There were three principal ones: the pro-Nazi German-American Bund, led by Fritz Kuhn; the National Union for Social Justice, led by Father Coughlin; and the Christian Front, led by Joe McWilliams. There was a fourth group that drew recruits from the other three; this was an organization of bully-boy street fighters who called themselves the Christian Mobilizers, roughly the equivalent of Hitler's Storm Troopers. The Christian Mobilizers brought terror to the streets of the South Bronx, and, one wild and bloody night, even attempted civil insurrection.

At the beginning, I watched fascism come slowly to the streets of my precinct with the same impersonal detachment I would have had if a gang of auto thieves moved in. It meant work to be done, countermoves to keep the streets peaceful and free of crime. If the Bundists liked Hitler and Nazi Germany better than America, that was their business, so long as they violated none of *our* laws. If the Christian Fronters cried against the Jews, under our Constitution they had a right to be crackpots, but let them beware of molesting a Jewish citizen. Street corner meetings? Very well, but don't block traffic, and don't incite to riot.

But then things changed and became worse. Copies of *Social Justice* began to appear on the streets; Coughlinites mounted boxes to shout their hate . . . all in the name of a Catholic priest. Here was my shame. Here was my responsibility, both as a cop and a Catholic. Yet I found it difficult to act in either capacity; that is, to act the way I wanted to.

The Coughlinites and the Christian Mobilizers began a campaign against Jewish merchants in the area, marching and shouting the slogan, "Buy Christian!" They concentrated a picket line in front of Sachs Quality Furniture Store on Third Avenue, trying to drive that concern out of business.

Captain Collins and I had a conference on this problem. He said, "Assign three men there during store hours, Bob. They should be able to handle things during the week. Maybe six men on Saturday."

"Captain, let me pick my men and move in there. I guarantee that by Saturday there won't be any picket line."

He shook his head and said sternly, "Now let's get this straight. We're to keep peace there, and see that those who wish to shop in the store are able to do so. We're not to take sides in this dispute. . . ."

"Good God, Captain," I exploded, "you're asking an awful lot of me. Those bums are acting in the name of a priest of my church, and you ask me to be neutral!"

Captain Collins laughed and said, "All right, you hot-headed Irishman, simmer down. I'm not asking you to *be* neutral, I'm ordering you to *act* neutral. I'm ordering you to be a cop and enforce the law, no matter what your personal opinions. Let those pickets march and shout all they want to, but keep them 10 feet from the building entrance and see that all customers have free access and exit. Now fall to!"

I fell to. I carried out my orders to the letter. The pickets were allowed to march and shout against the Jews; they were allowed to distribute copies of *Social Justice*, which charged that Jews were Communists and engaged in a conspiracy to take over the world; they were allowed to demonstrate to their hearts' content; but I saw to it that they didn't lay hand on a single customer who wanted to enter that store.

There are times when the strict enforcement of the letter of the law does not prevent the spirit of the law from being violated. This was such a time. The mere presence of the picket line had a disastrous effect upon Sachs' business, Jewish customers in particular staying away from the store in order to avoid unpleasantness. This success spurred on the anti-Semites, and picket lines began to appear all over the South Bronx. By observing the letter of the law, we cops hadn't kept the peace; we had allowed disorder to spread.

I turned now to my church for help. My parish priest explained he was powerless. The diocese told me that the church was deeply concerned about this distortion of her teachings, and the Holy Father in the Vatican was personally studying the matter. All well and good, but while the matter was being studied in Rome, I had a very pressing problem in the 40th Precinct in the Bronx. Finally I received support from the Society of Jesus, commonly known as Jesuits. This is a militant order dedicated to the propagation of the faith, and several of the young priests agreed to come to the Bronx and try to counteract Coughlin's influence among the Irish.

There were street-corner meetings almost every night, sometimes several in one night, and we decided that a Jesuit priest could stand up and speak in opposition to a Coughlinite whenever one raised his voice. I hoped that the appearance of these men in their clerical clothes, speaking the words of the church, would bring sanity . . . and peace. Vain hope!

When the first Jesuit spoke up, the crowd was surprised and for a moment respectful. But soon the muttering started. The priest said, "You misunderstand the teachings of the church, for never forget that Christ was a Jew, and his mother a Jewess." At that point the jeers and catcalls started, and not another word could be heard. It was the same throughout the Bronx, and several times I had to lead my men into the crowds to escort the priests to safety. When I saw this happen, saw the mob jeer men of the cloth, my heart hardened against them. I no longer considered them worthy to be called Catholic or Christian.

Conditions deteriorated month by month, with our police problems directly tied to political developments in Europe. Mussolini invaded and conquered Ethiopia in 1935; Hitler entered the Rhineland in 1936; both Hitler and Mussolini intervened in the Spanish Civil War in 1937. Each success of fascism abroad made the streets of the Bronx uglier.

I learned to read the European news headlines in order to know what I'd be faced with at home. In the summer of 1939, I read that Hitler had brazenly occupied all of Czechoslovakia without that country's British and French allies lifting a finger in her defense, and I knew we were in for trouble in the 40th Precinct.

In celebration of Hitler's latest success, the Christian Mobilizers announced a monster open-air rally. Captain Collins called me into his office to tell me our plans.

"We got word from the undercover squad that this is it," he said grimly. "For the past few weeks the Christian Mobilizers have been holding private showings of newsreel films from Germany, showing the Nazi Storm Troopers beating up Jews in the streets and wrecking their shops. They've got their mob worked into a bloodthirsty mood, and at the open-air rally they're going to work them up to an even higher pitch and then turn them loose. Joe McWilliams is going to tell them to do what the Nazis did—smash the Jewish shops."

"We gotta settle with this scum pretty soon, Captain. Looks to me like this is the time."

He paused a moment. Then, "I'm putting you in charge, Bob."

"That suits me," I said.

"I'm going to cancel all leaves, put the precinct on a twenty-four-hour basis, and bring in some reserves from the rest of the division. I'll give you a detail of fifty cops, and they're going to be tough ones. They may be Catholic, Protestant, Jewish, or Negro, but they'll be tough."

"The tougher the better," I said. "We won't wear gloves this time."

He pulled out a map of the precinct and, with a pencil, pointed out the area involved. "They'll meet here on the corner of East 140th Street and Crimmins Avenue at about eight o'clock. I want you to have your men dispersed and out of sight, except for maybe ten men. Put your detail in the basements of the surrounding buildings so they won't know our strength until it's too late. Now, it may be a perfectly peaceful meeting, and in that case we gotta let it run, but if the speakers begin to call for blood, incite to riot, we gotta break it up."

"We'll break it up all right, Captain," I said.

"Let me make this clear, Bob. I want the meeting *dispersed*. I don't want a fight if we can avoid it."

"Then we'd better not bottle them up."

"Exactly."

"I could do it this way," I said, pointing to the map. "I could hide my main reserves here on 140th Street just south of them. When it comes time, these men drive the mob northward on Crimmins toward 141st Street, which is a dead end on Crimmins and only exits to the west. Now, I place a cordon of men across Crimmins just north of 141st, and we got them bottled at both ends and they have to turn west and disperse to escape. Once they start to break up and run, we let them go."

"Sounds okay. Proceed along those lines."

"One more thing, Captain. News of this meeting is going to get around the neighborhood."

"I know what you mean. The Jews have taken a lot and are getting restless."

"Right. If they decide to show up at this meeting, we may have a riot despite anything we can do."

"Bob, they all trust you. Go and talk to them; convince them it's for their own good to let the police department handle this without any interference. You've got four days to make sure they all stay away from that meeting."

"Yes, sir," I said.

For the rest of that week I called on the rabbis and the social and business leaders of the precinct, promising them that the department would use all its resources to protect their persons and their property if they'd just keep their people from taking action on their own. I admitted to them quite frankly that there were times when it looked like the department wasn't doing enough against the mobs, but I promised them it would be different this time. I won their support, and they promised that on this Saturday night they'd keep their people off the streets and away from the meeting. I was pleased by their confidence in me, of course, but I had done only part of the job. There was still a large group of Jews not bound by this agreement—the Jewish gangsters.

There was a key man in the precinct, a goniff named Little Izzy. He had been part of the Rao mob until the Syndicate took over, and was now a runner for Luciano. I had sent him up once for felonious assault, but at another time had saved him from a pandering rap an ambitious young detective had wrongly brought against him. I thought Little Izzy trusted me. I hoped so, because the success of my plan depended on him. I sent word through a stoolie that I wanted to see him in a Manhattan bar.

He came into the bar at the appointed time, small and

dapper and furtive. He cased the place quickly with his flat blue eyes, decided it was no trap, and slid into my booth. I bought him a drink, which he tossed off, then a second one which he sipped.

"Izzy," I said, "do you trust me?"

He looked at me with a thin smile. "Yer a cop and ya sent me up fer a two-and-a-half to five. I should love ya?"

"Yeah, but that's not what I asked. Do you trust me?"

He studied his drink for a minute, then said, "Fer a cop, yer okay."

"All right, now listen. I'm gonna give you some straight advice. Stay away from the Christian Mobilizers' meeting on Saturday."

He looked up quickly, the startled expression suggesting that I had guessed right; the Jewish underworld was planning steps of its own. He sneered at me. "You cops protecting them bastards?"

"We're not protecting them. We're gonna collar them Saturday, but we can't do the job if your mob shows up and starts a riot."

"My people took plenty from them. Look what's happening in Germany, what they're doin' to my people there. It ain't gonna happen in the Bronx . . . not without a fight . . . not if I have to take a ten-to-twenty!"

He had become quite impassioned while he spoke, now he took a deep drink to calm himself. I let him think about it for a while before I spoke again.

"Izzy," I said softly, "I hate those Fascist bastards even worse than you do, believe me. I want to handle them myself, and I'm asking you to let me."

"What's the deal?"

"No deal, Izzy. Just a favor to me."

"Just this one meeting?"

"That's all."

"Lemme think about it."

I shook my head. "I gotta know now. If your answer is 'no,' then there's trouble, and I gotta arrange to have enough cops there to bag you all . . . you and Joe McWilliams alike."

He grinned. "Okay, McAllister, it's your show. But after Saturday, I ain't promising anything."

"After Saturday, things may be different."

He butted his cigarette and stood to go. I stopped him with a last question, a question I had asked someone every day for the past five years. "You know Joseph Dandio?"

Izzy said, "A punk."

"Yeah. . . ."

"A wop punk."

"Sure, a wop punk, but I want him. You know where he is?"

"Ain't seen him in years."

"If you get a line on him, let me know. It's worth a good deal to me, Izzy. Remember that."

"I'll remember," he said, and walked out of the bar.

Late Saturday afternoon I briefed my men in the muster room, using a map to show them how we were to drive the mob down the side street and disperse them. Then I sent the men, one or two at a time, inconspicuously into the neighborhood to hide in the cellars until the moment of action. I reported to Captain Collins that all had been done that could be to keep the meeting peaceful, or to disperse it with a minimum of violence. The rest was up to Joe McWilliams.

The mob began to collect on the corner at about eight

o'clock. It was surly, sadistic. It was bent on trouble; the mood was apparent at once. At 8:15, a speaker's platform was rolled into place and on it was mounted, of all things, an American flag! The speaker was McWilliams' right-hand man, Joseph Hartery. Captain Collins was present in full uniform; I was present with about fifteen patrolmen— visible. The crowd swelled to several hundred. I began to sweat a bit, wishing I had more reserves. I guess every military commander going into battle wants more troops.

Joe Hartery mounted the platform and there were cheers. Then he began to speak, or rather, to rant in a high-pitched style popular, it seems, among all crackpots. I toured the entire periphery of the crowd to check the placement of my men, and noted with satisfaction that the Jews had kept their word; nobody was here except bigots. I was glad to see them packed tightly into one spot. We could handle them much more easily.

Hartery had started out his speech by yelling about the need for Aryan racial purity; by the time I had completed my tour and returned to the platform, he had warmed up to the theme that there was an international Jewish con-spiracy to take over America, and from that he led to the rather amazing conclusion that the Jews not only controlled Wall Street, but also that the Jews were Communists. No matter what nonsense he shouted, the crowd howled in re-sponse. They pressed forward, eager, sweating, open-mouthed.

"But there's one place where the Jews have met their match," Hartery shouted, "one land, one people who have the guts to strike down the greasy kikes . . . and that's in Nazi Germany!"

The mob cheered hoarsely.

"Your brothers in Germany are striking at *your* enemy. Each dead kike means a live American. Are you going to let them fight the Christian battle alone?"

"No . . . o . . . o! No . . . o . . . o!" from the mob.

"Let the gutters of New York run red with the blood of the Jew . . . !" Hartery screamed.

His words were almost drowned by the mob's hysterical cries. At this moment Captain Collins jumped up to the speaker's platform, pushed Hartery away from the mike, and held up his arms for silence. He announced, "The speaker is violating the statutes of the State of New York by inciting to riot. This meeting is therefore illegal and ordered adjourned. Please disperse quietly."

Now was the moment of decision. I held my whistle close to my lips, ready to summon the reserves. Would the crowd disperse quietly, or was it to be a battle?"

There was a moment of stunned silence, then a low, nasty rumble began to rise, like thunder after a flash of lightning. Then, before my eyes, Captain Collins disappeared. Hands reached out to grab his ankles and jerk him down from the platform. He was beneath the feet of the mob. I blew a shrill blast on my whistle and charged, my nightstick swinging. I made it to Collins, got him to his feet, and we stood back to back for a moment fighting the encircling mob. In the distance, I saw my reserves pour out of the cellars and doorways. I prayed we could hold out until they fought their way to us.

There was an explosion inside my skull. Somebody had hit me with a lead pipe, and my knees went weak and I began to sink to the pavement. I knew what fate awaited me there; I forced myself back upwards, flailing with my club.

After a moment of blindness, my vision cleared, and in the grip of an icy rage I went after my attackers.

The fighting was general, but the momentum of the reserves was forcing the mob northward along Crimmins Avenue. In the wake of the moving battle appeared the wounded; dozens of men lying on the street, moaning or unconscious, bleeding and broken, cop and Fascist alike.

Within ten minutes, the mob had been driven west on 141st Street and dispersed. We turned to the wounded. A sector car had sent out a call for ambulances, and they descended upon the battlefield with sirens and flashing lights. I directed first aid and removal of the wounded, but there were many who crawled off into the night, preferring to nurse their own wounds rather than face arrest.

We had the ringleaders; I had seen to that. Handcuffed were not only Hartery, but Benjamin Stafford, a professional boxer, Louis Pepchinski, who had dragged Captain Collins off the platform, Jack Dougherty, an all-round bully boy, and William O'Connor, assistant editor of their publication, *Christian Mobilizer*. What a miserable-looking bunch of "supermen" they were now!

About half the wounded had been carted away when a sector car roared up, a patrolman jumped out to salute Captain Collins and say, "The mob is reforming, Captain."

"Where?" Collins snapped.

"139th Street. They've lit torches and are marching."

"Follow them. As long as they keep on the move, and don't molest anybody, let them march. Radio back their position every three minutes."

The sector car roared off. I said to Collins, "If they're marching, they probably have a destination."

"Maybe," Collins growled. "If they hold another meeting, we'll have to break it up. We'll wait and see."

We didn't have to wait long. Fifteen minutes later another sector car squealed to a stop in front of us, and a white-faced young patrolman shouted, "My God, Captain . . . they've laid siege to the station house! They've filled the entire block from curb to curb. They're waving their torches and shouting how they're gonna take the prisoners away from us when we bring them in."

Collins spat out an unprintable word, then turned to me. "How many men in the station house?"

I made a quick calculation. "A lieutenant, his clerical man, a sergeant, the attendant, couple of detectives . . . maybe seven in all."

The young patrolman said, "I could see the lieutenant had barricaded the doors, but if that mob takes it in its head to rush the station house. . . ."

He didn't have to finish the sentence. Collins and I looked at each other and knew what would happen to the outnumbered police officers inside. Collins had a choice of two actions; he could radio the division for reinforcements, but that would consume precious time. He chose the other alternative. He turned to me and snapped, "Take a sector car and proceed to the station house. We'll follow directly behind with the wagon and the prisoners."

I jumped into the white-topped police car and ordered the driver to the station house. As we approached the block in 138th Street, I saw the mob jammed solid, shouting and waving torches. As our car came into view they sent up a scream of hate. I said to the driver, "Turn on the siren and drive into them."

His hands, knuckles white, gripped the wheel. "You mean . . . ?"

"I mean that if they don't get out of the way . . . run them down." I repeated the order. "Run them down!"

The banshee cry of the siren split the night, and with a clash of gears we drove down upon the mob. They held for a moment, thinking we'd stop. They shook their fists, their clubs, their faces distorted by torchlight into something animal. They were beyond my understanding, beyond my pity or my hate, I felt only a deep revulsion as for something straight from hell. I cried hoarsely, "If they don't open up, run them down!"

They broke at the last moment. For some it was too late and our fenders caught bodies, sending them reeling and crying in anguish. We skidded to a stop at the station house steps; I sprang to the top of them, my gun drawn. I turned to face the mob. "The first man who puts a foot on these steps gets a bullet right in the gut," I shouted.

Captain Collins' car and the wagon with the prisoners had followed through the opened lane and now pulled to a stop. The prisoners were herded out of the wagon and into the station house, and not a member of the mob dared raise a hand.

Frustrated, the crowd broke up and dispersed, but all through the night segments of it formed and reformed, smashing Jewish shop windows and writing their foul slogans on walls and windows. Police reinforcements arrived and kept them on the run, holding the property damage to a minimum.

In the early morning hours, a police surgeon looked at the wound in my head and directed me to report to a hospital. "Nothing doing," I said. "It's never going to be said those bums put McAllister in the hospital." I continued on duty but two days later I fainted dead away. I had a concussion.

There followed the usual charges of police brutality, and the usual LaGuardia investigation of the charges. In my opinion, Mayor LaGuardia should have promoted Captain Collins on the spot instead of investigating him. The important thing is that the men we had arrested went to jail, and the back of the Fascist movement in the Bronx was broken. Never again did they dare to go hunting for Jewish blood.

Chapter Seventeen

DEBT OF SORROWS

Human suffering and death are part of a cop's job; he lives with them almost constantly from the day he becomes a rookie. Yet all this intimacy with death doesn't prepare him for it when it comes to his own family. At that moment he is as crushed and bewildered as any man.

Mabel died in the spring of 1941. The doctors had told me for almost a year that she was going to die, that the cancer eating her body could not be checked. But Mabel and I had faced and conquered so many evil things that I could not believe we'd fail this time.

We did fail. One day her wasted body was still and lifeless. Snuffed out were the love and limitless courage she had always given me. I was alone in a way I had never been and I was frightened. I even cried out against my God for failing to hear my prayers.

What caused this cancer? The doctors couldn't tell me; they didn't know all the secrets of the human body and soul. I evolved my own answer. It was not a very scientific answer, perhaps, for it was born out of my loss and my rage, but it took hold of me and never let me go. I reasoned that in the few years she had been married to me, Mabel Smith McAllister had known a lifetime of sorrow and terror. She had given all her resources to meet the emergencies of my life—she had simply used herself up.

But why had this been necessary? Was it my fault? For many long, black nights I was tortured by that question.

If I had been a butcher, like my brother George, it wouldn't have happened. If I'd been a streetcar motorman, like my father, it wouldn't have happened. If I'd been anything but a cop . . . ! But I couldn't have been anything else. Mabel understood that.

And other cops' wives hadn't had to face her ordeal. It was not my job, but my enemies who had killed my wife. It was Joseph Dandio and Dutch Schultz and Mamie Castro and Magistrate House and Joab Banton and the keepers in the Tombs and Tammany Hall. But most of all, it was Joseph Dandio!

I had already vowed to find him and bring him to justice, but now, with Mabel's death, a change took place within me, a frightening change. I wanted to kill Joseph Dandio!

At first I tried to ignore it—mentally look the other way until the grim desire disappeared. But it refused to go away; it grew inside me, crowding me. I knew this thirst for personal vengeance was a sin, yet whenever I went to confession, I always gave myself a long lecture to convince myself that I only wanted to see justice done, that I was only doing my duty as a police officer, and therefore had nothing to confess to my God.

And each time I came away from the confessional, having blinded myself momentarily to the truth, I was sick in my soul. At last, when I could stand it no longer, I went to my priest to discuss it. Even then I said to him, as I always said to myself, that I was only doing my duty as a police officer.

He listened patiently to my ramblings, then said, "You must search your heart, my son. If there is vengeance there, it is a sin."

"Justice, Father," I cried. "I want only justice."

"I'm not sure that is the truth," he said. "I can only give you conditional absolution. Go look in your heart, for God knows what is there."

I left the church, still without peace. Nor was I to have any, for to receive full absolution I had to confess the sin of vengefulness with the firm intention of ending it. This I could not do. I had to live with my sin, unable to free myself from it.

I plunged into my police studies with a cold relentlessness. Every hour, beyond my tours of duty and a minimum time for sleep, was spent in study for advancement. My ten-year-old son often came to the station house to sleep all night on a detective's cot while I worked. Honors began to come my way. Twice I received an official department commendation for good police work when I shot it out with holdup men and arrested them; I had even received a citation of honorable mention, the highest award in the police department. Above my gold sergeant's shield I wore the green-white-and-blue bar with the bronze star in the center that meant I was a member of the illustrious Honor Legion.

The examinations came for lieutenancy. Four hundred sergeants took the tests and when the results were posted, I was second!

Lieutenant Robert McAllister!

The city's underworld was changing; in fact, crime throughout the nation was changing. Up to now, individual gangs had flourished in various towns, even in various sections of a town, shooting it out with any rivals who might try to muscle in on their "territory." During the 1930s, it became apparent to the underworld leaders that these feuds resulted in their doing business in a very inefficient and wasteful manner. There was enough for everyone, so why kill each other off? All they had to do was reach a top-level agreement on territories. They did, and thus was born the Syndicate.

Everything was now run like a big business, with efficiency and a minimum of trouble. There was no more room for irresponsible killers. The life expectancy of the underworld leaders now lengthened, and they dared live in the open, buy expensive suburban homes.

There were some growing pains for the Syndicate, of course. There were a few rugged individualists who didn't want to be swallowed up by the big organization, who wanted to continue to play it alone. One such man was my old enemy Dutch Schultz. The Syndicate sent Charlie "The Bug" Workman and Mendy Weiss to a Newark tavern in 1935 to wipe out the Dutchman and three of his henchmen with a shower of machine-gun bullets.

Under the Syndicate's organization, "Buggsy" Siegel operated in California and Nevada; the Capone mob had Chicago; the Purple gang had Detroit and a piece of Miami; whereas New York was largely the bailiwick of the *Unione Siciliano* (Mafia) headed by "Lucky" Luciano.

Word came to me that Joseph Dandio was working for Luciano. He had been seen driving a Cadillac and was reported to be Harlem pickup man for Luciano's narcotic and white-slave traffic. I redoubled my efforts, spending my free time in the Harlem streets. But Dandio again dropped from sight, or else my stoolies became suddenly afraid. My vow of vengeance may well have reached Dandio's ears, and perhaps the powerful Syndicate was making this fight its own. Let them, I thought. In the meantime, I began my studies for a captaincy.

I was in the 40th Precinct in the Bronx in the spring of 1942. Pearl Harbor had come and gone, and the Japanese were following up their advantage and conquering the Philippines. Compared with the slaughter going on in the world at that time, a killing in the Bronx must seem insignificant. Yet, the murder of a child is an atrocity, no matter what might be happening in the rest of the world.

I was on the midnight tour, but I came into the station house at about four-thirty one afternoon to meet another lieutenant and go with him to the Schwartz Civil Service School, where we were to study until seven. When I entered the station house, I found it packed with brass, not only from the borough headquarters, but from city headquarters too.

"Dave, what's up?" I asked Dave O'Rourke, the clerical man who kept all the precinct records.

"A kid's disappeared. Maybe a kidnapping."

I whistled softly. Understandably, the disappearance of a child always galvanizes the complete resources of the department, and I was not surprised at the presence of so many inspectors and deputy inspectors. "Fill me in," I said.

He checked the blotter and said, "Name is Genevieve Connelly. Ten years old, blond, blue-eyed, Irish. Lives at 138th Street, just off St. Ann's Avenue. Mother sent her to the corner store yesterday afternoon. Hasn't been seen since. Parents are up in the detectives' office now. No good leads."

While he was talking, I looked over a man who was sitting quietly in a corner behind Dave's desk. He was slumped in the chair with arms crossed, staring off into space. His face was thin and sallow, his hair sparse and damply plastered to his skull, his hands large and work-roughened. There must have been something about him that made me do what I did, but I can't for the life of me figure out what it was. Anyway, I said to Dave in a low voice, "Who's that?"

Dave glanced over his shoulder and said, "Oh, that's the janitor in the building where the Connellys live. Name is Tom Conroy. In for a routine questioning."

The next moment I grabbed the janitor by the front of his shirt and jerked him erect with his face next to mine. His red-veined eyes were wide with surprise and fear. "You killed her," I growled at him. "You killed Genevieve Connelly." He shook his head. "Don't lie to me," I stormed at him. "You raped her, then you shoved her body into the furnace. You murdered the girl . . . didn't you? Speak up!"

Dave O'Rourke's amazed face came into my view. "Jesus, Lieutenant, you got something on this guy?"

Did I have anything on the janitor? Of course not. I had crossed the room and grabbed him without even thinking, driven by a blind, unreasoning hunch. I released my grip on him and he sank back down on the chair.

"Hey, Bob," came a voice from the door. It was the lieutenant I was to meet for school. "Come on or we'll be late."

I looked down at the janitor and said, "I'll be back in a

few hours. When I get here, I want the truth out of you."

During class that evening, I had difficulty keeping my mind on my studies. I tried to figure out what had made me go for the janitor; why I had this hunch about his guilt. I couldn't figure it. As class broke up and I headed back for the station house, the hunch was as strong as ever. I knew I'd have to follow it right to the end.

I reported for duty and took over the desk. The janitor was upstairs being questioned by Deputy Chief Inspector Johnny O'Conner, chief of Bronx detectives. I had nothing officially to do with this case, but the hunch rode me and I wanted to be in on the questioning. I put a sergeant on the desk and went into the detectives' room.

There were several detectives in the big office. O'Conner was alone with the janitor in the private office. After a few moments the detective chief came out, saw me, and said, "Bob, the clerical man tells me you were trying to break this guy. You got anything?"

I shook my head. "Not a thing, Chief. I just got a blind hunch when I saw him sitting down there."

"Damnedest thing," he said. "We only brought him in for routine questioning, but a little while ago I got a tip that he was seen with the child in the hallway late yesterday afternoon, long after she had been sent to the store by her mother. Maybe we got something here."

"What does he say, Chief?"   •

"Denies everything. But he's sweating."

At this moment several detectives entered the room. They had searched the janitor's basement apartment and the boiler room. They found absolutely nothing, no child's clothing, no sign of violence, no blood. A dead end. The detective chief returned grimly to the private office to continue the grilling.

There was no letup on that janitor, the detectives working on him in relay teams, but he held to his denial. I stayed on, unable to leave the squad office until my hunch had been proved true or false. At about three o'clock in the morning Chief O'Conner came out of the private office and slumped in a chair with a heavy sigh.

"He won't break," he said. "He's guilty of some part in this, as sure as God ever made apples, but he won't break."

"Chief," I said, "I've been talking to some of the men who questioned the parents, and they tell me that the janitor is a good friend of the family. In fact, Mr. and Mrs. Connelly brought him over from Ireland and got him the job as janitor."

"Yeah, that's right."

"He might break if you confronted him with the mother and father. Let them plead with him . . . and see what happens."

He thought a moment, then said, "All right, Lieutenant. I'll do it."

"I'll send a sector car for them," I said.

Within fifteen minutes the parents were in the office, pale and drawn. Chief O'Conner had them sit down, and told them very gently that in the next office was a man he suspected of being involved in their daughter's disappearance. Mrs. Connelly's hand sought her husband's. "Who is it?" she said.

"Tom Conroy . . . the janitor."

"Oh no!" It was a cry of anguish, but also of disbelief.

"No . . . not Tom. He couldn't! He . . . he was our friend, lived with us for a while. He loved Genevieve just as we did. No. . . ."

The chief said, "He may be innocent, but I want *you* to ask him. Think you're up to facing him now?"

She looked at her husband, then squared her thin shoulders and nodded assent. A moment later the janitor was led out to face the parents. He stood in the doorway of the private office, blinking his eyes to adjust them to the brighter light of the outer room, then saw the Connellys sitting in two straight chairs 10 feet from him. He stiffened slightly and grasped the doorframe to steady himself. There was a moment of silence. It was broken by the mother, and her voice was ragged.

"Tom . . . ," she said, then seemed unable to continue. She tried again. "Tom . . . they've been telling me things. I . . . I don't believe what they've been saying. I told them you're our friend. Tom . . . I told you loved Genevieve . . . you . . . you'd never hurt her."

For the moment she was unable to go further. We all watched the janitor. His face remained expressionless, but he swallowed often, his Adam's apple jerking up and down in nervous spasms.

The mother burst out, agony making her voice shrill. "Tom . . . if you know anything about Genevieve . . . in the name of God . . . tell us!"

The janitor gulped, made an animal noise deep inside him, and turned and staggered back into the private office. Chief O'Conner followed, shutting the door behind him. The mother broke down to sob in her husband's arms.

A few moments later the chief reappeared and motioned

me to follow him into the hall. He said, "He wants a priest."

"He's broken?"

The chief shook his head. "Won't say a word except he wants a priest."

"But that means he wants absolution. This proves we've got the right man."

The chief looked at me. We were both Catholics and we both knew what was involved here. He said, "His confession to a priest is not a confession to the police, Lieutenant. There's no way we can know what goes on in the confessional, no way we could use it if we did."

"Yes, sir," I said.

"Get a priest. Go to St. Jerome's over on Alexander Avenue."

It was now about four in the morning, and I had to pound long and loud on the door of the parish house. At last a sleepy-eyed young priest answered, listened to my story, and then quickly dressed to come with me. During the short trip back, I wanted to turn to him frankly and say, "Look, Father, the laws of our church are sacred, and I know you can't violate the confessional . . . but if you could just make him confess to *us* as well as to you. . . ." But I didn't say it.

The parents had gone home when we arrived back in the big office, the janitor was alone and silent in the private office. Chief O'Conner walked up to the priest and said to him what I had not found the courage to say.

"Father, that man in there has committed a most heinous crime. I hope you'll think twice before giving him absolution."

I saw the young priest's shoulders stiffen. He looked at the police officer, a public servant whose job it was to save lives, as it was the priest's to save souls. The priest finally nodded his head and said softly, "I understand."

The priest directed that all the lights be extinguished in the private office, all the shades drawn. Then he entered and closed the door behind him. There were a dozen police officers and detectives in the big room. They sat silently, Jew, Protestant, and Catholic alike, awed at the solemn moment of confession to God. In some of their minds, the thought probably occurred that we could have placed microphones in the room and overheard the confession, but none of them would have done so.

There was a low, indistinct mumble from behind the closed door. It went on for about five minutes, then abruptly stopped. We heard steps, the door opened, there was the priest. He said to Chief O'Conner, "He wants to talk to you now. I'll wait outside here and pray for him. Please let me see him again when you're through."

We all crowded into the private office, and the man who had been so impassive and remote for all these hours was now broken. Tears streamed from his eyes and he clasped his hands in prayer and said over and over, "I want peace with God . . . I want peace with God."

The story he told was fragmentary . . . and ugly. When Genevieve had returned from the store with a loaf of bread, she met the janitor in the lower hall and stopped to talk to him. He got the sudden impulse to kiss her and embrace her. She struggled free and cried that she was going to tell her mother, whereupon in a panic he choked her to scare her into silence. When she suddenly went limp, he carried her body to the coal bin and there tried to revive her. He denied raping her. When he couldn't revive her, he carried her to the big furnace and stuffed her in, head-first. With a poker, he shoved her body the rest of the way onto the bed of white-hot coals. He covered the body with a layer of coal, turned on the blower, then went to a saloon for a drink.

He returned in thirty minutes and opened the door to find the white-ash outline of her skeleton shimmering there on top of the red coals. Hysterically, he grabbed a poker and mixed it all up, added more coal, and then returned to the saloon to get really drunk. It was the vision of that powder-white skeleton that had burned into his brain and finally made him break.

The next day we sifted the ashes from the furnace and could find only the smallest chip which might be an elbow bone. Then we found a tooth. With these two bits of evidence, a curator at The American Museum of Natural History and a dentist reconstructed a body. It was the body of a ten-year-old child. The janitor was convicted and died in the electric chair in Sing Sing.

The janitor's confession conformed almost 100 per cent to that blind hunch I had had when I first looked at him. This gave me a sort of surprised satisfaction, but it was short-lived. I didn't try to account for the phenomenon, I only wanted to forget it. There are times when a cop's job is loathsome.

Chapter Eighteen

NOTHING

EVER HAPPENS

IN CANARSIE

It seems to me that life has a way of evening things. If I had received more than my share of sorrow, I also received more than my share of goodness and love.

When my wife died, I thought I would never marry again. I would never again know the security I had with Mabel, never again know such depth of mutual love, never again have the support of such steadfast courage. But I was wrong. I was to marry again and to a woman who gave me all these things.

With so much unhappiness in the world, with so many men and women failing to find love, it would seem that I received more than any one man is entitled to. I can only conclude that this is the way in which life balances the scales of suffering.

In the spring of 1942, my son Bobbie and I decided to visit LaGuardia airport to watch the planes land and take off. Like all boys, he was fascinated with planes, and though I had been in the air service during World War I, all I had for him were stories of digging latrines. If there was humor in my stories, it was lost on Bobbie.

We spent a large part of the afternoon at the airport observation ramp, then went into the hangars and climbed through several of the grounded planes, sitting in the pilot's seat and pretending to fly. Bobbie was discovering that there were some advantages in having a father with a police lieutenant's badge in his pocket.

At last he tired of the planes. I remembered that an old friend of mine named Grace Widli lived near LaGuardia and decided to drop in on her. I suppose that all women, given the right moment and situation, are eager match-makers. Grace welcomed us cordially, but there was a with-drawn and contemplative air about her; her mind was obvi-ously on some private plan.

Finally she said, with a bright smile, "Bob, I've got some dear friends I'd like you to meet . . . the Olsens. He's a policeman, too, and they don't live far from here."

"Okay by me," I said. "I always like to talk shop. How about you, Bobbie? Want to meet another cop?"

"Sure," he said agreeably.

On the way to the Olsen house, Grace casually dropped the information that the Olsens had a daughter named Marie. "Good," I said, "Bobbie will have somebody to play with."

Mr. and Mrs. Olsen received us cordially. It turned out he was a patrolman in Brooklyn, and we began to talk about men on the force we knew in common. Mrs. Olsen said her daughter was upstairs and would be right down. In another moment or two she came down the stairs and . . .

well! She was nothing for Bobbie to play with! She was in her late twenties, a statuesque girl with soft brown hair curly and shoulder-length and a broad, friendly smile on her face. At once I felt all hands and feet. I caught Grace Widli's sly smile of satisfaction and I knew she had planned this, that she was trying to promote a wife for me. And I didn't mind it at all.

I had a higher rank than Marie's father, and I'm afraid this gave me a feeling of overconfidence. I talked long and loud about my experiences both as a runner and a cop. I was conscious of the fact I was talking too much, but I couldn't seem to stop. I wanted to impress Marie Olsen with Bob McAllister. I was impressing her all right; I was running over her.

I took Marie out to dinner that night, and the next night, too. On the third night I proposed to her. I guess I expected her to fall into the arms of such an ardent and famous (or infamous) character as me, but she didn't. She drew back to look at me with amazement.

"Bob McAllister," she said, "what in the world are you saying?"

"I'm asking you to marry me."

"I've known you *three days!*"

"Well, I'm the impetuous type, I guess."

"Impetuous is hardly the word for it."

"I've got a future in the department, Marie."

"I don't doubt that, but. . . ."

"Honey, I love you."

She shook her head in bewilderment. "But how do you know?"

"I don't know how . . . but I do. I know what's in my heart."

"I don't know what's in mine, Bob. You just can't expect to bowl a girl over on the third date."

"I'm sorry. I didn't mean to take your breath away."

"Well, you did. The 'flying cop,' indeed. Wow!"

Under Marie's stern admonition, I agreed not to mention marriage again for a month. But I couldn't quite make the distance, and at the end of the third week I brought it up again.

"I like you, Bob," she said. "But give me a chance to know you a little better before I decide to spend the rest of my life with you."

What could I do? I waited. It took Marie ten weeks to realize what I had known at the end of seventy-two hours—that we should be married.

I wanted to marry Marie, my son Bobbie wanted me to marry her, but neither of us were fully aware of the wonderful wife and mother we were to receive. I knew there could be dangerous pitfalls in this marriage; a ready-made family, a dead wife who had been adored—these were things a young second wife might find difficult. But not Marie! She loved Bobbie as her own son; she revered Mabel's memory as I did, and for the same reasons. She was able to do all this because she was a wonderful woman in her own right and had no need to fear the shadow of another. Our life together became a special and precious thing.

Our first daughter, blond Judith Ann, was born on May 2, 1943. Two years later, on May 3, 1945, a dark-haired colleen joined the family. We called her Kathleen. Now I had a son, two daughters, and a devoted wife. Life was full.

Yet, there remained a shadow. There remained Joseph Dandio. Even my happiness in my second marriage failed to make me forget him, failed to ease the need for revenge. If Marie and I were enjoying comparatively serene and sunlit years, it was because Mabel had sustained me in the shadowed ones. And with the desire for vengeance, there was agonizing guilt. Marie was of my own religion, and I think she guessed some of the torment I was suffering, but she never pried, never reproached me. She knew it was something I had to fight in my own way. She gave me her love and her confidence and helped in my studies for advancement in the department. Night after night she would quiz me on the material I had read. She became almost as well prepared for captain of police as I.

I took the exam and passed it. On July 17, 1946, we all went to headquarters where Marie and the children watched proudly as Mayor William O'Dwyer, an ex-cop, led the ceremony that made captains of about fifteen lieutenants. After the ceremony was over the mayor stopped to pat Judy's golden hair.

She looked up and said, "You made my daddy a captain."

"Did I now?" the mayor exclaimed. "And what's his name?"

"Bob McAllister."

"Sure, the flying cop. And do you know something else, honey?"

"What?" Judy asked.

"I know your grandfather, Marty Olsen. We were partners on a beat in Brooklyn years ago. You give him my best wishes."

Judy suddenly felt very important.

But so did I. A captain at last. Those two gold bars . . . that precious insignia! The commander of a precinct!

But what a precinct! I was sent to Canarsie!

This command covered mostly a dump along Jamaica Bay. Here was where Murder, Incorporated, dropped the bodies of their victims . . . but never murdered them here. There was a saying in the department that "nothing ever happens in Canarsie." Okay, so I was in command of a graveyard and a hundred acres of rubbish . . . I'd police it as it had never been policed before.

A couple of things *did* happen in Canarsie while I was in command there, and they threatened to blow me right out of a job.

As I mentioned before, events in Europe often had their echo in the streets of New York. Three months after I assumed command of the Canarsie district, the Nuremberg trials came to an end and the top Nazi war criminals were condemned to the gallows. There was a great outburst of thanksgiving among the New York Jews, and a big drive for funds to help build their new "homeland," Israel.

There came into my office a young Jewish patrolman named Morton Silver (I've changed the name) who saluted smartly and said, "Sir, I'd like permission to raise funds in the precinct for the United Jewish Appeal."

I looked at him closely and said, "You mean during your regular tour of duty, I suppose."

"Yes, sir."

"And in full uniform, of course."

"Well . . . yes, sir."

"And you also know it's contrary to regulations, I'm sure."

"Well, sir . . . I thought . . . I mean. . . ." He stammered to a halt and stared at his highly polished shoes.

"Son, I know exactly what you thought. You were thinking that I'm an Irish Catholic, and there's probably been many a time when I went out in full uniform to shake the can for some Catholic charity. Isn't that it?"

He didn't speak, but a blush spread over his face and answered for him.

He was absolutely right in his surmise, of course. And how could I deny him permission to do something I had often done? Still, it meant trouble from the borough inspectors if I gave permission and was found out. I looked up Silver's record and found that he had six department commendations for good police work. That settled it.

"All right, Silver," I said. "Go raise your money and good luck. I'll carry you on the book as on special assignment for the captain."

I was not only violating regulations in regard to fund collecting in uniform, I was falsifying my own records to cover it. What a way to start out my command of the precinct!

You never knew when an inspector or deputy inspector would drop into the station house to look things over, you could only sweat it out and hope things would be in order when the surprise visit came. Three days later I reported in to discover that during the morning an inspector had signed in the book, and signed out again. He left behind no complaints. Silver and I were safe for the moment.

But now something new and really ominous pressed upon me. Something that made me completely forget Silver and his fund raising. Several officers reported they were missing the small caliber guns they carried in civilian dress. I put this down to negligence at first, but then several more made the same report, and it was clear that their guns had been stolen out of their lockers.

This was a most serious offense in the eyes of headquarters, and rightly so. Each man must account for his gun at all times, and he receives at least a department complaint, a black mark on his record, if he is careless enough to lose it. I should have issued such complaints against these men at once, but I stalled, hoping to solve this mystery. I stalled also because the captain himself is responsible for the department equipment in his command. I was in no position to survive such an official dereliction of duty. I had a record, and it would always weigh against me.

Let me explain about that record. Every policeman has a "Record of Charges" on permanent file in police headquarters. On my record was the charge of demanding a bribe (Mamie Castro), the charge of perjury (Zittel case), and the charge of murder (Dandio-Fighera). That I was subsequently proved innocent of these charges did not wipe them from the record. They were permanent, ineradicable; they would go with me to my grave. And they would be bound to influence any inspector or deputy commissioner or commissioner who might have me on the carpet for future infractions of the rules.

No, I wanted to solve this gun disappearance on my own. I put my best men to work on the case and prayed news of it wouldn't get to headquarters.

Because of this cover-up, I had forgotten all about Silver and my slight distortion of his record until one day when I was informed that he had failed to report for duty. That afternoon I learned he had died of a heart attack while shaving. He was a young man and a good cop and I was sorry to hear this news.

In due time a memorial dinner was arranged for Morton Silver. All the leaders of the Brooklyn Jewish community were to attend and I, as his commanding officer, was asked to speak. I accepted tentatively, knowing I'd have to clear my appearance and my speech with headquarters. Marie and I worked together over that speech, and I rehearsed it in front of her and the children. I sent it off to headquarters and it came back unchanged and approved.

The banquet room at the St. George Hotel was packed. I shared the speakers' platform with the Jewish political, civic, and religious leaders. One by one, they rose to speak and lauded some phase of Morton Silver's life. It came my turn and I stood. I was a police captain in full uniform, an Irish Catholic about to talk to the Jews concerning one of their own.

I had researched Morton Silver's police career thoroughly and told the audience about his fine work and his official commendations. I concluded with the statement that the city would be a lot safer and better place if every cop on the force was a man of Morton Silver's character and courage. When I sat down, the applause was thunderous.

The last speaker was a rabbi, and he told what Silver had done for the cause of Israel. He said that for several years Silver had devoted every waking hour off police duty to the cause. Of course, *I* knew he had also spent more than a few hours *on* duty for the cause.

"Morton Silver was a soldier of the front line just as much as the pioneers in the Negev," the rabbi intoned. "The life's blood of the new state, hard American dollars, came from Morton Silver. In his brief lifetime, he collected over thirty thousand dollars—not from the wealthy and renowned, but from the small shopkeeper, the laborer, the housewife. Thirty thousand dollars in nickels and dimes and quarters. But even that is not the full measure of his

contribution. He supplied the very sinews of self-defense
—he supplied pistols that were smuggled to the homeland!"

At that moment my uniform collar clamped hard on my
throat, choking me, turning my face scarlet. The pistols
missing from the lockers in my station house had been
stolen by Silver and smuggled into Israel! Aghast, I looked
at the press table where a half-dozen reporters were scribbling notes. By tomorrow, the whole town would know.
My concealment of the thefts, my falsification of Silver's
assignment in the precinct blotter . . . it would all come
out. My career was ended!

I didn't hear the rest of the rabbi's speech; I slumped in
my chair, my mind full of bitter self-recrimination. Applause told me the speech had ended, the meeting was over.
I turned to the rabbi, clutching him by the arm, and said
hoarsely, "My God, man, do you know what you've done?
You've broken me."

I explained the situation to the rabbi, and when he understood, he was extremely upset and apologetic. He said,
"Captain, we'll hush this all up."

"There were five reporters at that table," I cried. "You
can't hush this up."

"I'll talk to the reporters," he said.

"Look, Rabbi, I know something about newspapermen.
They're very touchy about being told what they can and
can't write. You'll never muzzle five of them. It's just
impossible."

"I'll talk to them nevertheless," he said firmly. Then
with a dignified stride, he descended upon the press table.

Well, he pulled it off. Not one word of this mess ever
got into the papers, or to headquarters. I found out later

that every newspaperman present at the meeting happened to be Jewish. They saved the hide of an Irish cop.

I've often heard it said that it's human nature to gamble, and that cops should stop wasting time trying to stamp it out. I don't know about the human-nature part of the problem, but I know firsthand why we had to battle illegal gambling in the city. We fought the numbers racket in Harlem because it victimized the poorest of our citizens, taking money that should have gone for meat and milk. We tried to smash the floating crap games because they led inevitably to fights, knifings, and gang feuds. We made constant war on bookies because they were a source of corruption. Let me give you an example of the disease a bookie can bring to a city. Let me tell you about one of the biggest, Harry Gross.

After World War II, Harry started out as a small-time, drugstore operator in north Brooklyn. He'd take $2 bets and phone them to his Manhattan boss from the pay telephone, and occasionally, when the bet was on a long shot, he wouldn't phone it in at all, but pocket it. He built up a bankroll, and pretty soon he was making his own book and accepting $5 and $10 bets. He was hard-working, ambitious, and unscrupulous, and within a short time he had his own room and his own runners.

By 1950, Harry Gross had become a big shot in the Brooklyn underworld, riding in a Cadillac with a chauffeur and bodyguards, wearing $200 suits, wintering in Florida. All this time he bribed and corrupted public officials so that he could continue his operations.

Harry didn't operate in my precinct—there weren't enough horse players in the dumps along Jamaica Bay—

but north, around Ebbets Field. Occasionally when I went to see the Dodgers play, I'd spot him lounging in a box, a plump man in his thirties, sleek and arrogant, with the hard, complacent eyes of a despoiler. I heard he was too friendly with the cops in north Brooklyn. I didn't want to believe it; I knew firsthand what a vicious thing that sort of gossip could be; but the fact remained that he continued to operate in the open. He was the kind of man any honest captain wants to drive out of his precinct, but Harry Gross wasn't being driven anywhere.

He had a face that made you want to plant your fist in the middle of it. But it wasn't any of my business. My job was to run the 69th Precinct, and as long as he stayed out of there, there was nothing I could do about him. He never did step into my territory, but I got into the fight anyway.

As the months passed, the name Harry Gross spread through the department like a contagious disease. We all realized that some of the men were taking bribes, but we didn't know who. I suspected it might be some of the precinct commanders, but one day, a few months before the case broke wide open, I found I was wrong.

Captain Johnny Egert, commander of the 67th Precinct, where Gross operated, came to me in a great state of agitation. He said, "Bob, you know who Harry Gross is?"

"Yeah," I said cautiously. "I know who he is."

"He's got connections in the department."

"So I hear."

"Jesus, I don't know what to do about him."

"If he ever steps foot in *my* precinct, I'll bounce him on his ass."

Egert shook his head sadly and said, "You don't understand."

"Don't understand what?" I snapped.

"Mac, don't get your Irish up. I'm in a jam and I want your advice."

"Sorry, Johnny. I didn't mean to climb on you. What's the trouble?"

"I found out who Gross is doing business with."

I tried to conceal my surprise at this. I had thought Gross was doing business with Johnny Egert, among others. But the man's sincerity and his agitation were too obvious to leave any doubts on that score. I sat quiet and waited for him to continue.

He said, "This morning at two o'clock I was taking a wrap-up of the precinct and I went by Garfield's Restaurant on Flatbush, and through a gap in the curtain I saw Harry Gross and his kid brother, Jackie, giving a party in the private dining room. They were entertaining three headquarters men!"

I whistled softly, said nothing.

"I recognized them all," he continued, "and I wish to hell I hadn't. A captain and two plain-clothes men from Jim Kennedy's confidential squad."

"My God . . . are you sure?" I exclaimed.

He nodded miserably. Now I could well understand his concern and apprehension. James Kennedy was supervising assistant chief inspector of the entire department. Only the chief inspector and the commissioner were above him. Jim Kennedy had a reputation for being a tough disciplinarian, but an honest and just man. This news was a great blow to me, as it was to Johnny Egert.

"Johnny," I said at last, "you've got to play this one by the book."

"What do you mean?"

"Report what you saw to Mike Murphy."

Inspector Michael Murphy was Brooklyn's 18th Division commander, our immediate superior. This case was too big and too hot for a precinct captain to handle, and the correct thing to do was to pass it on to the next in command. There was danger, of course, because there was no telling who was on the Gross payroll, but the book was still the book, and it seemed the safest procedure to follow. Johnny Egert and I discussed it a long time, and he went away still undecided. He delayed his decision too long. Three months later District Attorney MacDonald broke the whole case wide open.

It turned out that MacDonald's staff had been working on this case for almost a year, in fact they had tapped telephones in every station house, and this became one of the most heartbreaking scandals in the history of the department. Actually, the corruption was nowhere near as extensive as the newspaper headlines indicated. Almost all those who had taken bribes were headquarters men, and many of them were on Jim Kennedy's confidential squad. Kennedy himself was completely innocent and went on to higher advancement in the department. When Mayor Wagner appointed Stephen Kennedy (no relation) police commissioner, Jim Kennedy became first deputy police commissioner and, as these words are written, still holds that post. His responsibility in the Gross affair was only that he trusted his men too much.

When something like the Gross case breaks open, there are bound to be angry reactions which can lead to many injustices. It was over such an injustice that I became involved.

Right after Gross had been arrested and placed in Riker's

Prison to await trial, a shakedown racket burst upon the
department. Jackie Gross, Harry's brother, began to approach Brooklyn cops to demand money for Harry's defense. Jackie threatened that if the cop refused to kick
through $500 or a $1,000, Harry would name him as bribe
taker.

I first learned of this from a friend of mine who was a
deputy inspector. He said, "Bob, that little bastard Jackie
is going to every cop who was ever assigned to this borough. Last week he came to me and asked for fifteen
hundred dollars, and he knew damn well I had never taken
a cent from Gross. A lot of innocent men are going to be
smeared before this thing is over."

That inspector didn't pay off Jackie, but unfortunately
he didn't arrest him either. He had been a headquarters
man all his life, with no street experience, and he didn't
think fast. If he had only grabbed Jackie and pulled him
in for attempted extortion, the whole case might have
shaped up differently and many innocent men might have
been saved. I walked the streets of my precinct hoping that
Jackie Gross would try to shake *me* down, but he never
came near me. And so it became possible for a good cop
and a friend of mine to be framed.

Morris Coon was a deputy inspector in the Bronx when
the Gross case broke. He and Gross had lived in the same
neighborhood, but he had not seen Gross or passed a word
with him in years. Yet when Gross took the stand, he
testified that he had given Coon ten dollars to buy himself a hat. Now, Coon was not in the precinct, or even
in the borough where Gross operated, and therefore could
not do him the slightest favor. There could be no possible
reason for Gross to try and bribe him. When asked about

this during cross-examination, Gross merely shrugged his shoulders and said he had given the money "just in case" he might need Coon in the future.

And on this flip word of a gutter-creature, Coon was brought to departmental trial. He came to me in tears and said, "Bob, I swear to you I never took a cent from Gross. I haven't laid eyes on him since he was a kid. I can't understand why he's doing this to me."

I patted him on the shoulder. "You don't have to convince me, Morris. I know you'd never be on the take."

"Thanks, Bob."

"If there's anything I can do, just name it."

"That's why I came to see you, as a matter of fact. Bob, will you appear at my trial as a character witness?"

"You're damn right I will," I said.

As Coon's trial approached, several of my friends in headquarters advised me not to testify. An inspector said, "Bob, don't go down there. No cop is safe and you especially. You've got a police record, and if you ever take the stand, they'll crucify you. For God's sake, be smart and protect yourself."

But I couldn't play it that way. All my life I'd called them as I saw them, and this was no time to change . . . not with an innocent man's reputation and career at stake. I had been railroaded too often myself to be able to stand by watching it happen to a friend.

The day of the trial I presented myself at the Supreme Court Building. I wore full uniform, and above my gold captain's badge I pinned my six decorations for bravery and good police work. The departmental trial was presided over by Judge Delahanty who had been appointed a deputy police commissioner just for this purpose. The prosecutor was Corporation Counsel Hurwitz. When I took the stand, I gave my testimony in a loud and uncompromising voice. Let them smear me after I finished, let them try and discredit me with old slanders and frame-ups, but in the meantime, let them hear that Morris Coon was an honest cop.

When it came time for cross-examination, Mr. Hurwitz looked at me closely without rising from counsel table. He tapped the point of his pencil and studied my decorations, my belligerent jaw. Then he said softly, "No questions."

Morris Coon was found guilty, discharged from the force, and stripped of his pension rights. He had devoted over thirty-five years of his life to the department, had risen to the high post of deputy inspector, but had been brought low by Harry Gross. Why judges are so often ready to take the word of criminals the moment they make a charge against a cop is something I'll never understand.

We finally discovered what had motivated Harry Gross in this frame-up. A year earlier young Jackie had swaggered into a neighborhood candy store to boast that every cop in the city was on his brother's payroll. Coon's seventeen-year-old son entered the store at that moment, heard the tirade, and with a single punch flattened Jackie. Jackie and Harry Gross's revenge was to destroy the father.

The last I heard of Morris Coon he was a broken old man, a night watchman on the bleak Brooklyn waterfront.

God must have a special kind of punishment waiting for men like Jackie and Harry Gross.

I was in command in Canarsie for five years, during which the swamps and dumps gave way to housing developments and a burgeoning community. I had pretty much resigned myself to spending the rest of my career in this rather peaceful backwash of the great city when, in the spring of 1951, I received notice of transfer to the 25th Precinct in Harlem.

This Harlem precinct has more crime per population, and more population per square mile, than any other precinct in New York City. Here is one of the toughest police jobs in America. The 25th is known in the department as a "captain breaker," because no man ever commanded there without his full measure being taken. Captains who left the 25th always went up—or down; they either became deputy inspectors or were sent to Staten Island or Prospect Park.

Why was I being sent to the 25th, I wondered. It seemed unlikely that headquarters had plans for my promotion. I had been the cause of too much trouble, I had stepped on too many toes to win advancement beyond my mandatory civil-service rank. Suddenly a thought occurred to me that ended all speculation, a thought that bathed me in a cold sweat. The 25th Precinct was where Joseph Dandio operated!

Chapter Nineteen

A FURNACE

FOR MY FOE

As captain of the 25th Precinct, my station house was on East 126th Street, and I commanded the following: 4 lieutenants, 9 sergeants, 190 patrolmen, 2 plain-clothes men, 1 acting captain of detectives, and 14 detectives, first, second, and third grade.

With this pitifully small force, I was expected to keep peace in a jungle of fetid tenements and squalid streets. Here was a wasteland of tuberculosis, hookworm, and syphilis. Mothers hung their cradles on ropes from the ceiling to protect their babies from rats, but they were powerless to save their grown children from what waited in the streets—the prostitutes, the dope pushers, the perverts, the teen-age gangs in peg-top pants who lounged in the doorways and alleys.

This area had once been Italian, but these people had been pushed to the eastern fringe blocks by Negroes. Now the Negroes were being pushed by Puerto Ricans who were crowding northward from Spanish Harlem at 104th Street.

No race or nationality wished to live in the same building, or the same block, with another. Wherever the pressure of the city forced them to do so, there was hate and cruelty.

And somewhere in this wilderness lurked Joseph Dandio.

This was my personal hunt and I couldn't throw my command into it, but no officer in my precinct ever made an arrest or an interrogation, even for a traffic violation, without seeking information about Dandio. And during my off hours, I took to the streets myself in a block-by-block search. My sergeants and my patrolmen never knew when their captain might appear, at any hour of the day or night. It kept them on their toes.

I was no stranger to Harlem, having worked in both the 32d and 28th Precincts as patrolman and throughout the area as a plain-clothes man. Bit by bit, I picked up my old contacts and made many new ones. The leads on Dandio were elusive, but enough to keep me eager.

One day a regular stoolie of mine sidled up to me in the street and said, "Cap, there's an old man who suns himself every day in front of a candy store, corner of Second Avenue and 116th Street. He might know something about Dandio."

"Yeah? Who is he?"

"A retired leader of the Mafia."

"Retired?" I snorted. "They don't retire, unless they're full of lead."

"This one did," the stoolie insisted. "Just sits in the sun all day. His name is Joey Rao."

Joey Rao! What echoes that name set up. My very first assignment as a plain-clothes man thirty years ago had been to investigate the Bronx gang led by Dutch Schultz. Vince

Coll and Joey Rao had been Dutch's two top lieutenants. I remembered Rao at the beer drop where I worked as a driver, thin-faced and taciturn, suspicious, efficient. Later he had his own mob, allied with Schultz, and had hired the killers who went for me when I was a bus driver. Joey Rao, an old enemy of mine!

Yet, I didn't feel vengeful toward Joey Rao. The war between us had been between gangster and cop, impersonal. He hadn't framed me or disgraced me the way Dandio had. Now he might even help me. I was eager to see him, if in truth it was he.

It was indeed Joey Rao. Of all the old-time, Prohibition-era gangsters I had known, he alone had survived to a peaceful, almost philosophical retirement. When I went up to him, he smiled quizzically at me and said, "Hi ya, Cap."

"Hello, Joey. You know who I am?"

"Sure. McAllister."

"It's been a long time."

"Yeah," he agreed. "A long time."

"First time we met was at the beer drop you and Dutch Schultz ran in the Bronx back in the twenties."

He grinned and nodded.

"And in 1923, you and Dutch sent a couple of torpedoes to rub me out when I was driving a bus through Central Park."

The smile remained but it thinned. He shook his head and said, "You got me wrong, Cap."

"I got you right, Joey."

He shrugged his shoulders. "That was a long time ago. I don't remember everything that happened in those days."

"What are you doing now?" I asked. "Keeping your nose clean?"

"I'm retired, Cap. I just sit in the sun."

"When Vince Coll was gunning for you and the Dutchman, you didn't sit in the sun, Joey."

As I walked on down the street, I heard him chuckling over the memory of Vince Coll, the mad-dog killer. Joey had outlived him and would die peacefully in his bed. He could afford to laugh.

I hadn't asked him about Dandio because I wanted first to establish our relationship. I wanted him to realize that I was ready to let bygones be bygones. He also had to know that as long as I commanded this precinct, he'd better stay straight.

I stopped by to see him again a week later. He was in the same position, tilted back in a chair in front of a candy store, absorbing sun into his brittle bones.

"Hi ya, Cap," he greeted me.

"Hello, Joey. How things?"

"I'm livin'."

"More than some of your old friends can say."

"Yeah," he grinned.

"Joey, I had you tailed last week."

"I'm clean, Cap. I told ya, I'm retired."

"I had to be sure. I guess you're retired all right, but a lot of people talk to you."

"I gotta be deaf, too?"

"What I mean is, you know what's going on in the neighborhood. I want some information. I want to know about Dandio."

"Joseph Dandio?"

"That's right. A few years ago he was a Harlem bag man for Luciano. Where is he now?"

"Forget him, Cap. You'll never find him. He's sleepin'

with Bo Weinberg . . . in a cement overcoat in the bottom of the East River."

I thought about that for a moment; then I said, "I don't believe that, Joey."

He shrugged his shoulders and said, "That's what I hear."

"See if you can hear something else," I said.

Rao's information should have jolted me, but it didn't. I just couldn't believe that Dandio was dead. My quest had become a fixed idea in my mind, and I knew I'd have to see his dead body, even at the bottom of the river, before I could give up the search.

Dandio was soon shoved into the background, however, by some very disturbing developments. Headquarters squads began to make gambling raids in my precinct.

The first one occurred on Election Day. I had all my men covering the polls and was in the station house with a skeleton detail when the headquarters men marched in with sixty prisoners they had bagged in a loft on Second Avenue. Leading them all was Supervising Assistant Chief Inspector Jim Kennedy. I knew I was in for it.

Kennedy followed me into my private office, fixed his cold blue eyes on me, and made the classic taunt. "My men can knock over the crap games. Why can't yours?"

"This is Election Day," I bristled. "I haven't got enough men to raid a tea party." It was a poor excuse, I suppose, but it was the truth.

"McAllister, you'd better wise up. The Syndicate is operating a big game somewhere here in the twenty-fifth. Trigger Mike Coppolo and Eddie Coco are the cutters. Break 'em up or you won't last long as a captain in this precinct."

During the following weeks, I stripped the precinct of every available man; I put patrolmen into plain clothes, I even put my clerical man and the attendant on the streets in my war on the crap games. I began knocking them over, but it was the small stuff. The Syndicate game eluded me. Two months later the headquarters men were back. I received a call in my office from Kennedy who had raided a game on 120th Street and wanted a patrol wagon sent to pick up the prisoners.

When I arrived on the scene, I found not only Kennedy, but Chief Inspector Rothengast and Commissioner George Monoghan. CBS television cameramen were there to film it for news showing the next day. I was really on the spot now. To emphasize their dissatisfaction with me, the top brass decided to take the prisoners down to the district attorney's office for booking instead of doing it in my station house. I could see my transfer looming. And once I was broken out of the 25th, there would never again be an important assignment. All that remained would be Staten Island and retirement.

I fought back, trying to stave off disgrace. I drove my men and myself, hounded the stool pigeons. I got a lead on a game that was to be played in an undertaker's parlor. The operator was named the Cat, and the undertaker was the cover. If the place was raided, the players were to pose as mourners come to pay last respects to a friend. The games were only run when there was a dead body available for this sham. I raided the place and caught the Cat, but it was a cheap game. This was not Syndicate money.

Headquarters continued to breathe down my neck. I doubled my efforts. I was getting practically no sleep now, napping on the cot in my office instead of going home.

It was tough on Marie and the kids, but I had to locate the Syndicate game. Marie understood.

Then I got a lucky tip. It came from Marie's brother, who was a plain-clothes man in a West Side division. One of his stoolies told him that a Syndicate man called The Shark was bankrolling a 40- to 50-thousand-dollar game in my precinct. The money was strapped to his chest with adhesive tape and he traveled with Tony Lumps, his cutter. An armed bodyguard always trailed after the two of them.

I knew these two. The Shark was a short, fat man with oily manners; Tony Lumps was lean, with quick reflexes, a knifer who was as mean as they come. The night I got the tip, I replaced my uniform with a regular suit, took an unmarked police car, and began to tour the precinct. Several hours passed and I saw no sign of a game. Every thirty minutes I called the station house, but nothing was happening. It looked like a quiet night.

At 4:30 in the morning I decided to take a final swing through the precinct before turning in. I was coming across 120th Street when I saw a small group of men duck into a tenement. One of the men began to walk quickly on down the street and I recognized the hen-shaped body of the Shark. As I pulled the car to the curb he began to run.

"Stop or I'll shoot!" I yelled after him.

He stopped and I went up to him with drawn gun and frisked him. The money was there all right; thousand-dollar bills taped to his chest. I pulled them loose and shook them under his nose.

"Okay, where's the game?" I demanded.

"Now look, Cap . . . ," he began.

"How do you know I'm the captain?"

"You kiddin'? I know you're McAllister."

"Then tell me where the game is."

"Cap, you know better than to ask me that. You know I can't tell you."

"You're gonna tell me," I said grimly.

"Nothin' you can do to me would be as bad as what would happen if I told you. It's worth my life, Cap. I tell you where the game is and in twenty-four hours I'm at the bottom of the East River. You know that, Cap."

He was right, of course. I could beat him within an inch of his life, but at least he'd still be living. Yet, I had to force his mouth. Then it occurred to me there's one thing a gambler loves more than his life.

I took a thousand-dollar bill from the big wad, held it by the corner, and ignited it with a match. It burned briskly and fell at our feet, a white ash. I selected a second thousand-dollar bill and held it before his face and said, "Where's the game?" He shook his head with a sad smile. I ignited this bill and we watched it burn to a crisp.

"Shark, I'm gonna burn every last dollar of your money if you don't tell me."

A third bill went up in flames. And a fourth. And a fifth. Each one making a bright little orange flame in the middle of the black Harlem night, then disappearing in ash. Five thousand dollars was sifted gray ash about our shoes. It was illegal to destroy United States currency, but I did it anyway. I was desperate. I reached for the sixth bill. As it burned, he broke his silence.

"I know your reputation, Cap. You're not on the take but . . . don't get sore but . . . you can keep half the money if you don't burn no more."

My answer to the attempted bribe was to reach for the seventh bill. I was sweating now. In a few minutes I had burned up almost the equivalent of a year's pay. I struck the match and heard him nervously clear his throat. I paused a moment, the match dancing brightly an inch from the edge of the bill.

"Cap . . . ," he whined. "Don't burn no more money."

"You gonna tell me?"

"I'll make a deal with you."

"What kind of a deal?"

"Don't burn no more money and we'll never run another game in your command. I give you my word. Not only this precinct, but any precinct you're ever in . . . no game."

I looked at his oily face and considered what to do. The match sputtered against my finger and went out. We stood in darkness and considered. At last I said, "It's a deal."

He kept his word. From that day on, the Syndicate never ran a game where I was in command. Yet this didn't help me in my trouble with headquarters. They kept riding me to knock over the big Syndicate game and I couldn't tell them there wasn't any in my precinct because I had burned $6,000 of the Syndicate's money.

On April 9, 1952, I received an order to report to headquarters. I stared at the order, then closed the door of my private office and sat down to think things through. I was fifty-two years old—thirty years a cop. There comes a time when you say, "Enough." I picked up the telephone and called Marie.

"Honey," I said, "how would you like to go to Florida?"

"Bob, what are you saying?"

"I just received an order to report to headquarters. This is probably it, hon. A transfer. I'm awful tired and I think I'd like Florida better than Staten Island. How do you feel about it?"

"Whatever you decide is all right with me, you know that. But, Bob, think about it carefully."

"I have. I've made out my retirement papers and they'll be in my pocket when I go down there. If they start chewing me out again about those goddamn crap games, we'll head for Florida."

I don't know whether I was really serious about those retirement papers; maybe I was just momentarily weary of the job. Anyway, I never got a chance to use them. As the commissioner shook my hand, my old friend, Chief Clerk Vince Finn, handed me a brand new deputy inspector's shield. I had been promoted to deputy inspector!

I opened my mouth and then closed it. I had to swallow all those words that had been waiting and find some new ones. Finally I managed, "Thank you, sir."

I left the commissioner's office with an assistant chief inspector. In the hall I turned to him and said, "I can hardly believe it."

"Why, Bob?" he asked. "Don't you think you earned it?"

"Sure, but I always thought you headquarters men had the knife out for me."

"You're thinking about twenty-five years ago."

"Yeah," I said softly, "twenty-five years! All this time I've had a persecution complex about the brass. You know, Inspector, now that I've got the promotion, I'll tell you the truth. Sometimes I'm a thick-headed Irishman."

He laughed. "Sometimes we all are."

That summer, on a day when the heat pressed down upon the city in thick, hard layers that made it difficult to breathe, I received a telephone call from a Federal narcotics agent down in Foley Square.

"Inspector," he said, "we've got a friend of yours down here."

"A friend of mine?"

"Yeah. He's such a good friend he once tried to send you to the chair. His name is Joseph Dandio."

In the sweltering heat my body went shivering cold. "I'll be right down," I said.

When I arrived at Foley Square, the Federal man had put Dandio in a private office. I said, "I'd like to see him alone."

The Fed looked at me closely and said, "Inspector, I'm responsible for him. Don't get me on a hook."

"Just five minutes . . . alone with him," I said.

He shrugged his shoulders and I walked into the office, shutting the door behind me.

He sat with his back to me, slumped in a straight chair. I saw the skeletal shoulders protruding through a filthy shirt. The head, sunk between the shoulders, was a tangle of long, matted white hair. In disbelief, I walked around him to stare into a ruined face. The flesh was suet-gray and sagging, the eyes inflamed, the mouth slack. A whitish tongue flicked constantly over the cracked lips, but left no moisture. A tic convulsed one side of his face, giving the effect of a monstrous, ghoulish wink. On his skinny left arm was a line of ulcerated sores. He was a dope addict.

"Dandio," I said. "Dandio, you know who I am?"

The lips worked soundlessly for a moment, then a voice came cracked and whistling through a tortured throat. "Doc . . . gimme a fix."

"I'm not the doctor. I'm McAllister."